BEGINNER'S GUIDES

PAINTING

Still Life in Oils

JENNY RODWELL

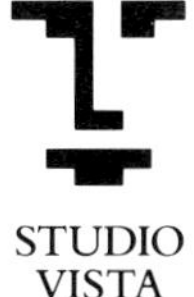

STUDIO
VISTA

ACKNOWLEDGEMENTS
The author and publishers would like to thank the following artists
who have allowed us to use their work in this book: Lionel Bulmer,
pp. 6-7, 9, 12-13; Fred Dubery, p. 8; Margaret Green, p. 7;
Brenda Holtam, pp. 4-5, 66; Ken Howard, pp. 10-11;
Celeste Radloff, pp. 7, 36-37. Special thanks to Winsor and
Newton for their generous help with materials; to Ian Sidaway for
his step-by-step demonstrations and artwork; and to Fred Munden
for taking the photographs.

Studio Vista
an imprint of
Cassell
Villiers House
41/47 Strand
London WC2N 5JE

First published 1994

British Library Cataloguing in Publication Data
A catalogue record for this book is available from the British Library.

ISBN 0-289-80083-8 (pbk)
ISBN 0-289-80118-4 (hbk)

Series editors Jenny Rodwell and Patricia Monahan
The moral rights of the author have been asserted

Series designer Edward Pitcher

Distributed in the United States by
Sterling Publishing Co. Inc.
387 Park Avenue South, New York, NY 10016-8810

Typeset by Litho Link Ltd., Welshpool, Powys, Wales
Printed and bound in Great Britain by
Butler & Tanner Ltd, Frome and London

CONTENTS

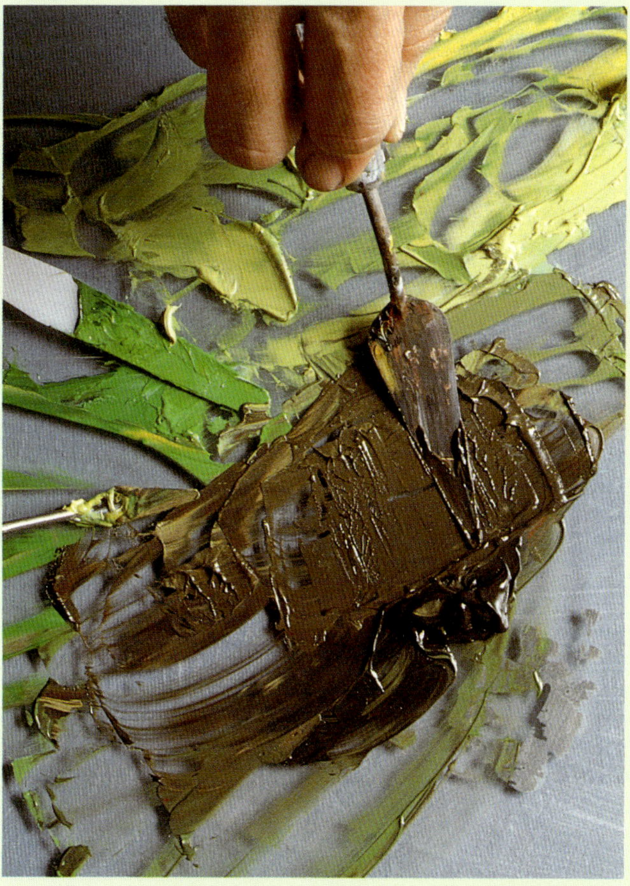

Introducing still life

S TILL LIFE developed almost unnoticed in the quiet
corners of great paintings. Early pictures often depicted
figures from history or religion, sometimes caught up in
dramatic events. But placed on the tables and shelves, or
maybe strewn on the floor, you will notice pockets of
tranquillity – clusters of objects which give a sense of place
and identity, just as a silent collection of possessions can
vividly recall an absent person.

Long before the term existed, therefore, artists had been
unwittingly painting still lifes. As religious themes ceased to
be a central feature of most paintings, the artists began to
focus on details in their own right – not only the
landscapes, flowers and buildings, but also the vast range
of objects which became the subjects of still-life painting.

Still life is now so generally accepted that many people,
when they first think of 'art', see in their imagination some
of the famous clichés of the genre – the fruit, the fish, the
game birds and so on – that grace so many art galleries.
Such old favourites can still be painted, with a fresh
approach, but you need not be restricted: as contemporary
paintings show, the range is infinite.

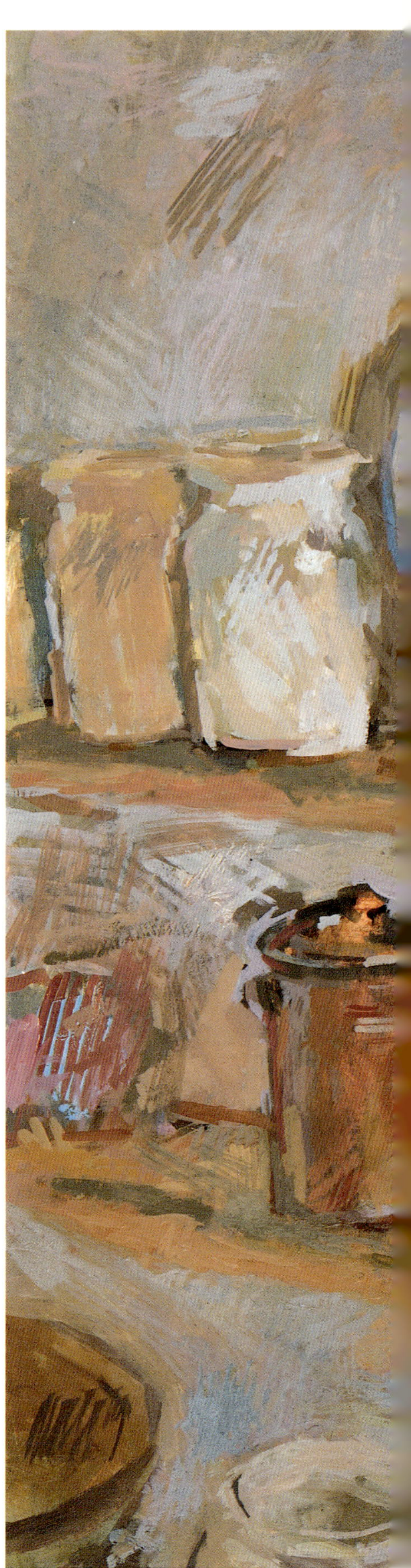

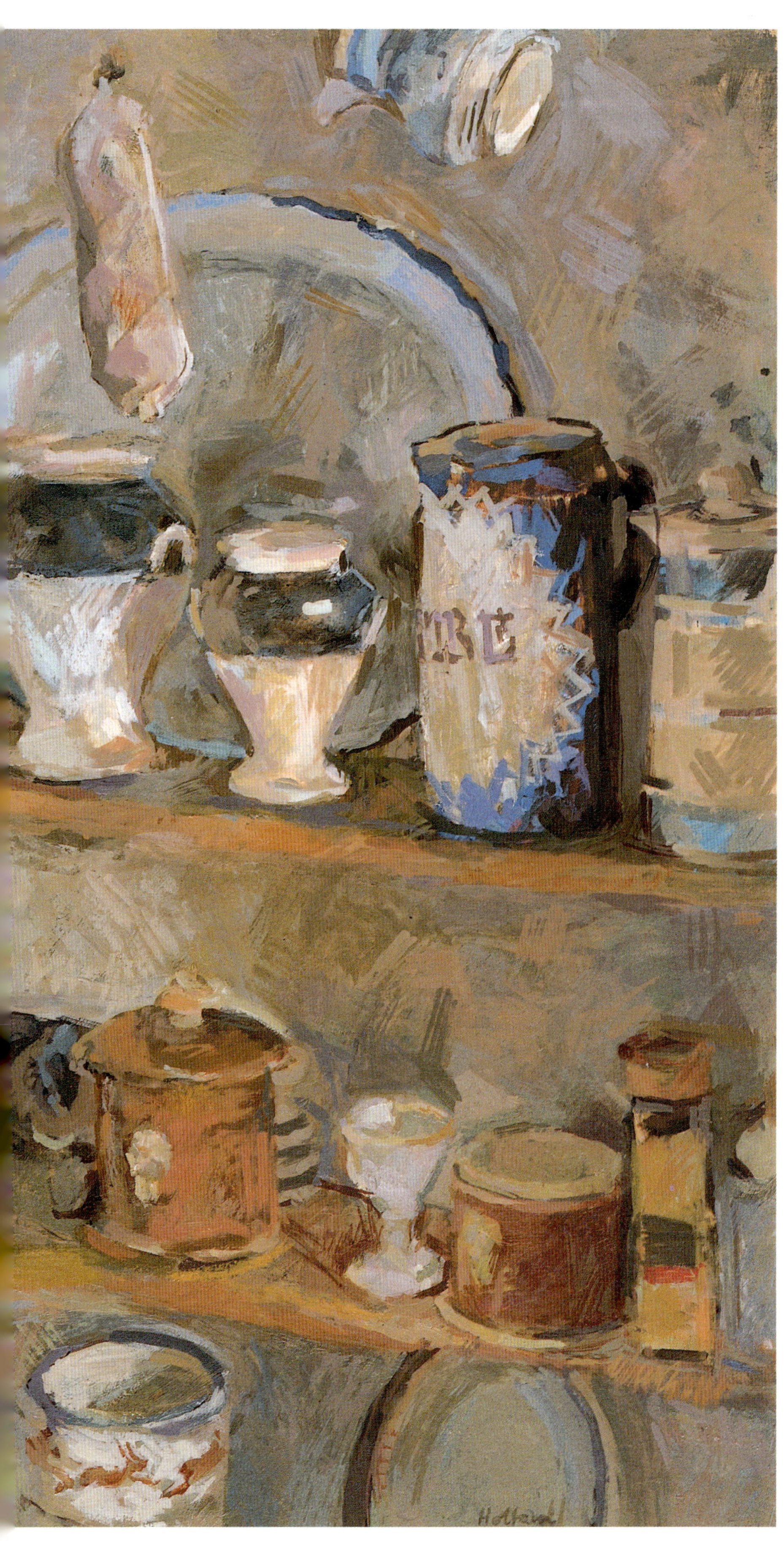

Early still lifes featured as details in religious and figure compositions. Often they were domestic objects — books laid out on a desk, or other items chosen to provide a clue as to the identity and occupation of the subject. In this informal arrangement, artist Brenda Holtam takes a detail and turns it into a painting in its own right. The dresser was painted exactly as it was, with the mugs, plates, jars and food randomly placed on the shelves. Nothing was moved or rearranged in order to manipulate or alter the composition.

THE VERSATILE GENRE

Still life suffers from much the same problem as Shakespeare. It is regularly 'done' – perhaps overdone – in school, so children grow up assuming it is boring. Later, however, if you are lucky, you discover its variety and worth. But because of its common classroom use, still life is regarded as academic and so takes on all the negative feelings associated with school. Familiarity, it seems, has bred contempt.

Why has still life been such a popular subject in the classroom? The main answer lies in its convenience and versatility. You do not have to wait for the weather; you do not have to trek into the countryside to seek landscapes; you do not have to pay for models to remain static for hours. Still life is chosen for art students in the classroom because it seems to be a simple matter of collecting interesting objects, spreading them on a table and letting the students get on with it. Some art teachers do operate this way; however, luckily many realize that still life has much more to offer.

In fact, still life is a very creative and personal field. It enables you to take objects and artefacts you like, and with which you have associations, and extend these into painting. You are not obliged to paint something with which you are uncomfortable. This does not necessarily mean that the objects should suit your personality, but rather that you are free to choose bright, cheerful subjects if you like them, or to pick atmospheric subjects or simple, formal shapes if these are more to your taste.

Still life and oils

Historically, still life and oil paints go together. Still life only really became a genre in its own right during the sixteenth century; it was almost always carried out in oils. It is mainly a northern European genre, coming into its own after the Reformation, when religious paintings almost disappeared.

Even then the subject matter was not painted for its own sake but was mainly symbolic. Many of these early still lifes were concerned with the transience of life, hence the commonly depicted objects like skulls, candle snuffers, butterflies, mirrors and so on.

Early masters

Wandering round any of the major art galleries, you can see not only how many still-life paintings there are but also how very different they can be.

During the sixteenth, seventeenth and eighteenth centuries, still-life paintings made considerable strides. They moved on from grim reminders about the shortness of the human lifespan to statements about how good that short life could be. Piles of fruit, food, silver tableware and other emblems of an opulent lifestyle are common features, particu-

▽ **Pattern and texture** *A varied subject gives the artist plenty of scope to concentrate on those elements which interest him most – in this case the colours, textures and pattern of a still-life arrangement.*

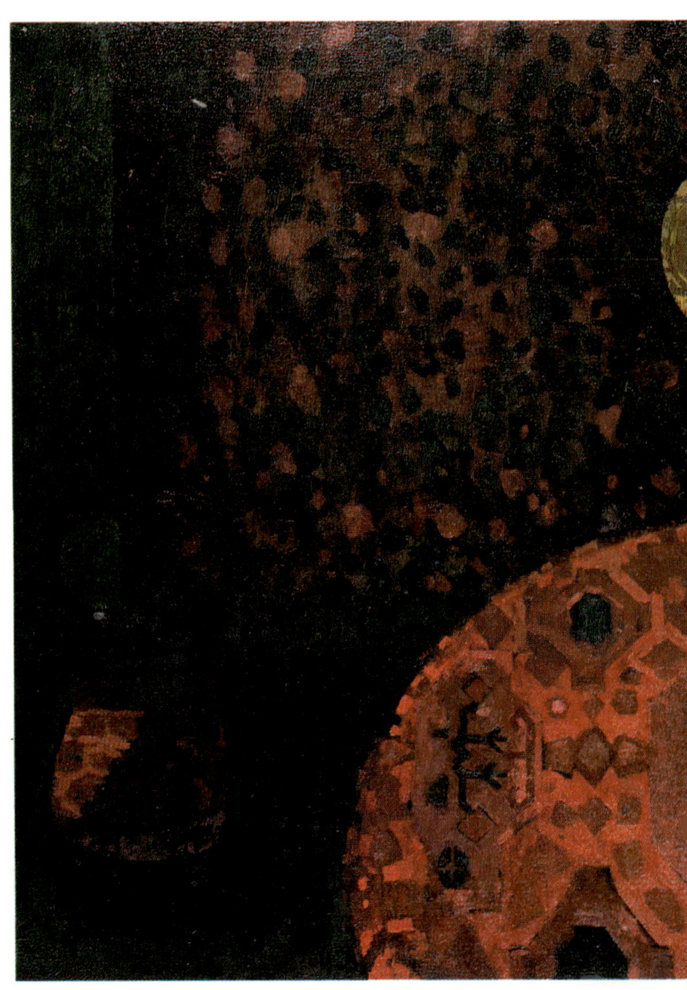

▽ **Colour and shape** *Celeste Radloff finds in her subject a series of flat, geometric shapes which are painted in pure, vivid colours. The perspective in this painting is flattened, so there is no illusion of three-dimensional space in the composition.*

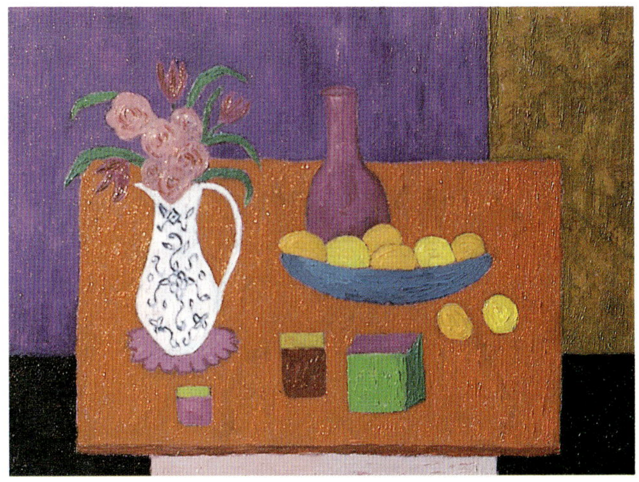

larly in paintings from France and Italy. Musical instruments, furniture and even the dogs and servants are included in many of these grand pieces.

More recently, still life has cropped up in all the major art movements. Notable exponents were the leading Cubists, Picasso (1881–1973) and Braque (1882–1963), whose major works were almost always based on arrangements of objects. In their search for colour and light, the Impressionists too brought still life into the centre of their world. Post-Impressionist giants such as Cézanne (1839–1906) and Van Gogh (1853–90) have made still-life paintings universally known and admired. They invited us to see apples, sunflowers, wooden chairs – everyday objects – in a new and magical way.

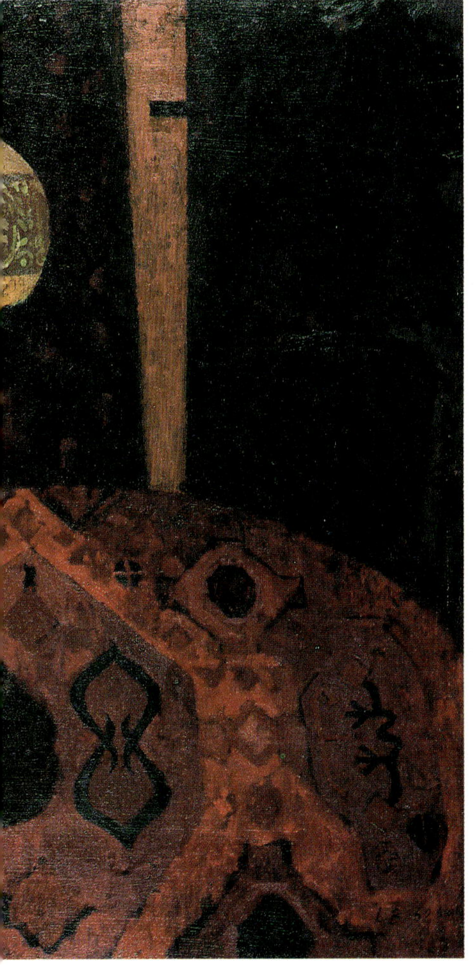

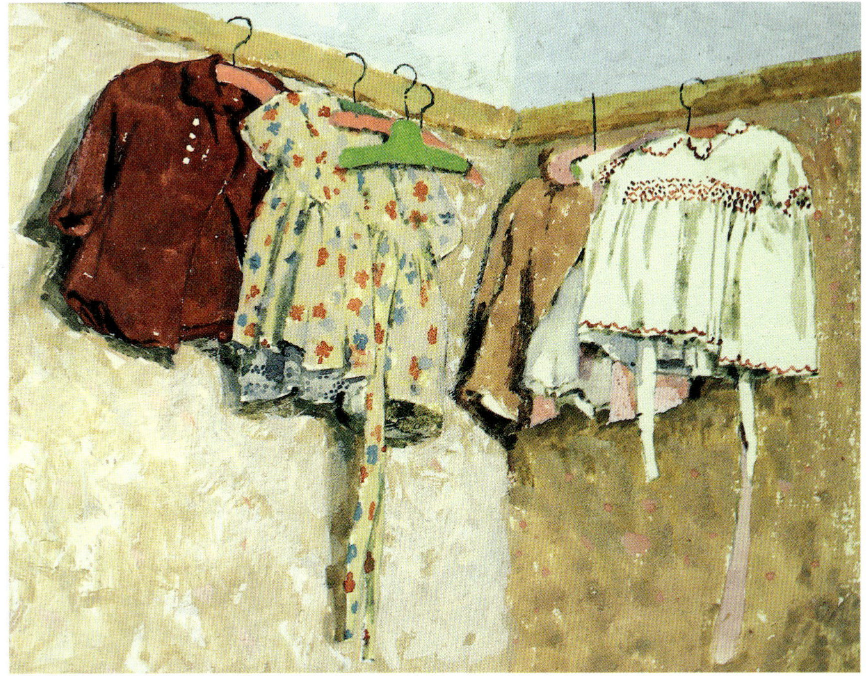

△ **Individual viewpoint** *A charming still life by Margaret Green. A child's dresses hang from a picture rail in the corner of a room. They are higher than the artist's eye level and she looks up at the subject in order to paint.*

THE PERFECT SUBJECT

For the newcomer to oil painting, still life is the best possible subject. Not only can you choose exactly what you want to paint, but you can arrange the subject as you like and can leave it alone for as long as it takes you to paint it. You are in absolute control.

Still life is especially suited to oils, which can be a slow painting process. With oils, it is usual to do a painting in several sittings, leaving the paint to partially dry overnight and then continuing next day – or whenever you can. With still-life painting, the subject will be there when you are ready to continue. The only unstable factor is the change in light during the day. There are suggestions later in the book on how best to cope with this.

Be selective
When painting a landscape, figure or portrait, you are stuck with whatever is in front of you. And because these subjects are rarely straightforward, it is up to you to select and simplify in the painting. The selection must take place as you work.

But with still life, if the subject is wrong, it can usually be changed. Objects can be removed, added and changed round.

Still life plus other genres
Still life embraces all other genres – as you can see from the pictures here. Often, other factors are added, so that a painting might not just be still life. It might incorporate a landscape, interior or human portrait. We frequently see still lifes, for instance, with a window or door in the background. The still life is thus placed in a broader context and we can see past the objects into the world beyond.

When still life encroaches on figure painting and people enter the picture, we find that the objects become more personal. They remain central to the picture, yet they are seen as belongings, or as part of a home.

Whole or part
Some still-life subjects take in a whole section of a room. Rather like a wide-angled lens, they might

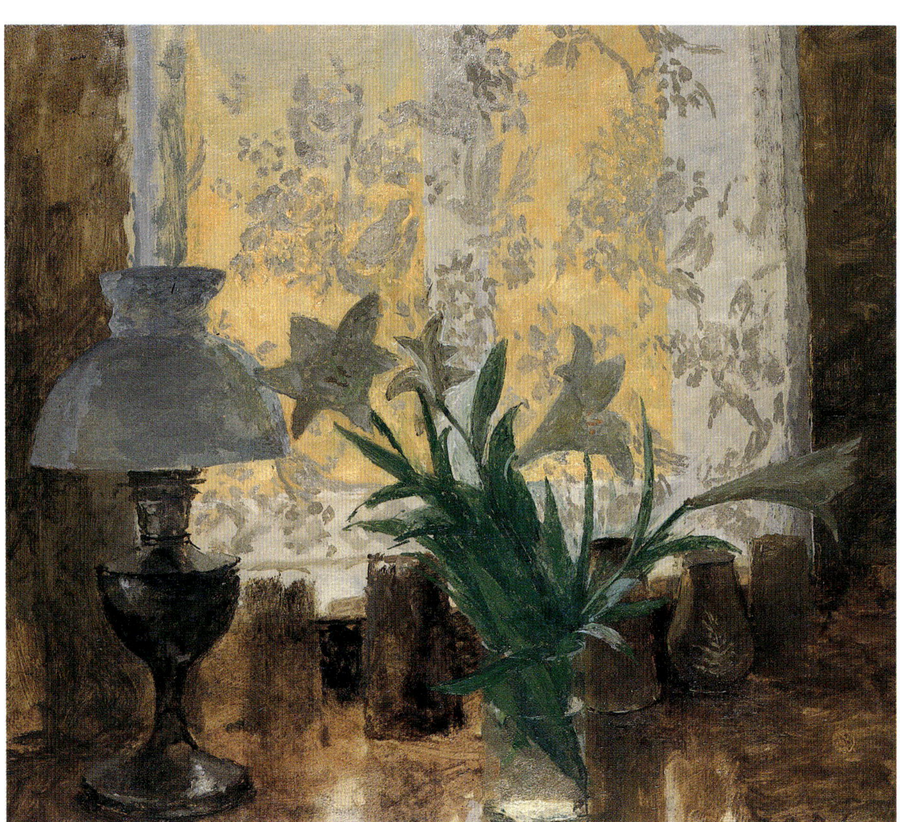

◁ **Subtle whites** *The choice and composition of these objects plays an important part in the finished painting. Fred Dubery chose objects for their light tones and subdued, warm colours. The arrangement includes a variety of different whites, including the lilies and floral curtains.*

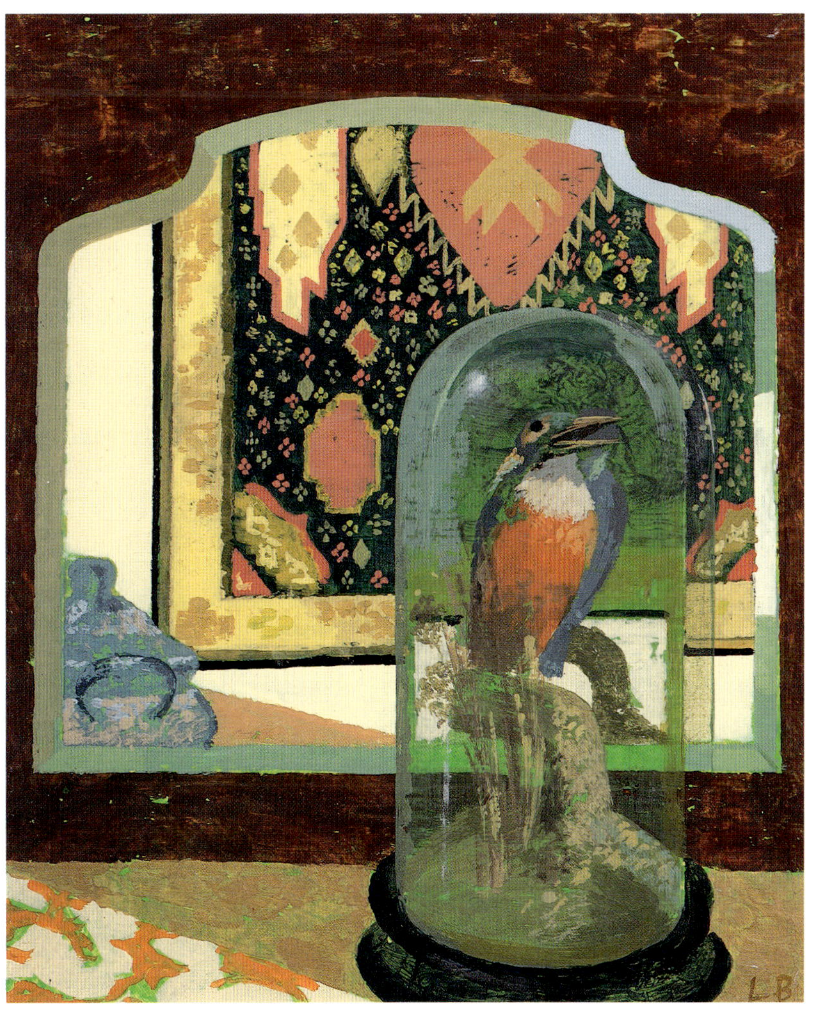

▷ **The impact of colour** *When Lionel Bulmer collected these objects together, colour was uppermost in his mind. Each item in the painting – including an exotic bird with vivid plumage, a patterned wall hanging and an eye-catching cloth – was chosen for the vivid contribution it made to the overall composition.*

include furniture, doors, windows, etc. In this way, a whole interior becomes a kind of still life, the study of a mass of objects relating to each other – a frozen moment in a room, perhaps. Even though the emphasis is on the objects themselves, the artist in this case would be concerned with the relationship of those objects not only to each other but also to their environment.

Conversely, a still life can be a microscopic part of a whole – the equivalent of viewing the subject through a magnifying glass. It might be a single flower or any other small object, enlarged so that every detail is visible.

Fruit, flowers and gearboxes

Jugs, jars, flowers and fruit are often associated with still-life painting, but an infinite range of objects can be gathered in. Natural forms such as shells and driftwood are fascinating subjects – and do not forget the mechanical world. Car parts and pieces of machinery are as exciting to one artist as a vase of flowers is to another.

Often the best still-life subjects are things that are so much part of our daily lives we have almost ceased to 'see' them. The still life gives them new meaning. Thus many of the objects we choose to paint are close to hand.

One of the most fruitful places to explore is the kitchen, as it is filled with an amazing array of shapes – probably why cooking utensils are among the most frequently painted subjects. Because they are so versatile, we turn to them again and again, and still find something fresh and interesting to paint. Some artists repeatedly paint the same item. It is not just a particular white jug or red ladle you are painting for the umpteenth time; it is an object that has a certain shape and colour, and that looks good in many arrangements.

PRACTICAL TIPS

Start simple and let this govern the choice of subject as well as your approach to painting. And be aware of the practical points that could cause hitches with even the simplest of choices: for instance, still-life objects do not always stay still – they can rot, droop and wilt.

The examples in this book range from very simple – a single piece of fruit – to quite complex arrangements. You too should begin with simple paintings and build up to more involved subjects as your skill develops, in a progression similar to the structure of this book.

In the pages that follow, a particular technique or aspect of still-life painting is demonstrated and then linked to a selected, appropriate subject. The subject for neutral colours, for instance, is a collection of shells. Complementary colours are then demonstrated, with oranges against a blue background.

You should adopt a similarly structured attitude, and make the subject matter work for you. In this way, you can decide on a theme before setting up the arrangement. If you want to use complementary colour, then choose your objects with this in mind. If you want to paint an arrangement of textures, then collect textured objects and nothing else. Work starts not with the first brushstroke but as you look around for something suitable to paint.

Despite the accessibility of objects for still-life painting, there are certain practical limitations which can be all too easily forgotten. Be aware of these from the outset and you will not waste time once you have started painting.

Food and flowers

If food, flowers or other perishable things are part of your still life, then you have to plan your work a little more carefully. Cut flowers can last several days, but they tend to open up in heat and light, and close as the light goes. They also droop and change position remarkably rapidly. These changes are not normally noticeable, but it is irritating when

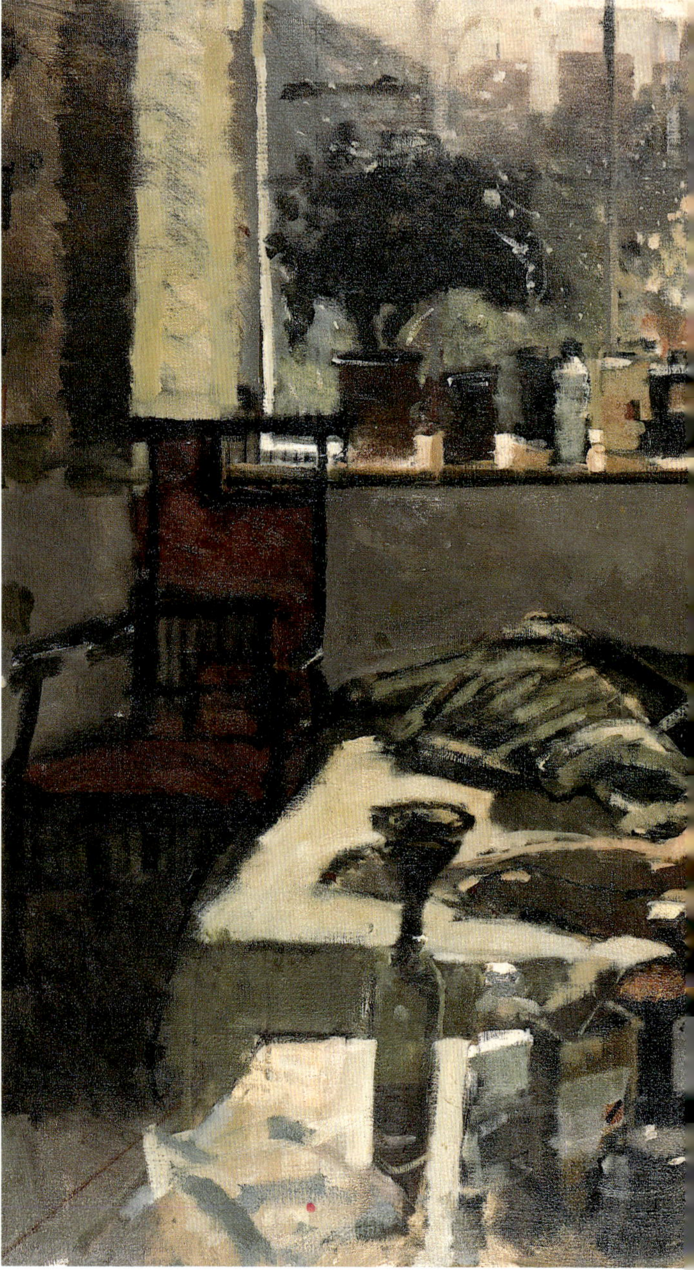

painting – you start with a closed tulip, for instance, only to find it has opened up and bent over a few hours later.

Painters sometimes replace wilting blooms with fresh ones. Others have been known to support the stems of the flowers with wire, but this is a fiddly business. Probably the most practical solution is to stick to potted flowers and plants, where change occurs much more slowly.

Food can also be tricky. Fish often starts as a favourite with still-life painters. Unfortunately, it is a particularly difficult subject, because it goes off

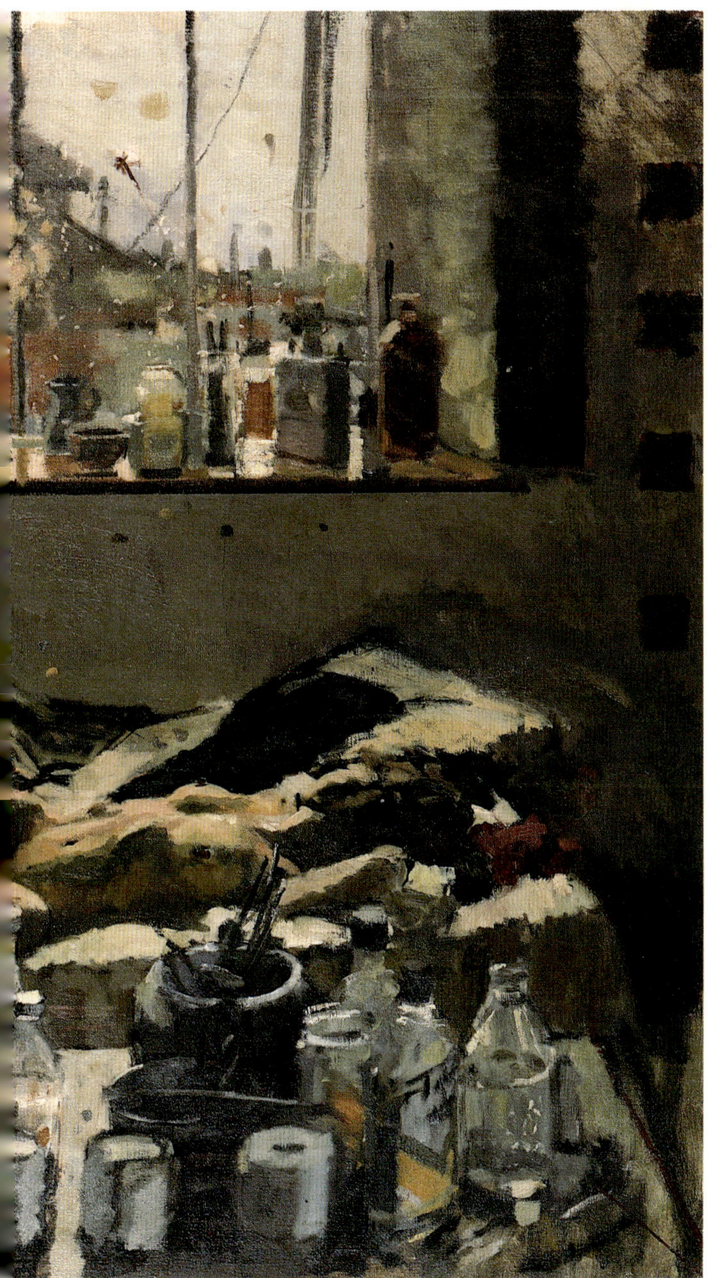

Continuity

If you have to remove part or all of your arrangement before you have finished work but intend to reassemble it at a later date, it is a good idea to mark the positions of the objects. Small pieces of masking tape adhere to cloth as well as to hard surfaces, and do not leave a mark.

If you do forget to mark the subject, your arrangement can be reassembled by referring to the painting. This takes patience. You will find it necessary to keep moving the objects, sometimes by a fraction of an inch. Do this, then keep walking back to the painting to check.

◁ **Still life with figure and landscape** *A truly 'combined' subject, the table scattered with bottles and jars dominates the foreground of this painting by Ken Howard. The viewer's eye is drawn back into the picture, first to the bed and reclining figure, then to the landscape – the view through the window.*

▽ **Composition and colour** *Jack Millar contrasts the strong, warm colours of this still-life arrangement with the cool lemons and greens of the view through the window. The window frame and the dark shape formed by the plate, vase and flower pot are important structural elements in the composition. Paint is applied as small dabs of pure colour.*

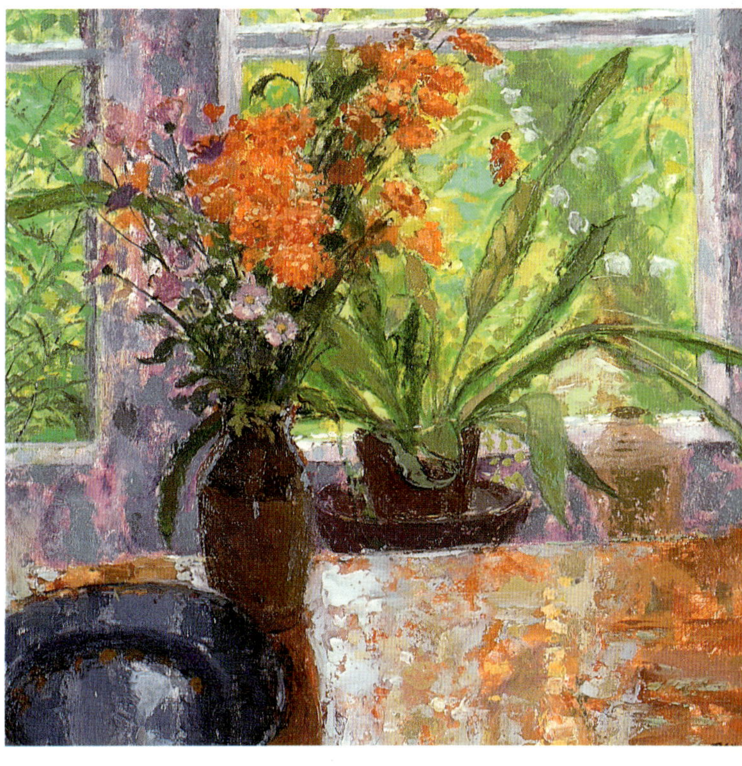

and starts to smell – very noticeably if you are closeted in the same room. You can stretch its painting-life by a day or two by putting it in the refrigerator between sessions, but this is obviously a temporary expedient. Fresh fish are very shiny, but their glossy surface and colours go dull after a short while. This can be remedied by frequent spraying with water or rubbing with oil.

Not all foods are so problematic. Bread and other baked items have to be fresh only if you want to eat them! For a painting, they can go rock-hard without changing appearance.

Before you paint

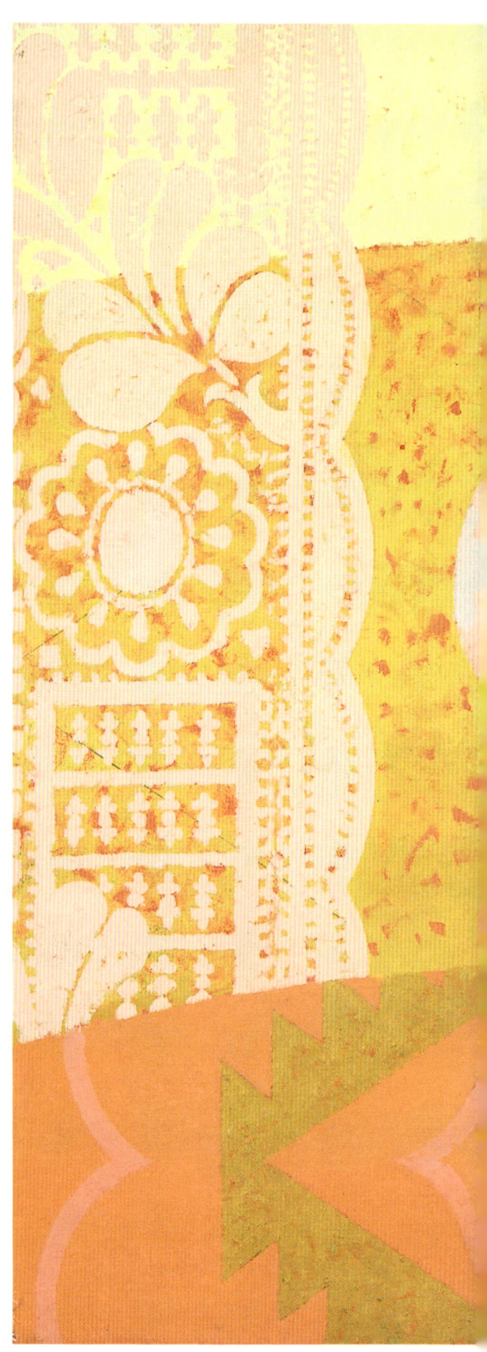

WHEN YOU PAINT or photograph a landscape, you automatically 'select' an area which will be portrayed. This is known as the composition and is a vital part of landscape art. You cannot change the landscape in front of you, although you can simplify it and change it in the painting. Still life, however, grants you enormous freedom. The composition is actually created by the artist before painting starts. Even pictures which depict an apparently accidental array of objects have often been carefully arranged.

This arrangement of objects is inseparable from the painting process. You are constantly thinking about how you will translate the composition into paint. Other important things need consideration before you apply the paint. This chapter tells you how to arrange your objects. It analyses the importance of composition, using photographs of objects set up in different ways and with different emphases, taking care not to lay down rigid rules but pointing out possibilities. The chapter also discusses lighting. It covers the preliminary process of sketching and how to enlarge sketches into full-sized compositions ready for painting. Perspective – an aspect which many do not expect to associate with still life – is considered as well.

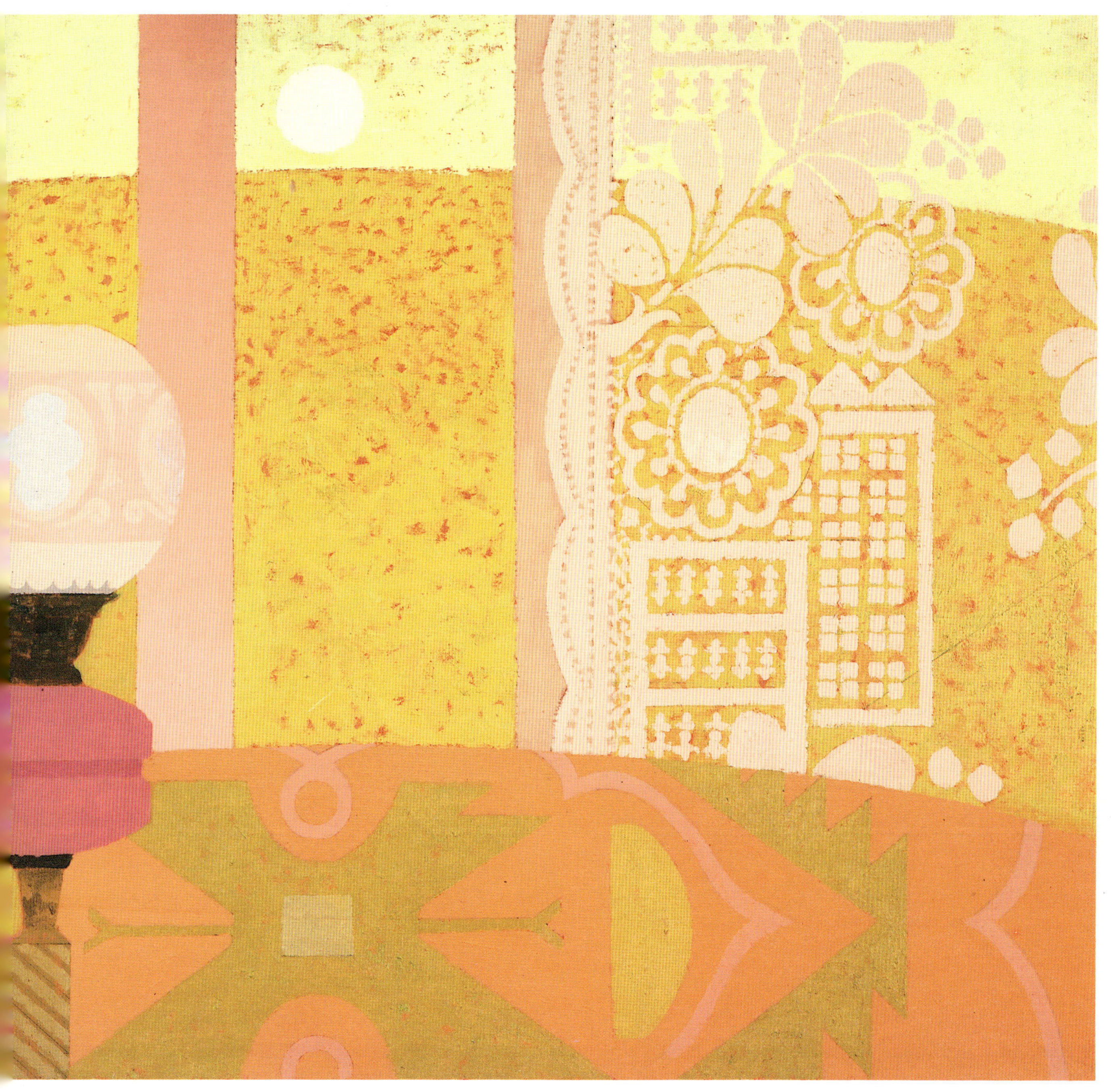

Lionel Bulmer interprets the subject
here in a creative and personal way,
with emphasis on both the colour
and pattern. The subject is handled
in a stylized rather than a literal
manner, with deliberately flattened
perspective and heightened colours.

ARRANGING YOUR SUBJECT

Composition is a vital part of a picture, and the arrangement of objects in a still life is a vital part of the composition. If you give no attention to this, the picture could end up dull no matter how well it is painted. In still life more than in any other sort of painting you are in control of what you are painting, and it is a pity to waste this opportunity.

Beware, however, of overdoing this aspect. Your subject may be quite simple – a few kitchen utensils or some pieces of fruit, perhaps. Even so, the possibilities are limitless, and you could end up taking more time to arrange the objects than to paint the actual picture. You need to be decisive as well as creative.

One good idea: tip all the pieces haphazardly on to a surface and take it from there. Move the objects around until you have an arrangement of shapes, colour, tone and texture you like the look of. Then start work before you lose confidence in the result.

There are no rules about still-life arrangements. You can see simply by looking at a subject whether or not it appears crowded, clumsy or contrived. However, as a general guide, objects look better if they are displayed in a natural manner, and for this reason geometric or symmetrical arrangements are usually best avoided – unless that is the particular effect you are seeking to create in the picture.

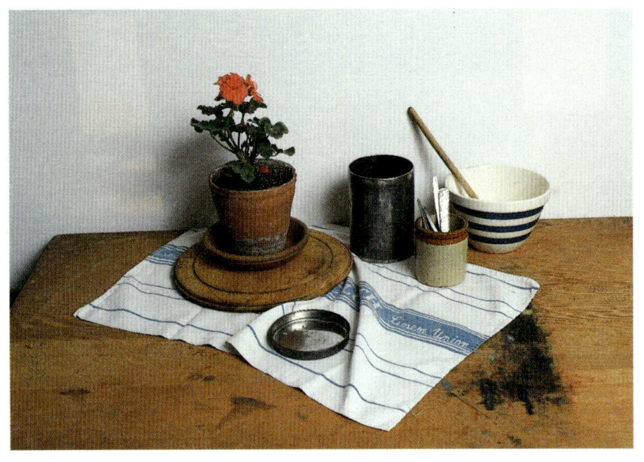

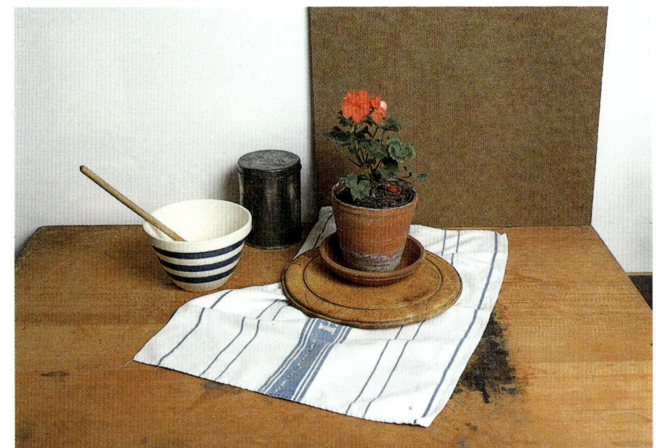

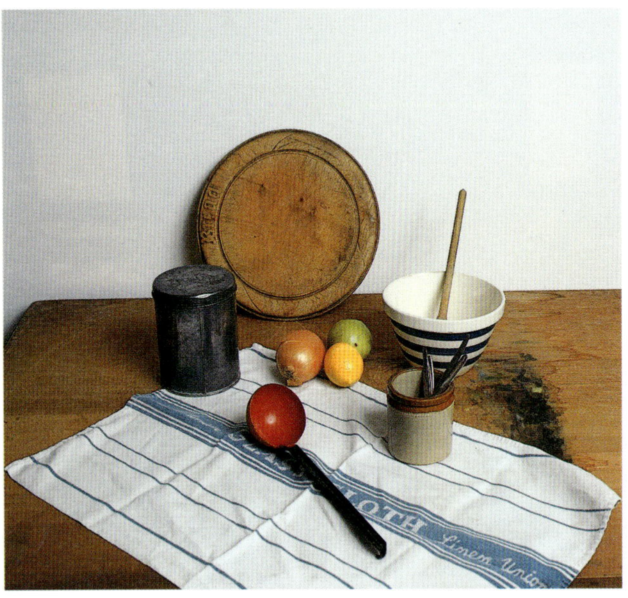

△ ◁ All the objects are arranged in a central cluster, with the white shape of the tea towel containing most of the darker shapes. There is no discordant element to take the viewer's attention away from the main group. The blue stripe leads the eye into the centre of the arrangement.

△ Again, the objects are arranged in a central cluster, but the artist has divided the background into two contrasting shapes – dark and light. This device breaks up the horizontal symmetry of the arrangement and provides a choice of background for the different objects.

◁ Here the white cloth is taken off the bottom edge of the arrangement, with the stripe and ladle handle positioned to lead the eye inwards towards the centre of the arrangement. The circular shape of the breadboard cuts into the white background, so transforming a blank wall into a positive shape in its own right.

The illustrations on this page show a selection of objects arranged in different ways, any one of which would be suitable for painting. The artist started off with a collection of kitchen items and laid them out in various ways. In some arrangements, everything is clustered in the centre; in others, one or more of the objects is only partially visible, with the rest being taken deliberately outside the picture area. Sometimes the artist uses all the objects; at other times certain things are discarded in order to simplify the subject.

Contrast and colour

As a general rule, the more variety you can include, the more interesting the subject will be. A mixture of light and dark objects, for instance, gives a greater tonal contrast to the painting than a selection of things which are all either light, dark or medium-toned. This is why the tea towel here is so important. The artist uses it as a stark white shape to break up areas of darker tones, either in the wooden table top or in the background.

The colours of the objects themselves are also important. If they are all warm reds and browns, for instance, the painting could be boring. As soon as you introduce a touch of blue or another cool colour – as the artist has done here with the stripes in the tea towel and the blue on the pudding basin – the whole arrangement comes to life.

Shape and texture

Inevitably, any subject is made up of lots of different shapes – including the shape of the table top and the shape, or shapes, of the background. You can control and change all these by moving objects around, placing one in front of another, altering the distance between each one and so on.

You can change the background by dividing this into two or more shapes, as you can see from the photograph, or by breaking up a bland expanse of background with a strong shape, such as the round breadboard illustrated.

A variety of shapes and textures usually makes for a more interesting still life and certainly gives you greater scope when you are putting the subject together. These kitchen utensils include angular, cylindrical and elliptical shapes, surface textures are reflective metal and porcelain, matt wood, soft fabric and the irregular natural surfaces of the fruit and foliage.

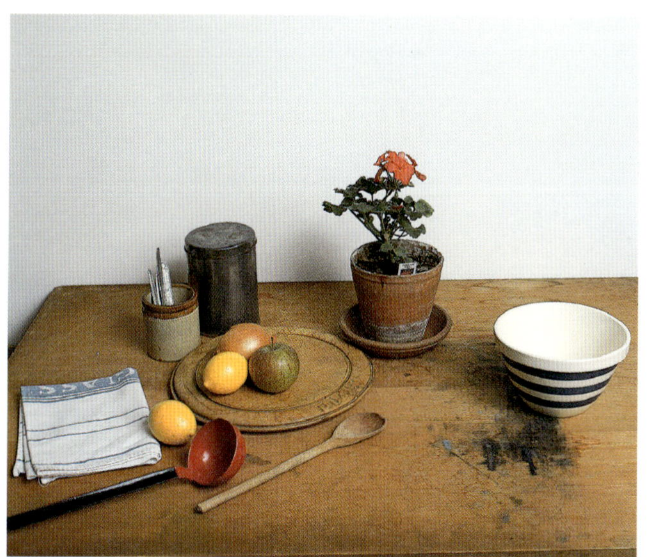

△ *The objects are spaced further apart. A scattered arrangement can sometimes isolate the objects and produce a bitty composition, but here the arrangement is held together visually by the strong diagonal movement of shapes from the bottom left-hand corner which leads the eye firmly into the centre of the composition.*

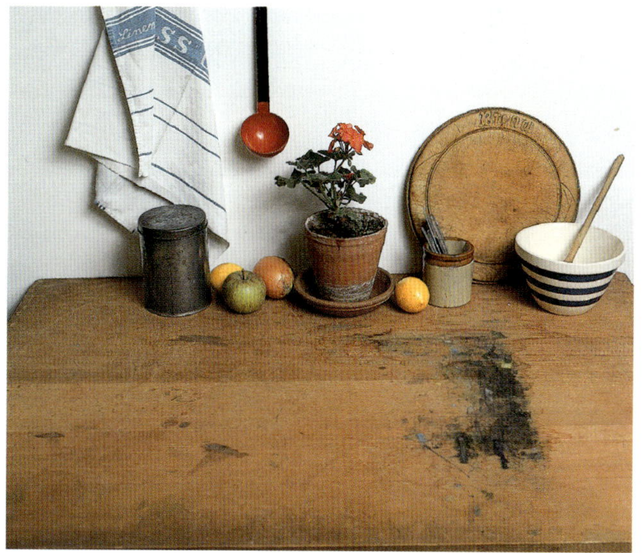

△ *Here the artist has created an unusual horizontal arrangement which obliterates the straight dividing line between the white background and the table top. Because there is very little sense of space in a single row of objects, the artist has created space by including a lot of empty foreground in the composition.*

SCALE AND PROPORTION

You have arranged the pieces and the background, but there is another important factor to consider when planning your composition, and that is the canvas itself.

Choosing a shape

The shape of your canvas is part of the composition. A rectangle is the most popular, because it is versatile and easy on the eye. You can also choose whether you want to use the rectangle vertically or horizontally, and this choice depends on the subject and how you want to depict it.

Bought canvases generally come in standard rectangular sizes, but if you stretch your own and buy your own stretcher pieces (see pages 32–3), the scope is wider. It allows you to make square or exaggeratedly long rectangles to suit your exact requirements.

The painting on this page was done on a bought, standard, rectangular canvas which suits the subject very well as the artist has painted it. But you can see from the illustration that the same subject could be treated in many equally interesting ways, simply by working on a different shape.

Big or small?

Most artists develop a preference for painting on a particular scale, and this need not necessarily be dictated by the size of the subject itself. One painter will feel comfortable working on a tiny canvas, even when painting comparatively large objects, such as giant plants or pieces of furniture. Another will take a small single item, such as a shell, and choose to paint it on a gigantic scale with large brushes in order to explore and emphasize the particular forms and patterns within the subject. It is very much a matter of personal taste.

The newcomer to still life, however, will probably find it easier to avoid extremes, at least initially. Most of the demonstrations for this book were painted on canvases measuring from 16 × 12 inches (40 × 30 cm) to 36 × 24 inches (90 × 60 cm), and certainly anything between these sizes is manageable and quite portable. Later you may want to experiment with larger or smaller paintings. Your work can only benefit from trying out new dimensions.

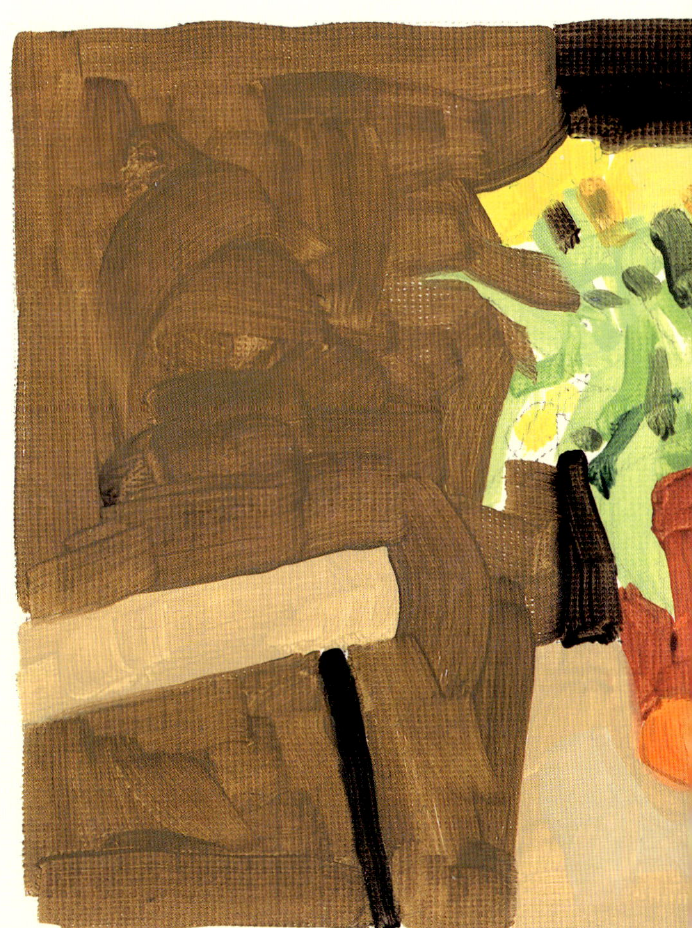

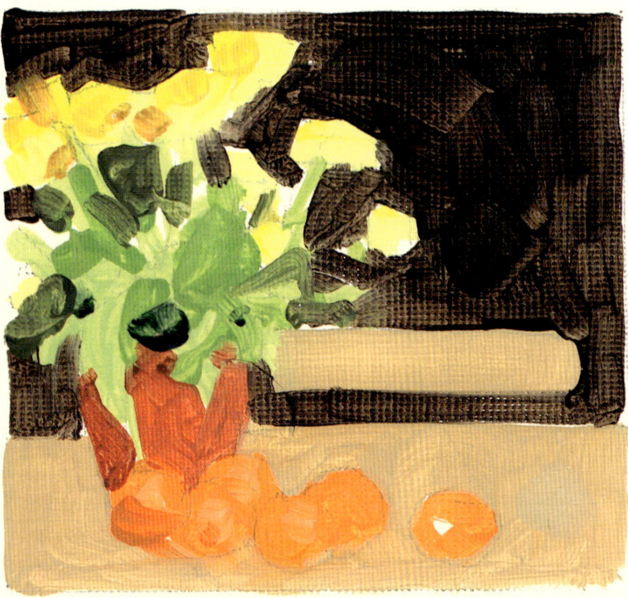

Infinite alternatives   *As you can see from these thumbnail sketches, there is no single 'correct' way to compose a picture. These sketches show just a few of an almost infinite number of possibilities. Your painting may be rectangular or square, upright or horizontal; the subject can be painted in its entirety, or you may decide on a close-up, using just one part of the subject.*

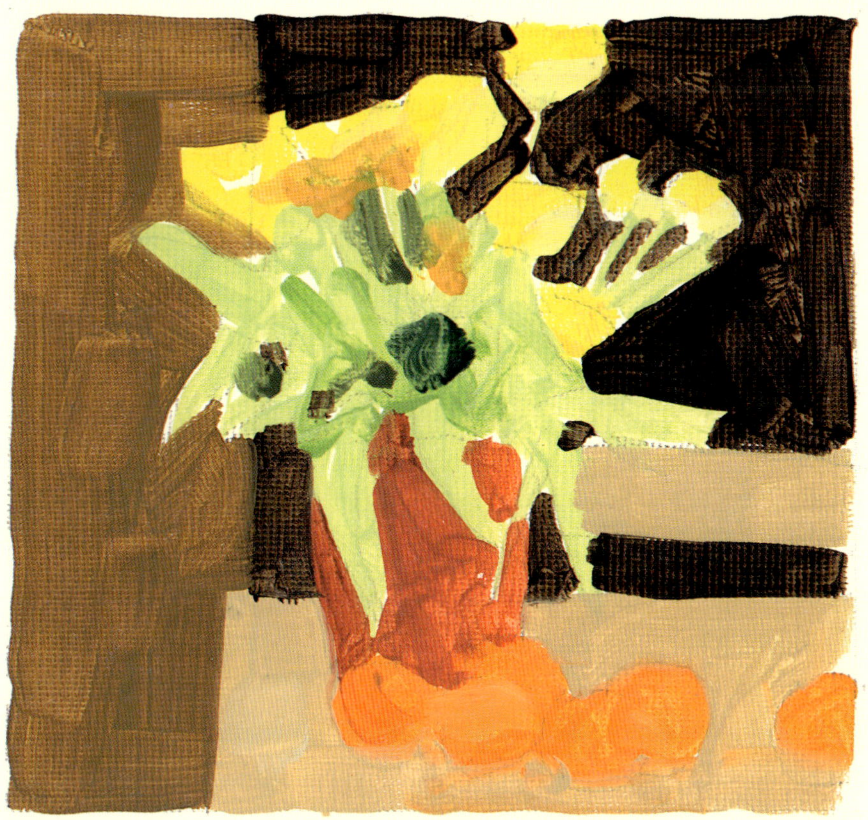

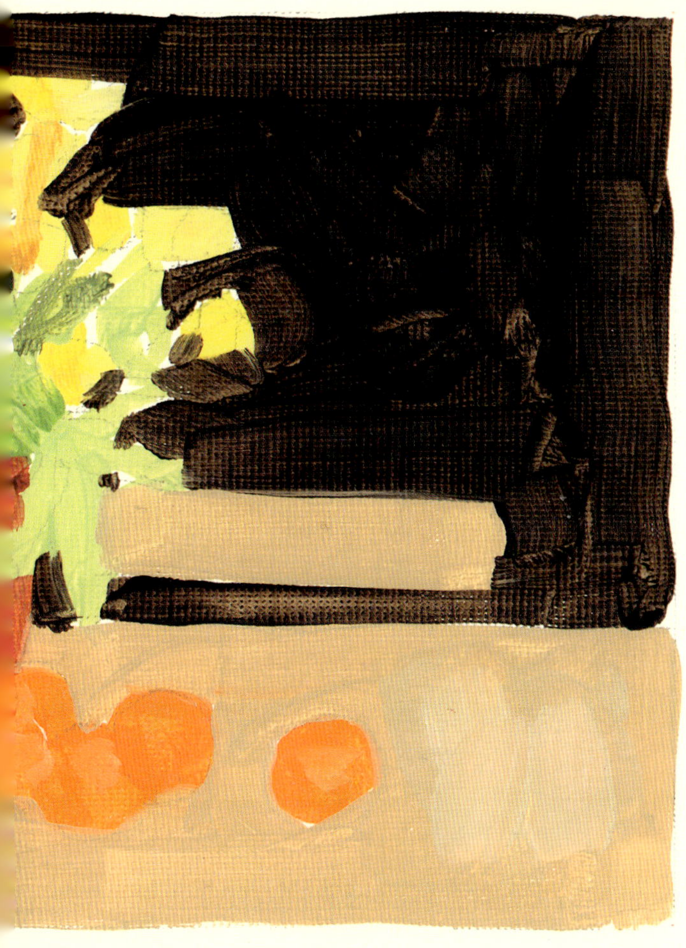

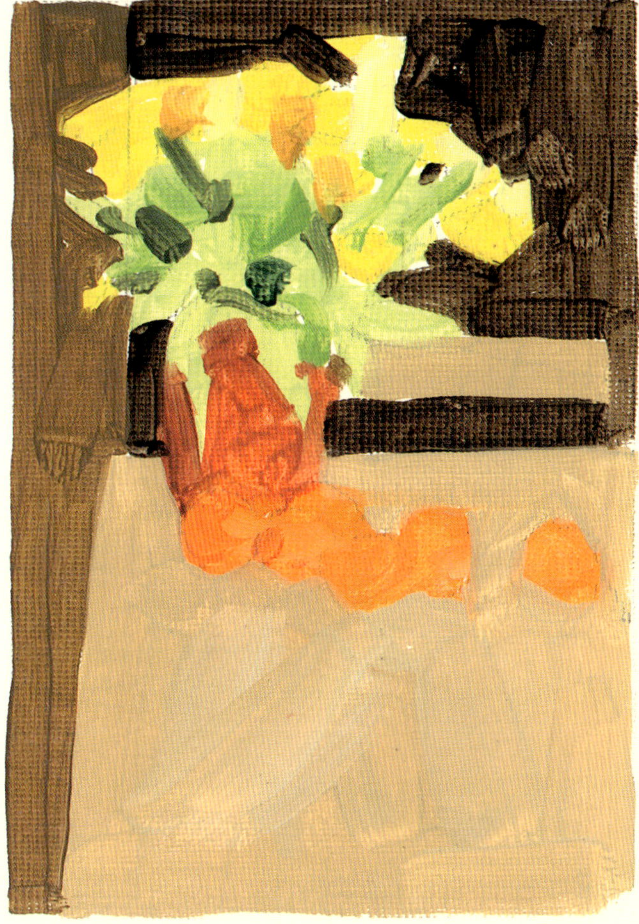

LIGHT SOURCES

A still-life subject can be totally transformed by a changing source of light or type of lighting. Those who have already tried to paint by natural light alone will have found to their irritation that sunlight is inconsistent. Daylight changes constantly – disappearing altogether just when you are in the middle of a particularly important piece of work.

One of the great advantages of still-life subjects is that they are stationary and unchanging. Flowers and food do gradually deteriorate, but even so they remain paintable for a reasonable length of time. This stability allows you to paint at odd times of the day or night if that is the only time available. But this advantage is lost if you are totally dependent on the vagaries of natural light.

With still life more than any other subject, therefore, it is well worth paying some attention to lighting, both for your own convenience and for getting the best from the subject.

Lighting the subject
No electric lamp is exactly the same as daylight, but 'daylight' bulbs produce a reasonably similar effect which at least has the advantage of consistency.

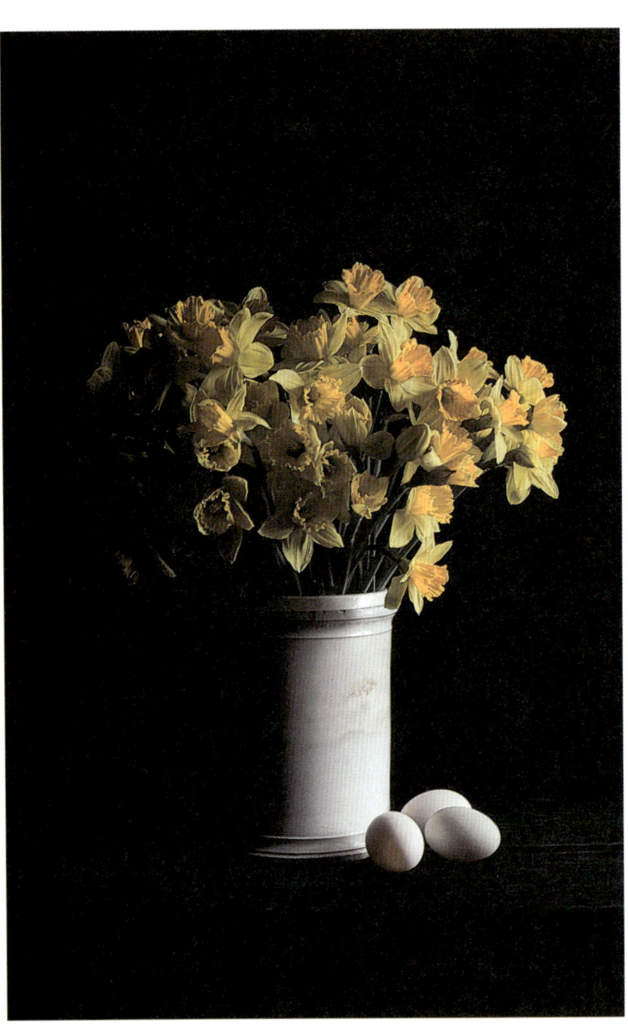

Transparent or translucent objects are less affected by the direction of light than opaque objects. These four illustrations show a still-life arrangement illuminated from different directions.

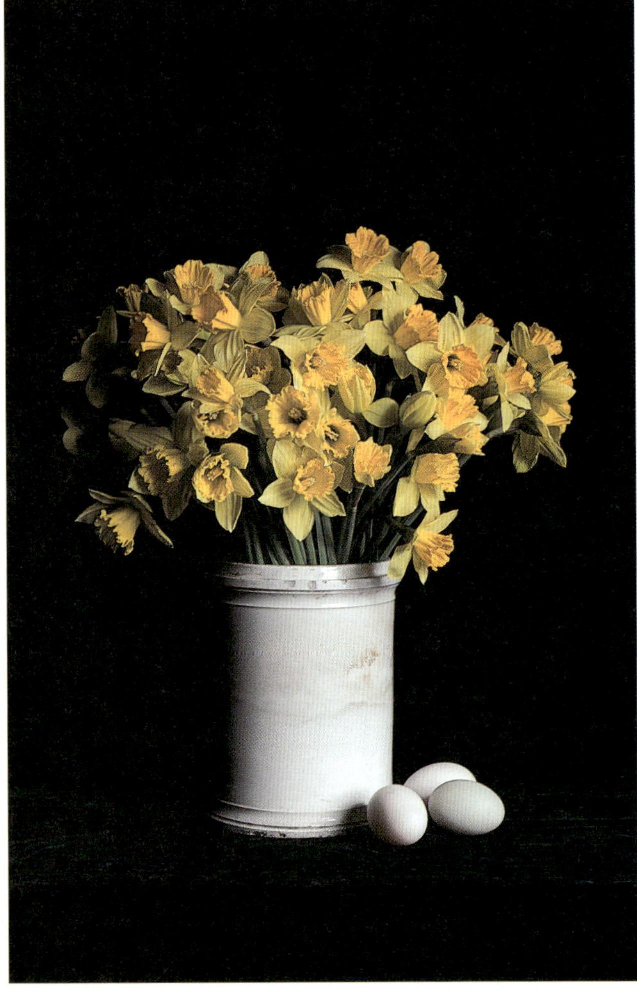

◁△ *Side-lit*
△ *Two-thirds side-lit*

These are available at art shops and most electrical shops, and can be used to replace natural light totally or partially. If you like to paint through the day and into the evening, a daylight bulb near the window can take over when the sun goes down without changing the light source and without affecting the shadows and highlights on the subject.

Many artists are happy to use electric lighting to illuminate their subject, preferring the warm tones of an indoor lamp to the cooler ones of natural light. Use an ordinary household lamp, spotlights or any other type of available lighting, arranging these and directing the light to suit the subject.

With spotlights and other direct lighting it is possible to change the colour emphasis and atmos-phere of a subject by placing a tinted filter over the bulb. The filter colour should not be too dramatic, but a pale pink or amber, for instance, can saturate your still life with a warm glow which will affect the overall painting.

Light to work in
Apart from lighting the subject, you also need a good source of light in which to work. Colours look completely different when seen in different lights, so if you start work in daylight you cannot easily change to electric lighting without affecting the colours in the painting. Again, a daylight lamp is a useful stand-by and will ensure colour continuity throughout the picture.

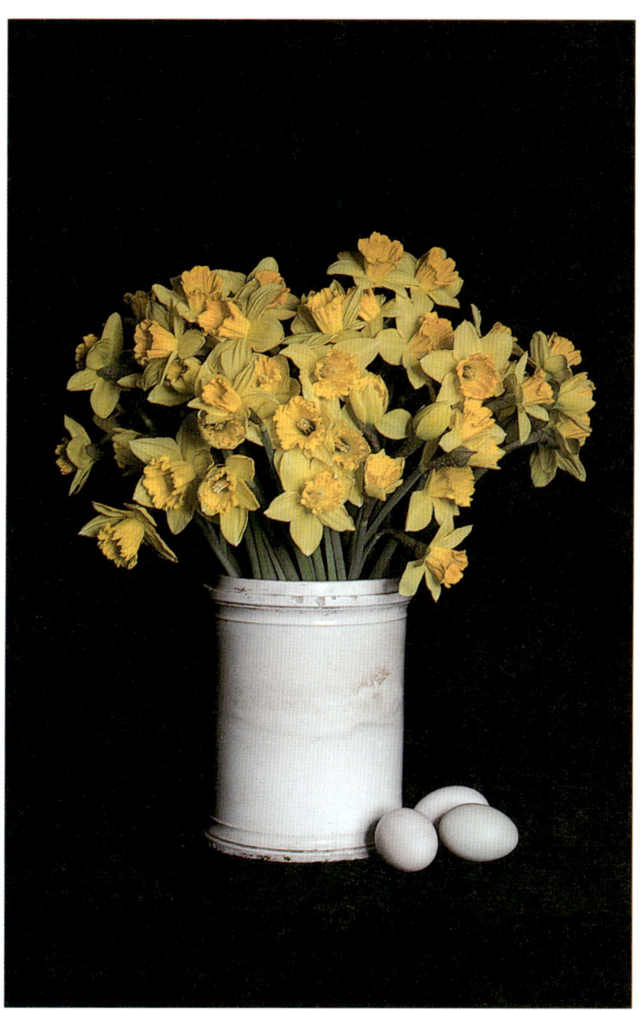

△ *Front-lit*

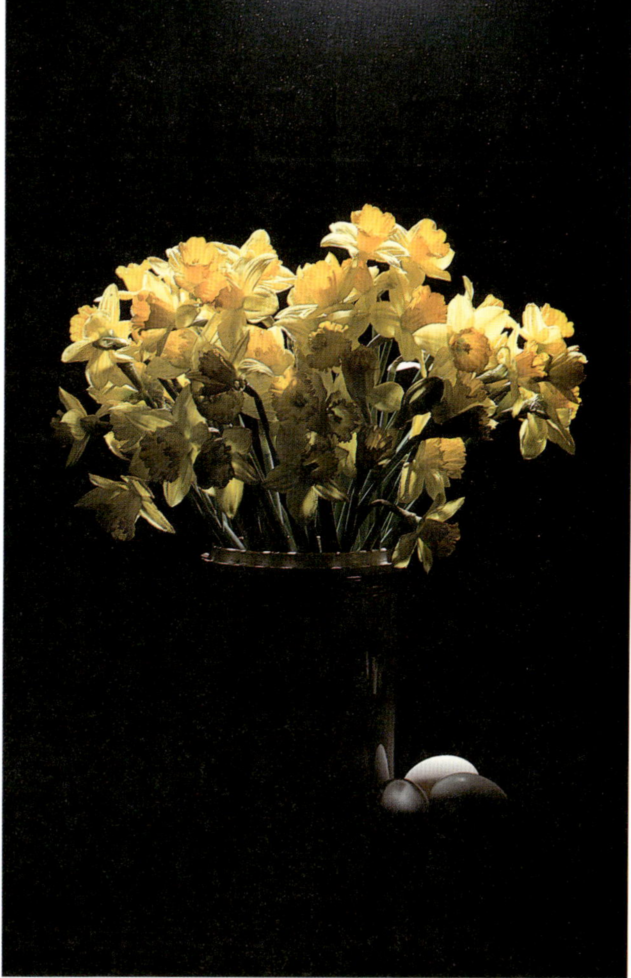

△ *Back-lit*

SKETCHES

There is more than one way of looking at a still life, and the best way to explore the variety of possibilities is to make sketches of the arrangement before starting to paint. This forces you to look for new things in the subject and to consider it from a number of different aspects and angles.

Ways of seeing
Walk around your still-life subject. You may find it is more interesting from the side than from the front. The composition might also look better from above or below, so experiment with your elevation. Keep an open mind at this stage, and do not be afraid to try out new ideas.

Our artist made three sketches of the still-life arrangement shown here, looking at the subject from various angles and exploring different elements and even materials. Each sketch shows the subject in a new or unusual light. Each one also tends to emphasize a different aspect of the subject, which may or may not be included in the final painting. They have served to broaden the artist's choice.

Sketching materials
Pen and wash proved the ideal method for capturing the tonal contrasts in the composition. A pencil sketch concentrates on the arrangement of both the various shapes within the subject and the incidental shapes these create in the background. Another sketch, done with graphite, shows the subject from above, with the artist looking down at the objects on the table top.

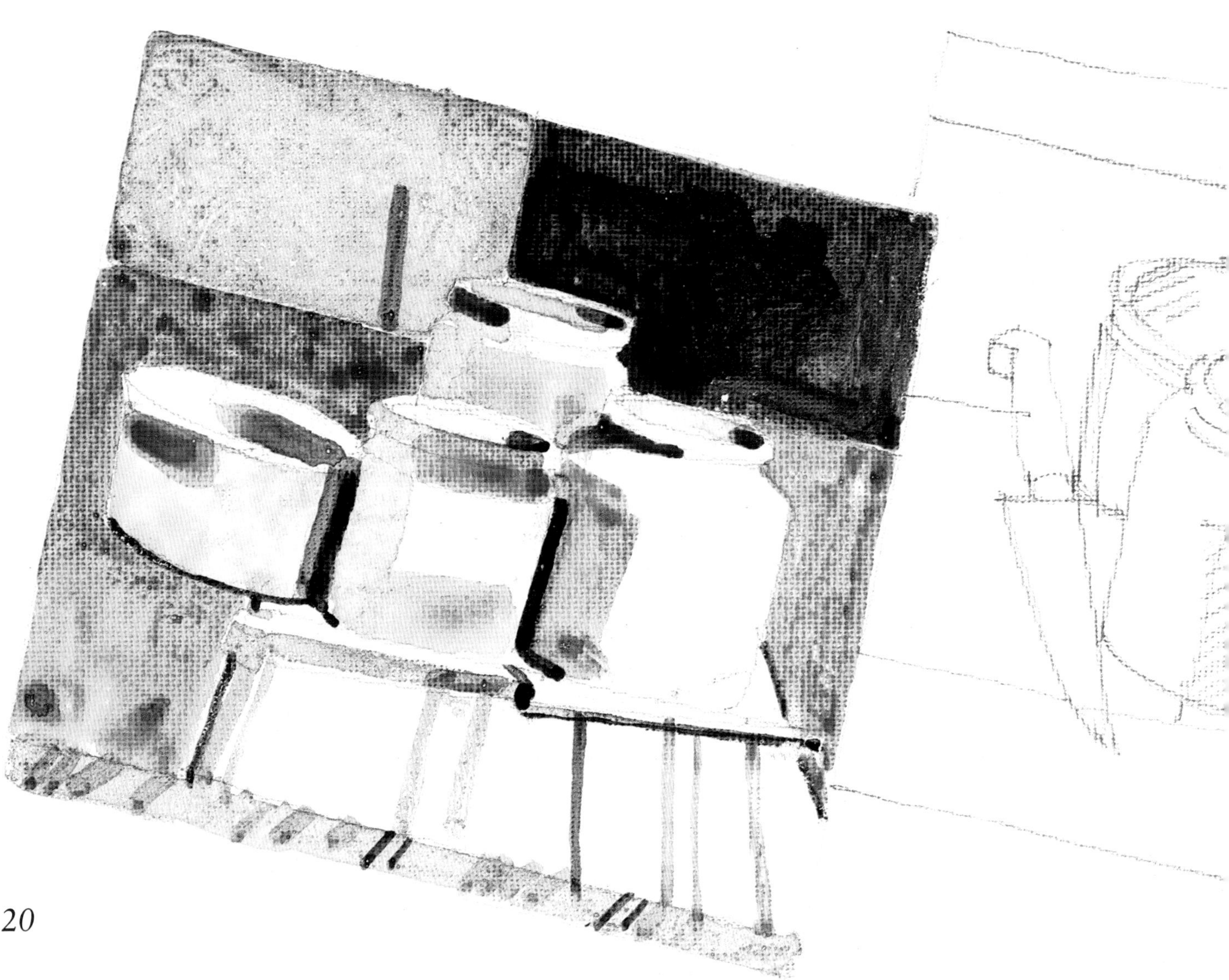

Almost any drawing or writing tool can be used for sketching – anything, in fact, that will make a mark. Pencils, ballpoints and fountain pens are all useful, and the sorts of thing we can lay our hands on at a moment's notice. Felt-tips, typewriter correction fluid and highlighter pens are among the more unlikely materials that have found their way into sketchbooks.

Lively sketches
You will probably be surprised at how good your rough sketches look. After all, they were done so quickly, and without any real thought or planning! Actually, it is this very lack of planning that makes sketches look so fresh and lively. The next step is to make sure you retain this spontaneity when you start to paint.

Left to right *Pen and wash, drawing pencil, graphite stick.*

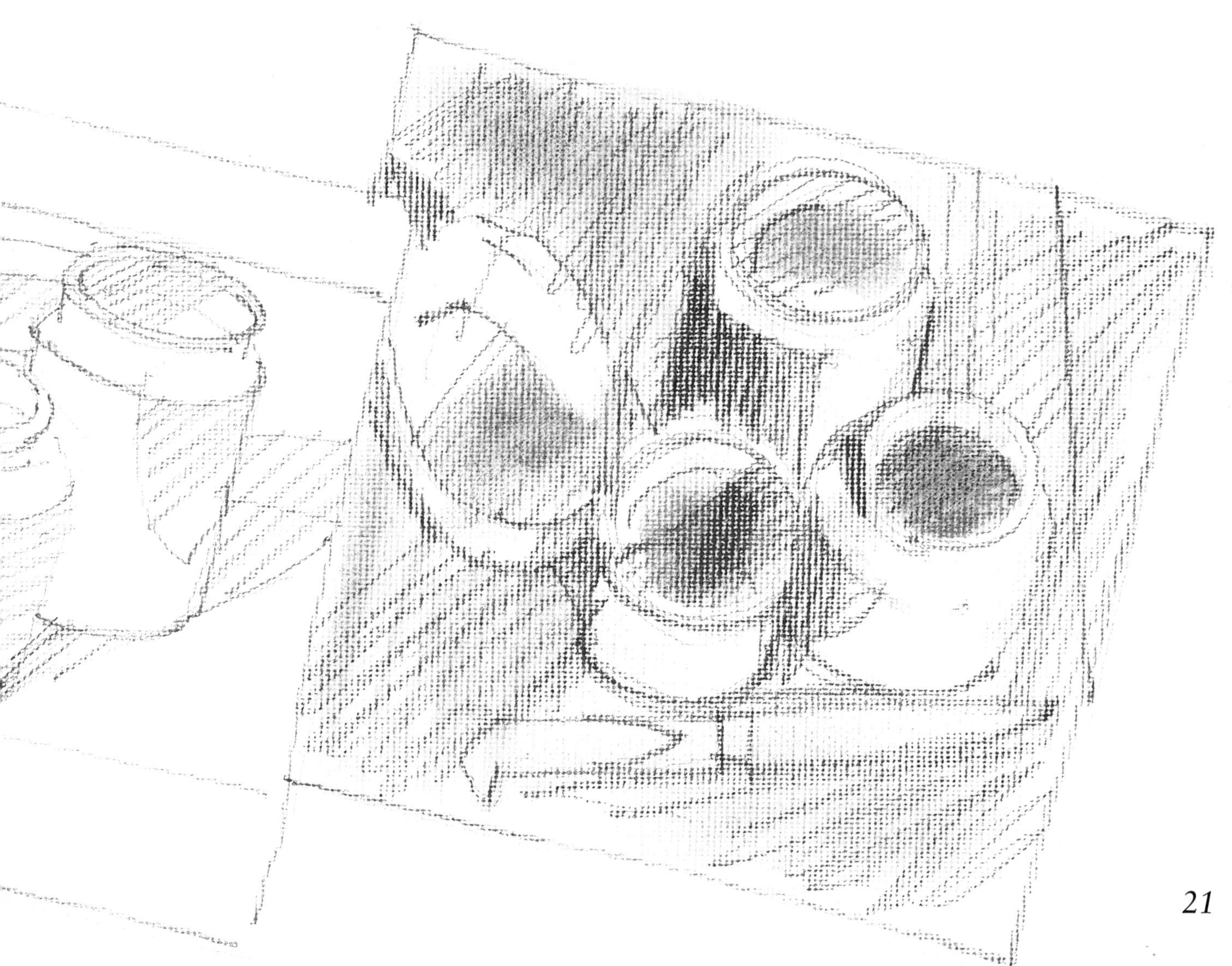

FROM SKETCH TO CANVAS

If we are going to keep our painting as fresh as a sketch, let us consider for a moment how we worked when sketching, so that we can capture the vitality that finished paintings sometimes lack. If the sketches did look lively, ask yourself why they were so unselfconscious. Perhaps it was because the sketches were a means to an end rather than the end itself. In other words, it did not matter whether they looked good, as long as they did the job. The lines, therefore, were confident and the drawing flowing and strong.

When confronted with a pristinely white canvas, however, the situation changes completely. Because this is the 'real' thing, it seems somehow important to be extra careful and to avoid making a mistake. Sadly, this caution often proves to be the biggest mistake of all, because the initial stage is that of transferring and enlarging a small sketch on to a bigger canvas. If the result is a timid drawing, the painting can look stilted from the outset.

Freehand drawing

Experienced artists often draw directly on to the canvas, referring to the sketch as they draw. Often they deliberately use paint or a thick stick of charcoal to avoid making the drawing too tight. They seek to work in the same free manner on the larger drawing as they did on the original sketch.

For the beginner, an over-cautious approach can lead to the enlarged drawing being too small in relation to the canvas, resulting in too much empty space around the subject. The remedy is to treat these background areas as actual shapes, paying as much attention to them as you do to the rest of the subject. These important background areas are often referred to as 'negative shapes', and there is more about them on pages 56–7.

It takes confidence and practice to make a freehand drawing directly on to the canvas in this way. But if you choose chunky charcoal or oil pastel, and refer frequently to your sketch as you draw, it is quite possible to copy and enlarge the

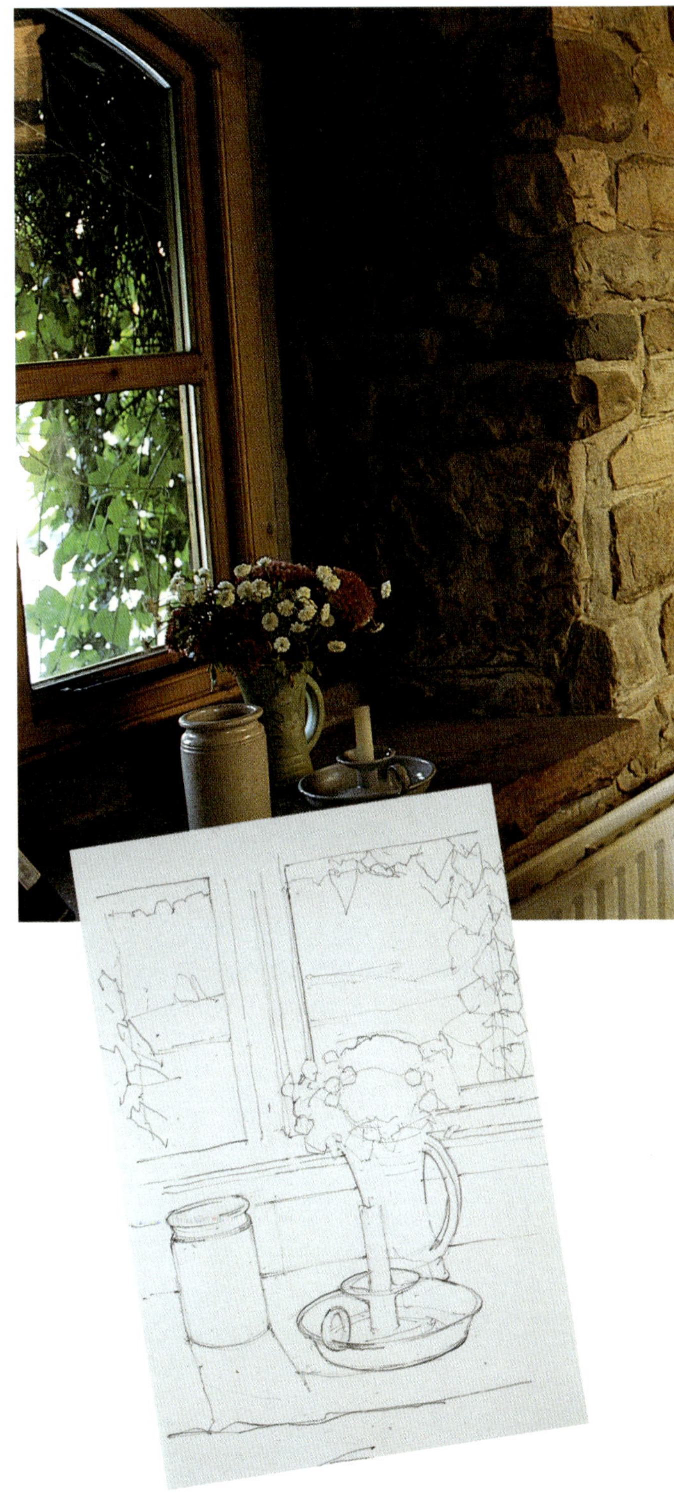

△ △ **1** *Instead of painting directly on to the canvas, the artist starts by sketching the subject. In this case, several sketches were made before a satisfactory composition was decided on for the eventual painting.*

△ **2** *The selected sketch may need strengthening so that the lines are clear enough to be transferred by copying on to the canvas painting support.*

image without losing any of the freshness of the original sketch.

Using a grid

A more accurate method of transferring the sketched image on to a canvas is to use a grid. The grid should divide the canvas into a number of equal squares or rectangles. A similar, smaller grid is drawn on to the area of the sketch to be enlarged. The image can then be copied section by section on to the canvas. It is important that the two grids are proportionately equal, otherwise the enlarged drawing will be distorted.

As with freehand drawing, it is easy to be over-cautious when transferring marks on to a larger canvas. It is still important to draw with decisive, confident strokes. And these are easier to achieve if you work with a chunky medium that encourages you to draw boldly.

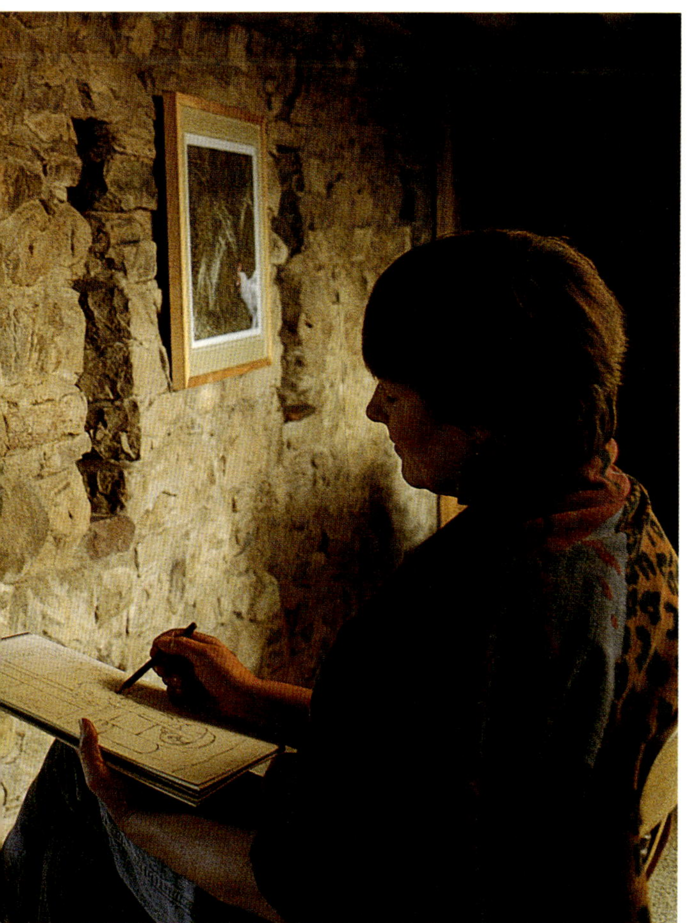

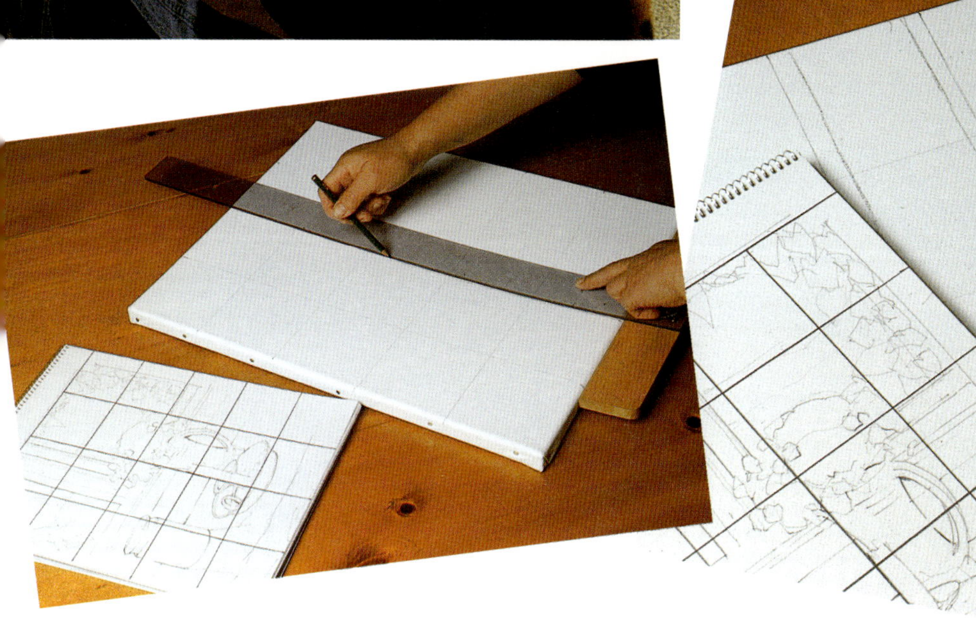

△ **3** *Using a ruler and pencil, the artist divides the larger canvas into a grid of equal sections. These may be square or rectangular, depending on the proportion of the canvas (in this case the canvas divides conveniently into twenty squares). A similar, proportionately smaller grid is also drawn on to the sketch.*

△ **4** *Using the sketch as a reference, the artist then copies and enlarges the sketched image on to the canvas. The image is thus transferred section by section, with each section being accurately and proportionately reproduced on to the larger-scale support.*

THE IMPORTANT DRAWING

As with any subject, the still life must usually be drawn on to the canvas accurately before you can start to paint. True, some artists paint without making an initial outline drawing; they begin by blocking in areas of tone and colour without bothering about a line drawing. In these cases, the first stage of blocked-in colour is itself a sort of 'drawing', with the paint being applied thinly so that overpainting, changes and corrections are easy.

Generally, however, the first marks on the canvas will be a line drawing. It is important to remember that this drawing should be as minimal as possible – merely a guide to establish the subject on the canvas. The rest you can do with colour and a brush. There is absolutely no point in putting a lot of detail into the drawing, because this will be completely lost when you come to start painting.

The basic forms

If you look carefully, you will notice that most still-life subjects are composed mainly of simple geometric forms. Your drawing need do no more than establish these fundamentals on the canvas.

As you can see here, the first stage is to simplify each object as a very basic structure. The plate is basically an ellipse; the jug, a cylinder with an elliptical top; the book, a cube; and so on.

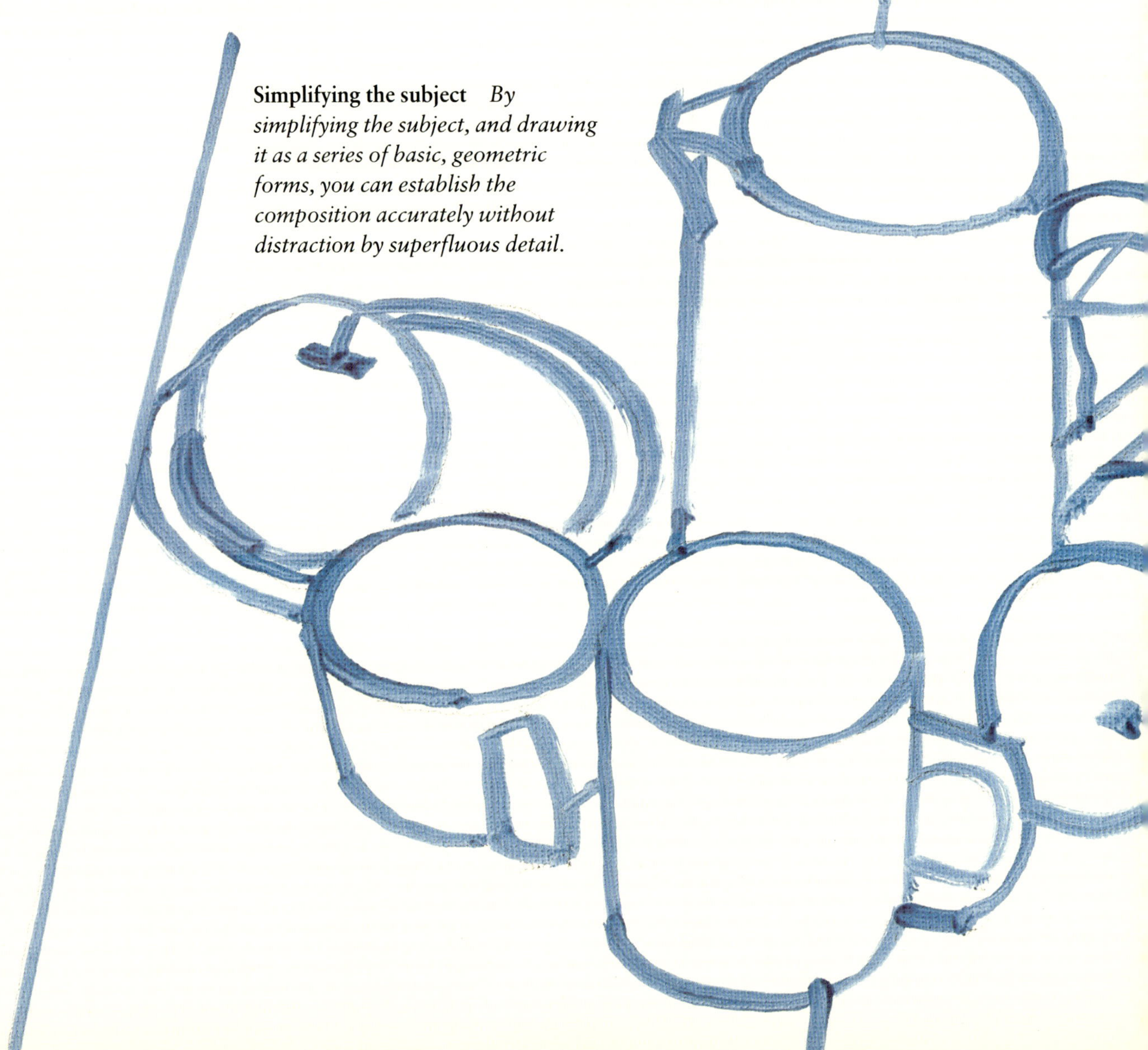

Simplifying the subject *By simplifying the subject, and drawing it as a series of basic, geometric forms, you can establish the composition accurately without distraction by superfluous detail.*

All these are particularly easy to simplify; but quite complicated structures, such as plants and other irregular natural forms, can also be broken down into a single, simple form or – occasionally – a series of simple forms. In fact, every item you will ever paint in a still life (or any other type of picture) can be treated in exactly the same way: it can be simplified.

Drawing ellipses

When looking at a flat, round object from the side, what you see is an elongated, oval shape, or an ellipse. In still-life subjects, ellipses occur time and time again – in bowls, jugs, plates, circular table-tops, mats and many other objects. They are not especially difficult to draw, but when drawn badly they are immediately noticeable and can spoil an otherwise successful painting.

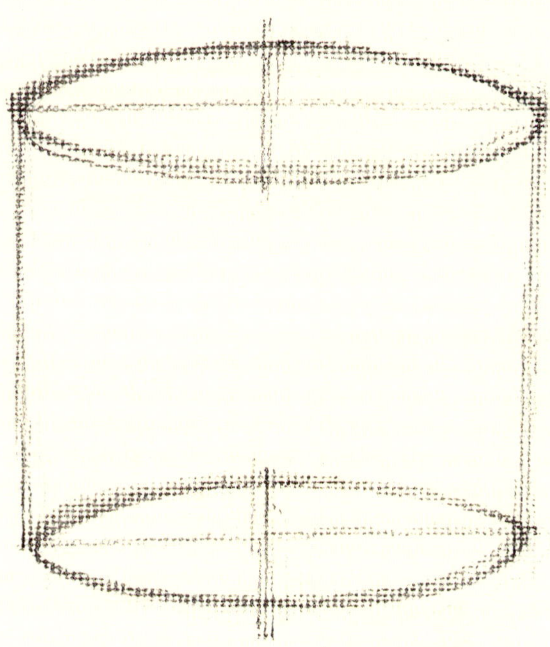

An ellipse can be drawn with the help of two construction lines, dividing the shape vertically and horizontally.

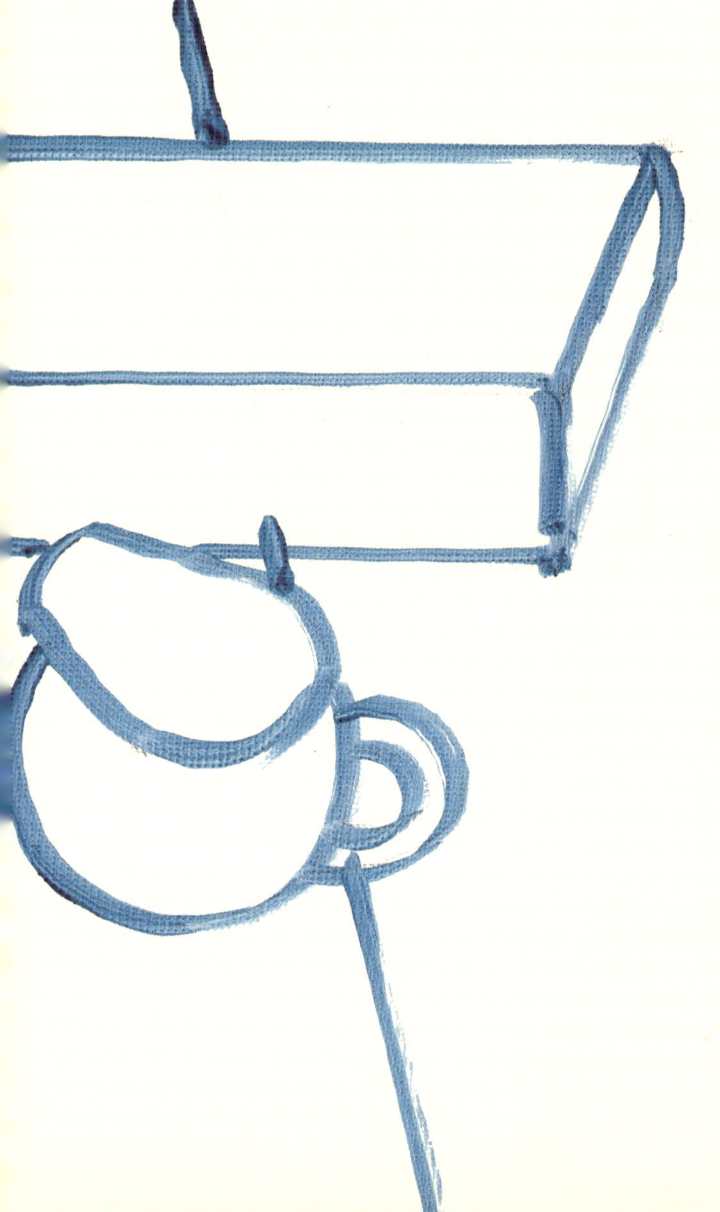

Therefore, it is well worth coming to terms with the ellipse.

The first thing to remember is that a true ellipse is symmetrical if it is divided vertically. If you draw a vertical line through its centre, the two halves become identical mirror-images.

If you draw a horizontal line through an ellipse, however, the two halves are not quite the same. You will notice that the top section is rather smaller than the bottom section, as well as being a slightly different shape. This is because the top section represents the part of the circle that is furthest away from the viewer's eye, and it therefore looks smaller as it recedes into the distance.

All this may sound rather complicated, but if you tackle the problem as the artist has done in the drawing here, using construction lines to help you with the rounded shapes, then an ellipse is actually quite straightforward. With practice, you will draw ellipses easily and automatically, without needing the structure lines at all.

PERSPECTIVE

When you paint three-dimensional objects on a flat canvas, you are actually creating the illusion of space and distance on a two-dimensional surface. Anything that contradicts this illusion will destroy the effect you are trying to create.

The crucial element in creating a special painting is accurate linear perspective: the idea that lines on the same plane will eventually meet at an imaginary point on the horizon – the 'vanishing point'. If they do not do so, the space in the painting will be distorted and look wrong.

Most of us are familiar with perspective diagrams showing streets or railway tracks disappearing as they converge. Consequently, we tend to associate perspective with landscape painting and forget that it is equally present in all other subjects.

Incidentally, we should also bear in mind the fact that the term 'horizon', as used by many artists, can be slightly misleading, because it actually refers to the eye level of the viewer rather than to any natural line. Thus the 'horizon' of a still-life painting is an imaginary line running at the same level as your eyes when you are in your working position.

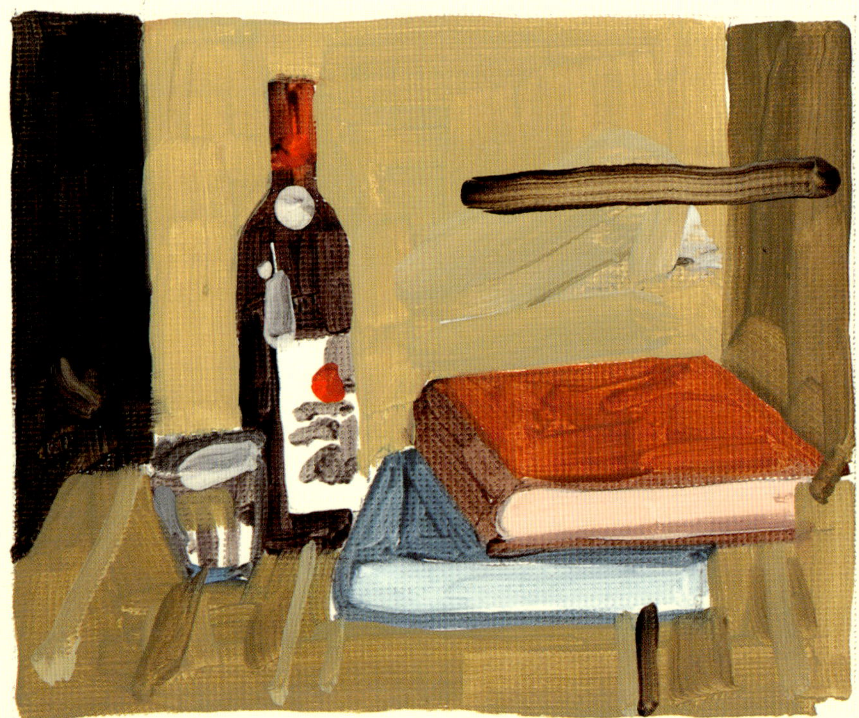

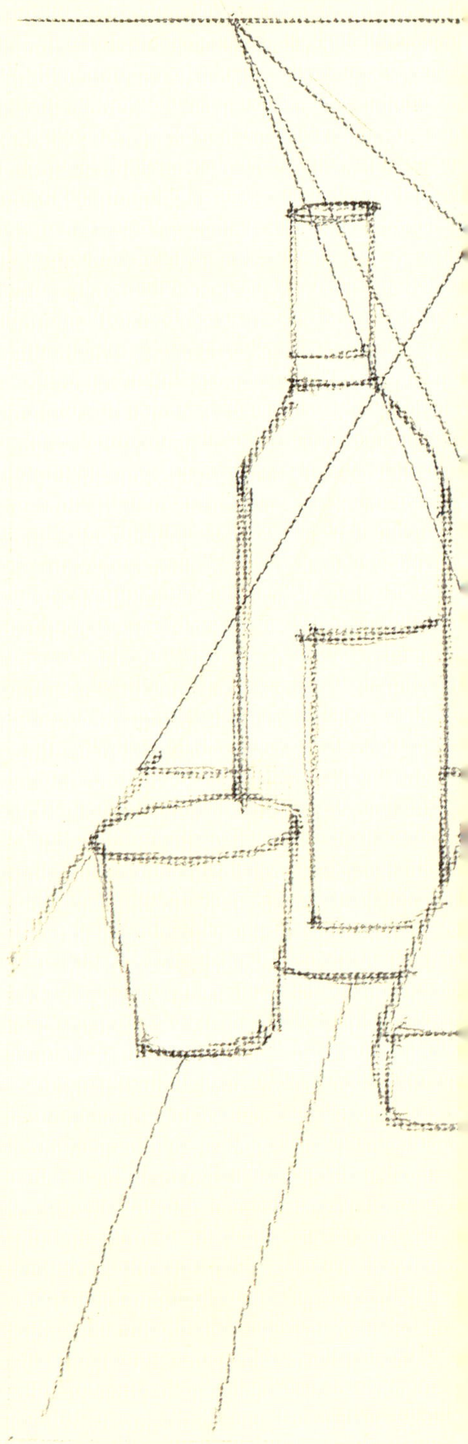

Linear perspective *The parallel sides of the table recede away from the viewer to meet at an imaginary point on the 'horizon line' – the viewer's eye level. This point of convergence is known as the 'vanishing point'. The parallel sides of a book or other object placed randomly on the table meet at a different vanishing point on the same horizon line.*

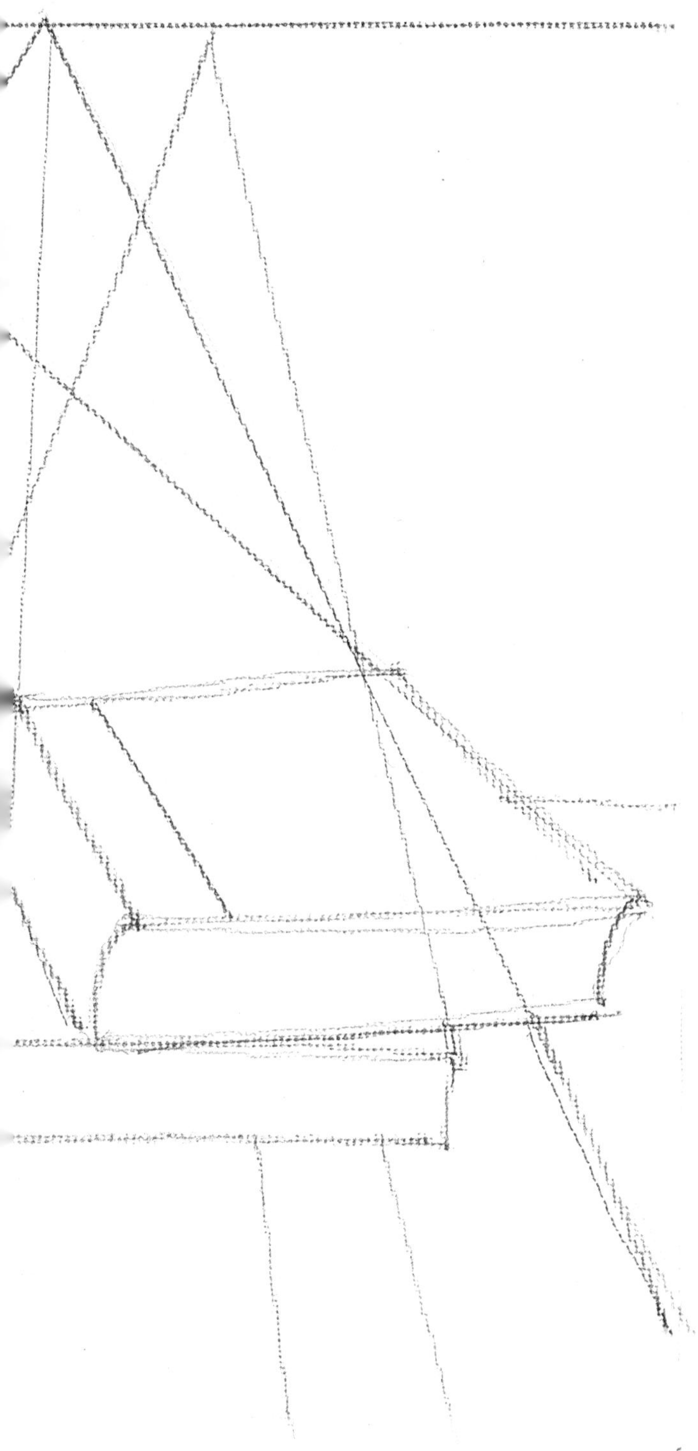

Table tops and surfaces

For the painter of still-life subjects, the most dominant example of perspective will probably be the table top or surface on which the subject is placed. If this is rectangular or square in shape, and the edges are visible in your composition, then the rules of perspective apply. You must make sure the edges of the surface are at the correct angle to each other, and that they converge at the same point on the imaginary horizon line which is your eye level.

If, as in the drawing here, a book or some other rectangular object lies on the table, then this too will have a vanishing point somewhere on the same horizon line.

Find the angles

There is a very simple way of drawing the edges of a table top or any other rectangular object at the correct angle. First, make sure you are facing the subject squarely. Now, take a pencil or brush and hold this up in front of you, tilting it sideways along the line you wish to draw. The brush or pencil must be held upright, at right angles to the floor. While tilting it sideways, do not move your brush or pencil either towards or away from the subject, but keep it upright, as if you were holding it against an imaginary windowpane.

Without altering the angle in any way, carefully lay the brush or pencil on the canvas along the line to be drawn. This should give you the correct angle and enable you to draw your table-edge in the right position, but you can always check the line by repeating the process.

You will need . . .

THERE IS an old saying that only a bad workman blames his tools, but don't you believe it. Without certain basics, it is impossible to produce the sort of picture you already probably see in your mind's eye. Any good artist or craftsperson will put a lot of effort into gathering a selection of reliable and workable equipment.

In this chapter, we give guidance on how to take the first steps towards setting up your home studio.

We begin with a palette. Choice of colour is obviously subjective and you will eventually develop your own ideas on this. However, the 'starter palette' given here is quite comprehensive. We have also included a few extra colours.

The 'support' is the surface on which you paint. It can be canvas, board, paper or other materials. As well as standard supports found in most art shops, we have suggested some surfaces which can be quickly made or improvised in the home. The supports used in the demonstrations include a few made by the artists themselves, such as the one of coarse hessian. This was done when the artist concerned sought a particular texture and colour.

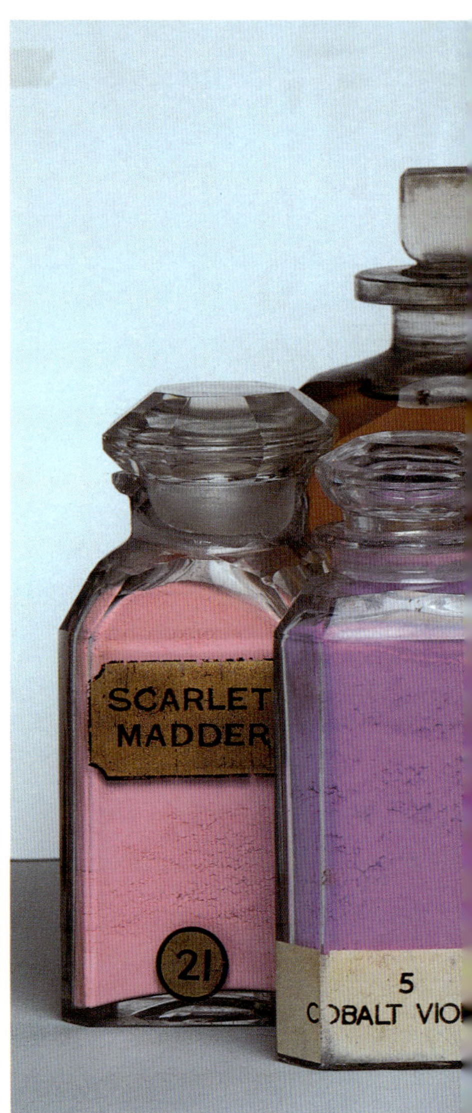

▽ *Paint pigments and brushes from the Winsor and
Newton factory in London. Some of the oldest colours,
such as the siennas and umbers, are natural pigments and
come from the earth. Others come from vegetable,
animal or mineral sources. Some of the more recent
pigments, such as dioxazine violet and phthalo blue,
have been developed in the laboratory.*

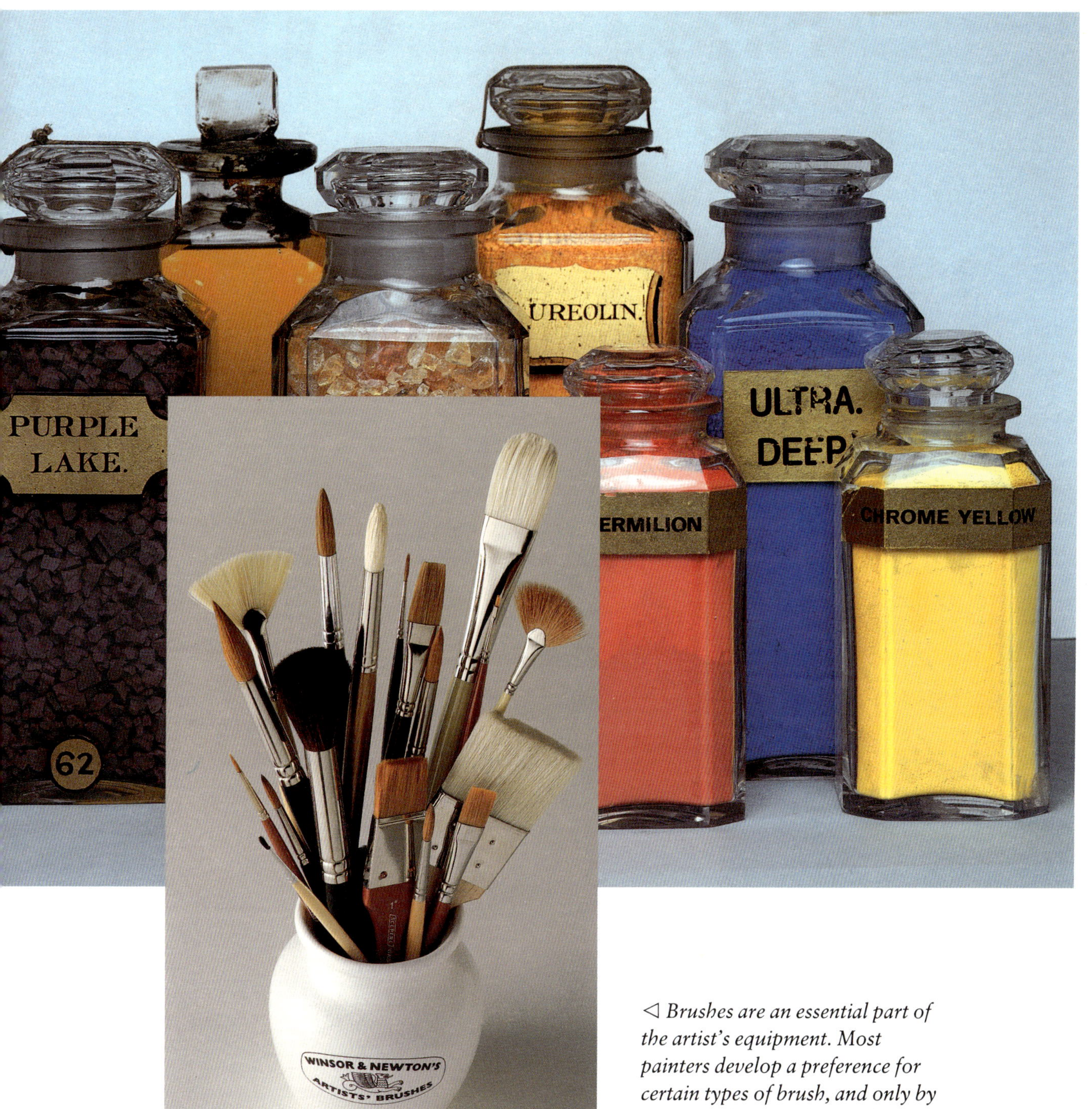

◁ *Brushes are an essential part of
the artist's equipment. Most
painters develop a preference for
certain types of brush, and only by
trying a selection of sizes, shapes
and bristle-types will you discover
which are best suited to your needs.*

PAINTS AND COLOURS

Oddly enough, it is often more difficult to paint with too many colours than with too few. With only a limited range, you can mix almost any colour you need from the few well-chosen basics, and because all the colours in your painting come from the same source, the picture will often have a harmony that more elaborate colour compositions can lack.

Choice of colour is ultimately a personal matter. For the newcomer to the medium, however, the range available can be daunting, so it is helpful to have a guideline – a list of specific colours with which to arm yourself before venturing into the art shop.

First-year art students are often given a suggested 'starter' palette of colours loosely based on those used by the English painter Walter Sickert (1860–1942). This palette has become a sort of yardstick for many painters, most of whom go on to make adaptations and additions to suit their own personal requirements.

Colours to start
The art school 'starter' colours are black, white, cadmium red, alizarin crimson, French ultramarine, viridian green, cadmium yellow, yellow ochre, raw umber and Indian red. Cerulean blue, cobalt green, Payne's grey and cadmium lemon have also been included here because they are helpful, personal additions used by artists for specific still-life subjects during demonstration projects for this book. All the projects can therefore be followed using the

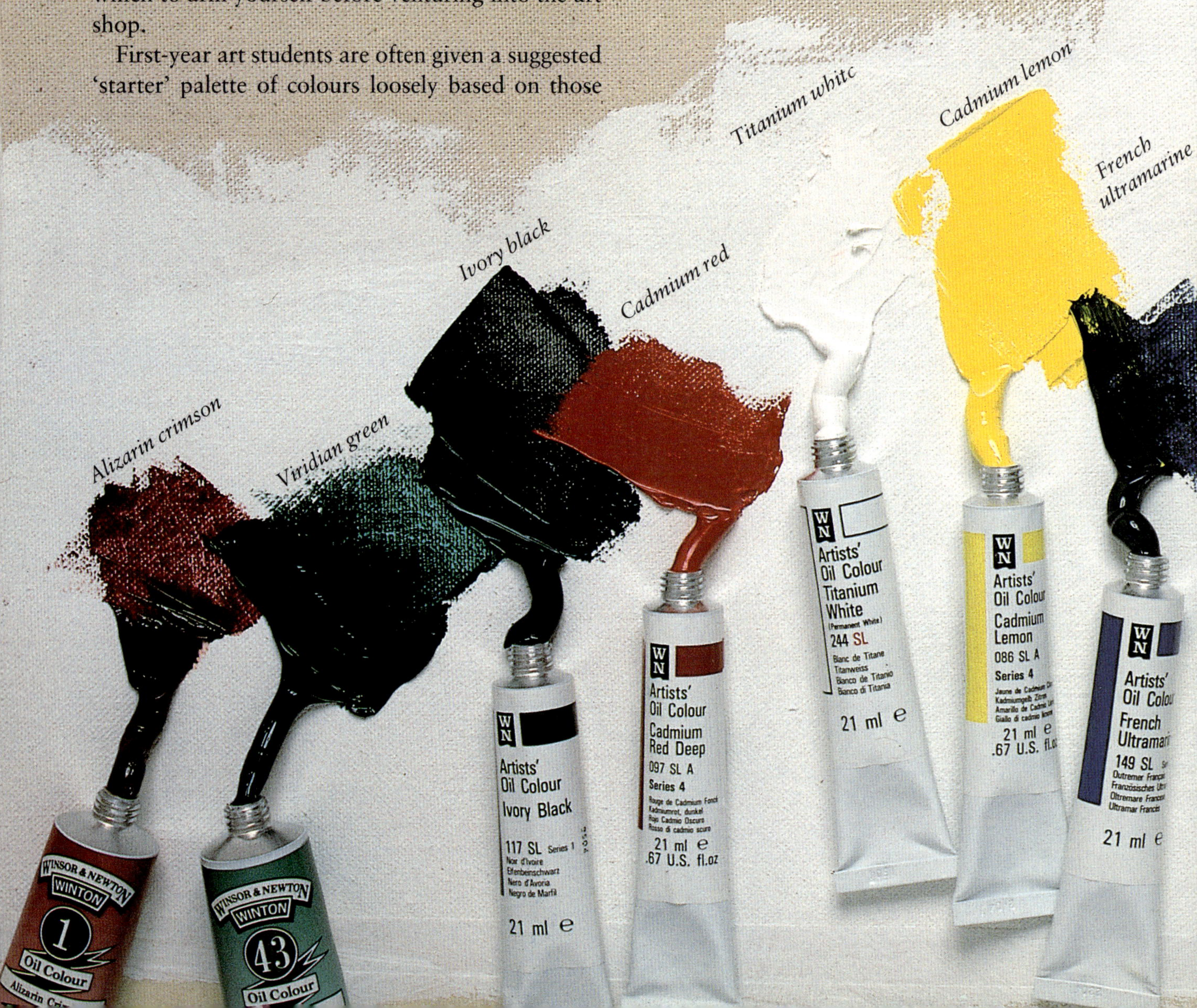

colours listed here, although you will by no means use every colour in every painting.

This selection is a general one, suitable for any subject, but the quantities used will obviously differ according to what you are painting. A landscape painter inevitably needs lots of blues and yellow, for instance. But with still-life painting, the subject is so varied that the amount of any one colour you use will depend on what you are painting at the time. However, every artist uses far more white than any other colour, so it is worth getting a large tube.

The paints
Most manufacturers produce two grades of oil paint: so-called artists' quality and a less expensive range. Artists' colours tend to be made from superior pigments. Many painters find the texture of these colours less oily and some of the pigments brighter. However, provided you buy an established brand, there should be no significant difference between the two. The type you choose will depend on how much you want to spend and, to some extent, on how you work. If you paint big, with very thick paint, for instance, quality colours could work out quite costly.

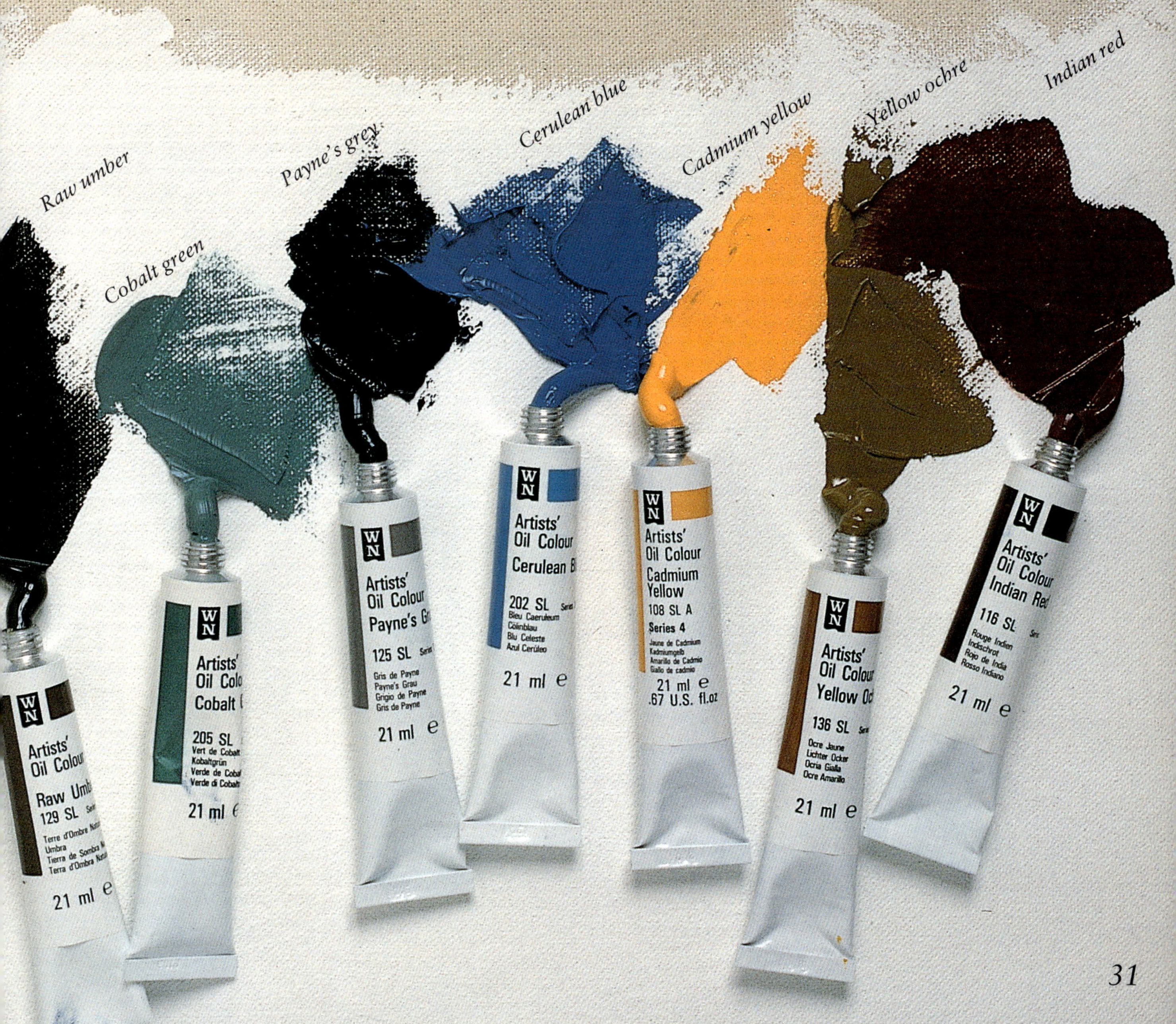

WHAT TO PAINT ON

You can buy primed canvases and canvas boards in all art shops, and these are without doubt the most convenient painting surfaces available. They come ready to use in a range of sizes and in various textures, from fine to fairly coarse.

Bought surfaces do have certain limitations, however, and for this reason you may sometimes want to make your own. A bought canvas or canvas board is primed in white, which is fine for most purposes and anyway can be tinted with a coloured ground if you prefer to paint on a toned back-ground (see page 84). But if you want the texture and colour of the canvas to show through and become part of the painting, as the artist does in the apple still life on pages 40–43, then you should make your own painting support.

Stretching your own

Many artists like to work on stretched canvas because it has a springiness and flexibility which a rigid board cannot provide. The illustrations here show how to stretch your own canvas, which is traditionally done with artists' linen (crisp, light brown) or cotton duck (softer and off-white). Both of these come in varying degrees of coarseness and fineness, and can be primed to provide a permanent, taut surface on which to paint. The prime can be acrylic gesso, which is brilliant white, or you can use acrylic medium, which dries to a transparent

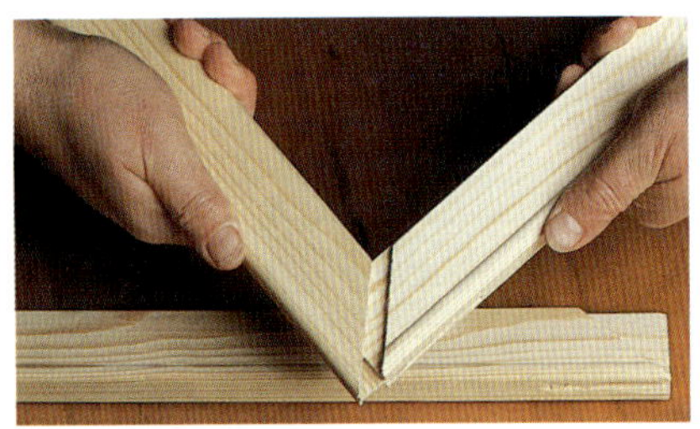

△ **1** *Assemble the stretcher pieces by slotting them at the corners. Some stretchers are bevelled (rounded) along the outside edge, so make sure all the bevelled edges are on the same side. Check the corners are at right angles before cutting and fitting the canvas.*

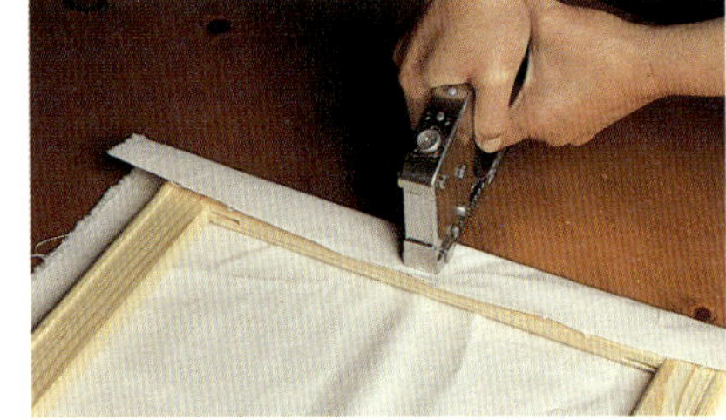

△ **2** *Cut a piece of canvas to fit the stretcher, with a margin of 3 inches (7.5 cm) all round. Place the stretcher centrally on the canvas with the bevelled side facing down. Start on one side, folding the canvas back along the reverse side of the stretcher, and staple this down at the centre.*

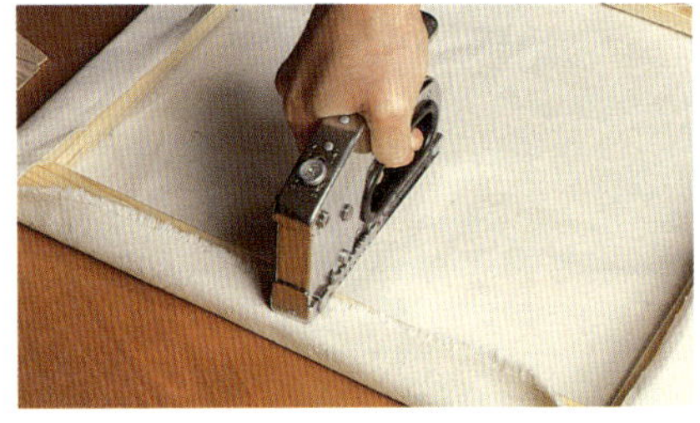

△ **3** *Staple the edges down at the centres on the other three sides. The canvas at this stage should be tight but not taut.*

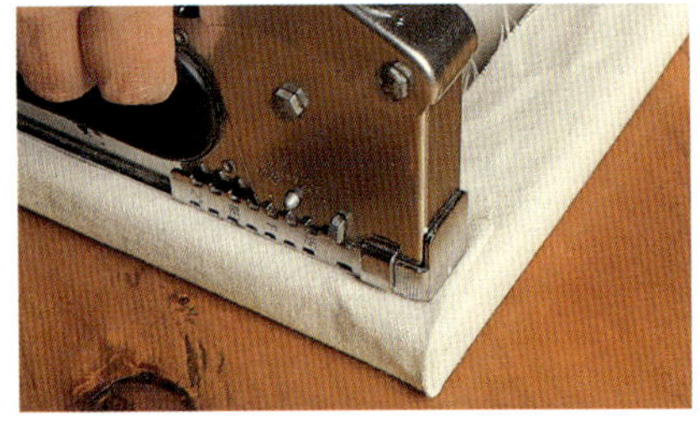

△ **5** *Secure each corner with two or three staples.*

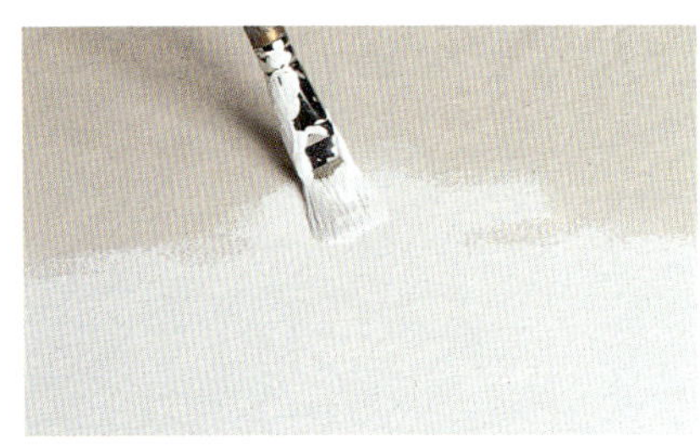

△ **6** *Using a large, flat artist's brush or a small decorator's brush, give the canvas a coat of acrylic gesso.*

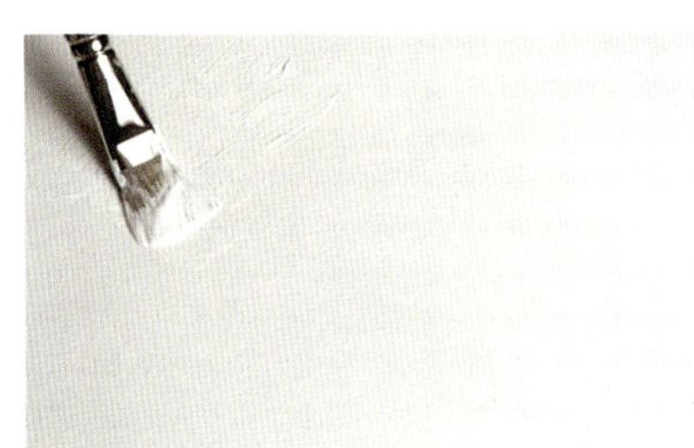

△ **7** *Allow the first coat of gesso to dry before applying a second coat. When dry, the gesso tautens the canvas to provide an opaque and receptive painting surface.*

finish and allows the stretched canvas to retain its natural colour.

Painting boards

For those who prefer a rigid support, both hardboard and plywood can be primed or sealed with acrylic medium to provide a smooth, receptive surface on which to paint.

Alternatively, if you like a rigid support but prefer a fabric surface, you can stick canvas, cotton duck or any other type of material directly on to the board. Most fabrics are suitable, depending on the surface texture or colour required. Hessian, as used in the apple still life, gives a coarse, granular finish – ideal for thick, textural painting; muslin has a finely woven surface which many artists prefer to traditional canvas.

Whichever fabric you choose, it should be stuck to hardboard or plywood with a liberal amount of acrylic medium, PVA glue or rabbit-skin size. Cut the fabric slightly larger than the board and fold back the edges, sticking them down to the reverse side of the board. This gives a neat edge to the painting surface. When the adhesive has dried, the painting surface should be sealed with the same substance and allowed to dry before you start work.

Alternative painting surfaces

Oil paper, available in pads, is an inexpensive alternative to canvas and board and is ideal for oil sketches. Other good and instant alternatives are cardboard and stiff brown paper, both of which can be sealed with one or two coats of acrylic gesso or medium, making them sufficiently tough and impermeable to be used with oil paints.

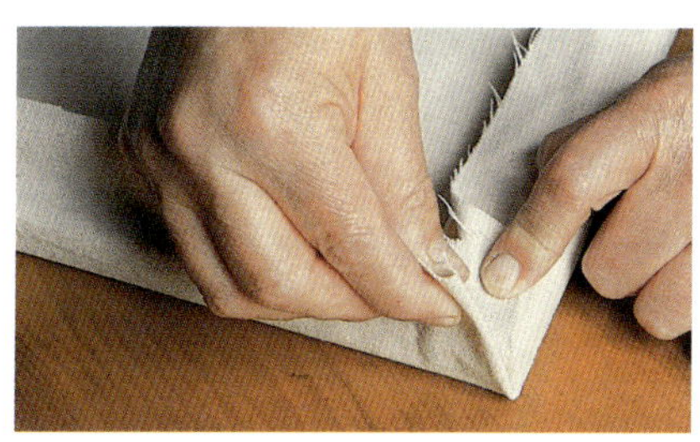

△ **4** *Staple each edge, starting at the centre and stapling at 1-inch (2.5-cm) intervals until you reach the corner. Fold the corner by overlapping the meeting edges and tucking in excess canvas.*

Top to bottom:
Oil paper
Cotton duck
Plywood
Artist's linen
Cardboard
Hessian

ROUNDS, FLATS AND FILBERTS

Apart from the paint and a surface to paint on, other essentials for your still-life painting are some brushes, linseed oil, turpentine and, if you like painting thickly, painting or palette knives. You will also need a palette and an easel to support your work.

Brushes
Brushes for oil painting come in three main shapes and a range of sizes. 'Rounds' have a rounded ferrule (the metal part that holds the bristles) and rounded bristle-head. Their full bristle-head holds a lot of colour, so you don't have to load the brush with paint very often. They are versatile: smaller sizes are good for detail and larger ones are used for spreading areas of colour.

'Flats' have a flattened ferrule, with the bristles cut to a straight, square shape. You can use either the narrow or the broad side of the bristles, allowing you to cope with fine detail or broad areas of colour. Short flats are often called 'brights'.

Flats with longer bristle-heads, slightly tapered, are called 'filberts'. These are a cross between flats and rounds. Many artists like them because they are literally flexible and combine the functions of other brush types.

Despite the characteristics described here, bear in mind that most painters develop their own preferences and can make one type of brush fulfil many roles.

Oil-painting brushes are traditionally made from hog's hair or other natural bristle. Today there are synthetic equivalents on the market, which some painters actually prefer. Until you have tried them both, do not buy a large number of either.

To start with, choose a small selection of brushes, both synthetic and natural, including a few from each category and covering a range of sizes. You will soon find out which you like best and use most

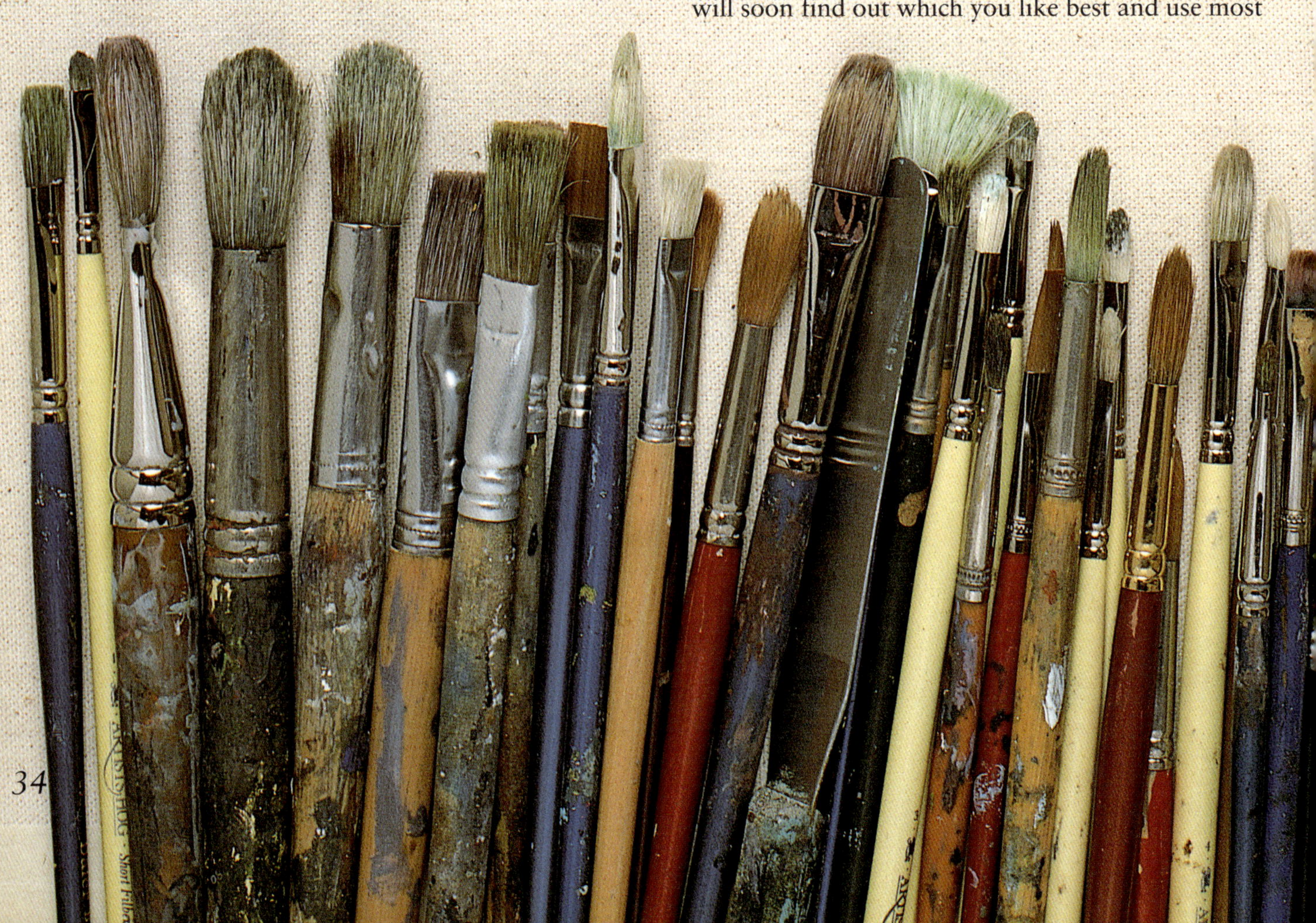

frequently. Other useful additions are a small decorating brush, for priming and for applying large expanses of wash or underpainting, and a 'fan' brush – with bristles spread out like a fan – used for blending colours smoothly.

Knives

Painting knives have cranked (bent) handles which keep the artist's hand clear of the painted surface. These come in various shapes and sizes and are used mainly for applying areas of thick paint, with either a smooth or a textured finish.

Although palette knives are made specifically for mixing, artists often paint with them, just as they sometimes use painting knives for mixing. Packs of disposable plastic painting knives are now available.

Oil and turpentine

Various additives can be mixed with oil paint to speed up the drying time, to add texture, to make the colour more transparent and so on. All these media have a place in still-life painting because the subject is often intrinsically so rich and varied in texture. There is no reason why you should not experiment with these additives from the outset – particularly with the glazing and thickening media, which are good for creating textures and subtle overlaid colours.

The only really essential additives are turpentine and linseed oil. Oil paint is diluted with turpentine, a spirit which also makes the paint dry more quickly. The initial stages of your still life should be blocked in with diluted paint, giving you a fast-drying layer of colour on which to develop the painting. As the turpentine dries, the picture surface will look dull and matt. This is countered by adding a little linseed oil to the paint, giving subsequent colours a glossy, succulent finish.

Palette

The traditional oil palette is kidney-shaped, with a thumbhole for easy handling. This design has evolved over the years because it is portable and easy to hold while working at the easel. If you like to stand at your work, stepping back from the picture at frequent intervals as you paint, then the traditional palette is ideal. If not, you do not need a portable palette for still-life painting and might do better with a large piece of wood, glass or perspex placed on a nearby stand or table.

A still-life subject can remain in place for a long time, but the paint on your palette cannot. After a day or so, a thin skin forms over the paint which eventually makes the colours bitty and difficult to use. Most oil-painters clear their palette every night, scraping it first with a knife, then wiping it clean with a rag and some turpentine. New colours are squeezed out at the start of the next work session.

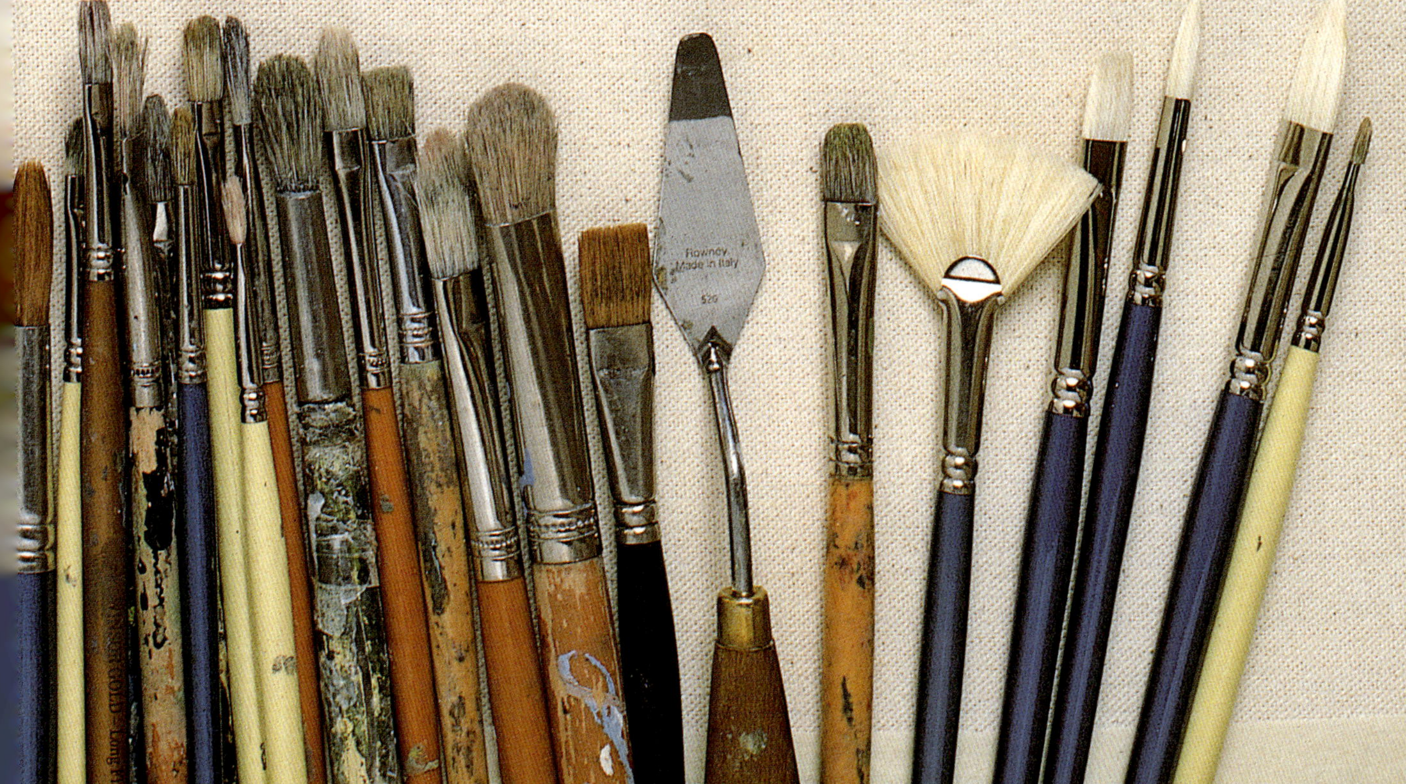

Basic techniques

WE HAVE divided our analysis of techniques into two, this chapter covering the basic stages and Chapter 5 covering the more complex ones. Yet a textbook start has been avoided. This chapter launches you straight into the possibilities of texture, deliberately taking it to the extreme, with impasto – thick strokes of paint – applied with a knife. The objective is to explore immediately the furthest limits of texture-making. Even if you never again apply paint with a knife, you will be acquainted with the process, which is after all a classic oil-painting technique used by many professionals.

We then move into the decorative, again taking the subject away from the academic and showing where the limits exist and how broad they are. This allows you to go directly for bright colours, patterns and jazzy outlines, rather in the way that Matisse (1869–1954) and some of the Fauves did. It reinforces the important idea that there are lots of different approaches with still life. Starting with some very different ones will help you escape from preconceived rules of thumb.

The basic drawing techniques are not ignored, and the chapter demonstrates 'negative shapes', a useful way of learning to draw.

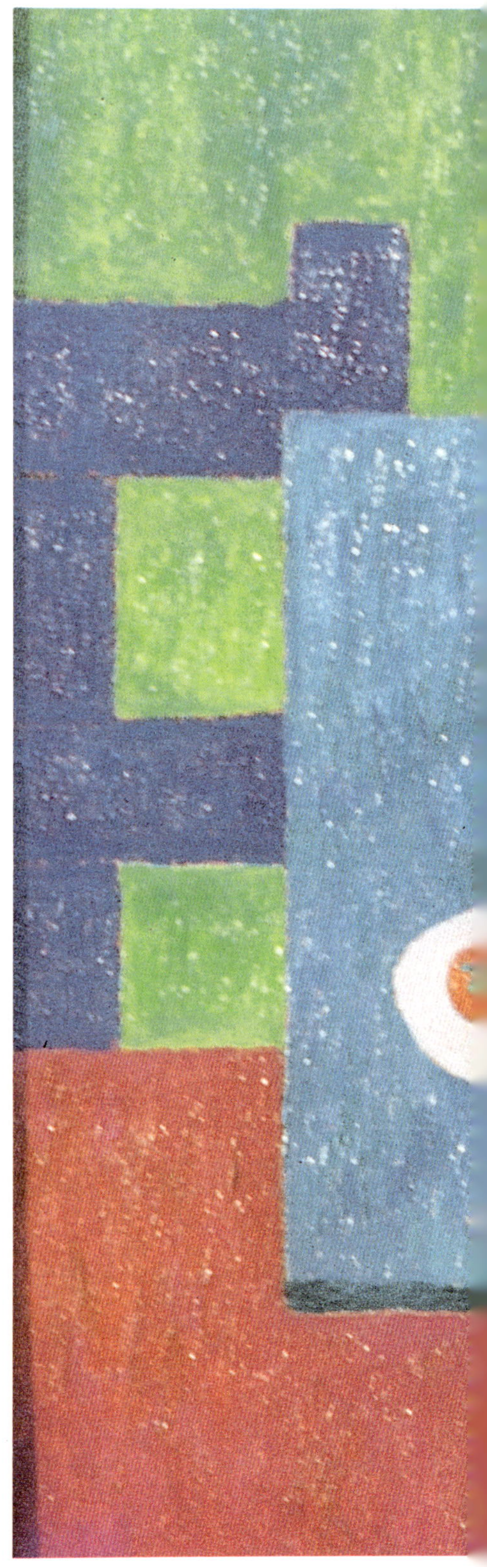

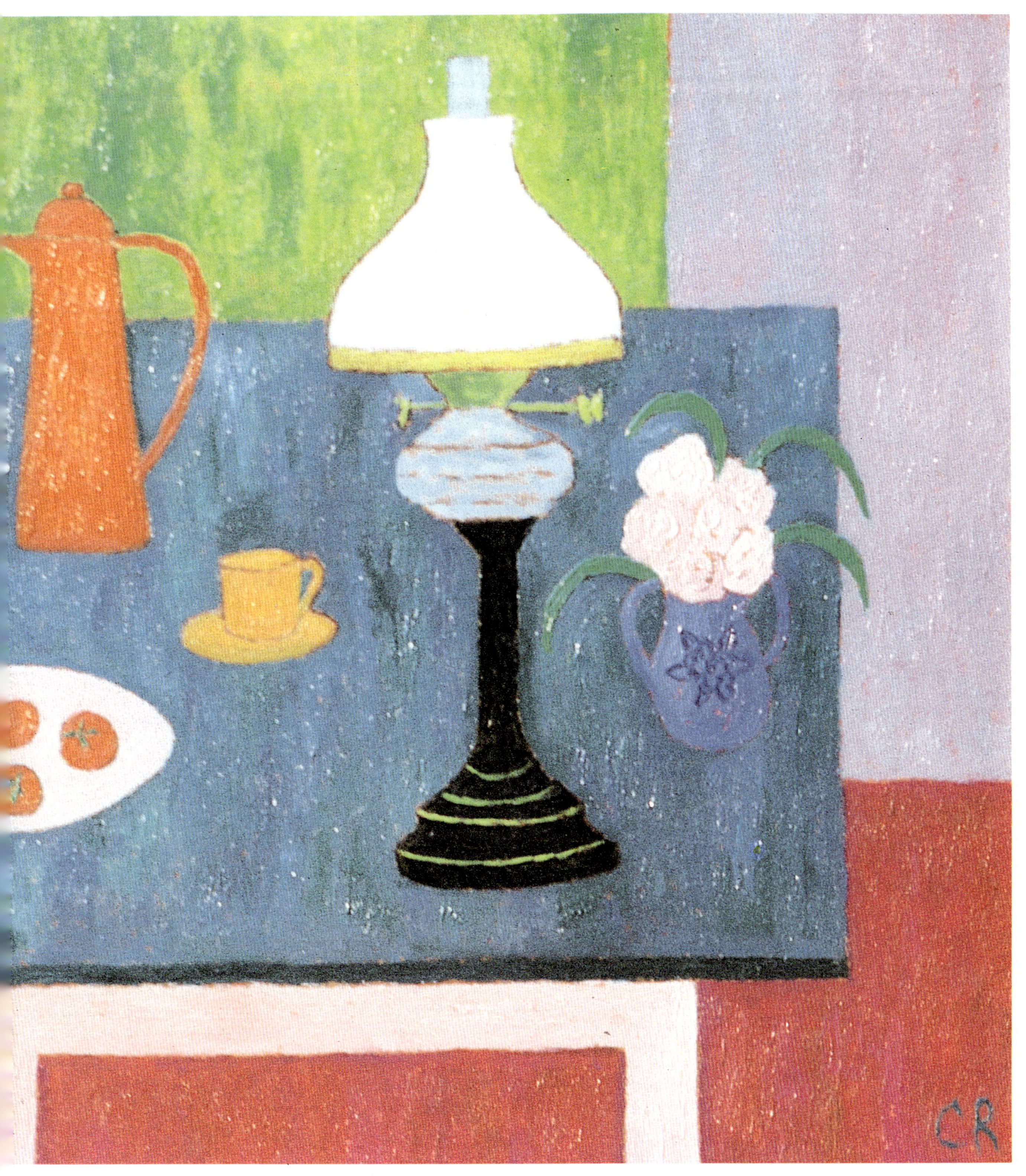

In this still life by Celeste Radloff, the blue table, white lamp, pink floor and green background are painted as an arrangement of bold, flat shapes. The emphasis here is on colour, and on how each colour reacts with its neighbours. Other pictorial elements – texture, tone and form – play a comparatively minor role in the painting.

TECHNIQUES

KNIFE PAINTING

Typically, a painting done with a knife has thick, built-up colours, often applied in chunky ledges or wedge shapes. The knife strokes are usually visible in the finished picture.

Impasto

Thickly applied colour is often referred to as 'impasto'. Paint thickness varies, depending on how you work, but knife marks tend to start with a squidge of thick colour which tapers off to a thin scrape, revealing the canvas texture underneath. These contrasting effects can be exploited to introduce different textures into your subject.

Thick paint gives lots of opportunity for scratching back to make patterns and textures in the painted surface. You can do this using the tip or side of the knife blade, or any other suitable implement.

There is an immediacy and directness about knife painting. The paint can be quickly mixed on the palette, and just as quickly and robustly applied to the picture, often using the same knife. This tends to make for fresh colour and a lively, interesting paint surface. The bolder you are, the more pronounced these qualities will be. In fact, the greater your confidence, the easier it is to paint with a knife. If you are fussy and pernickity about detail, if you try to get a neat finish on the paint marks, then not only does knife painting become unnecessarily difficult but you can also lose the rugged qualities inherent in the technique.

Size and shape

Because knives are available in different shapes and sizes, you can vary the scale of the paint marks to suit the size of your painting. A large area can be quickly blocked in using a long, broad knife, and the knife marks will be appropriately chunky to suit the scale of the painting.

For smaller pictures, painting knives are also available in quite tiny sizes. These enable you to work on a small scale without jeopardizing the

Laying colour

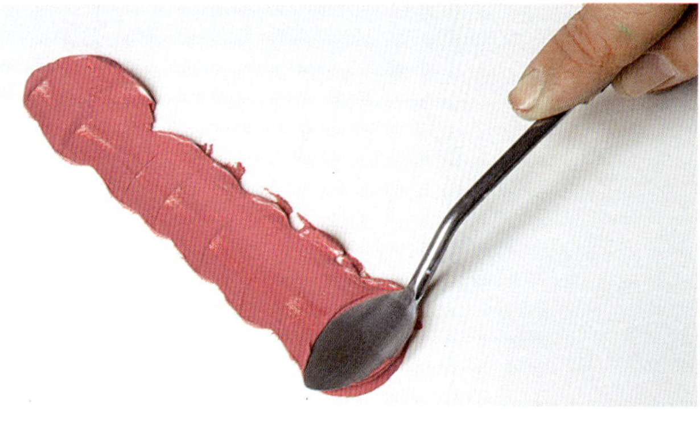

◁ **1** *The rounded edges of this oval painting knife give the wedges of paint a slightly concave shape, causing the edges of colour to stand up in pronounced ridges.*

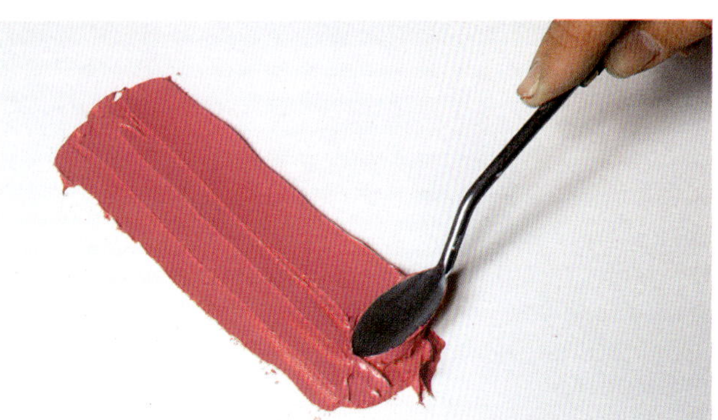

◁ **2** *The same oval knife is used to lay long, overlapping blocks of colour. Again, the rounded blade creates a concave mark with ridged edges.*

Mixing paint

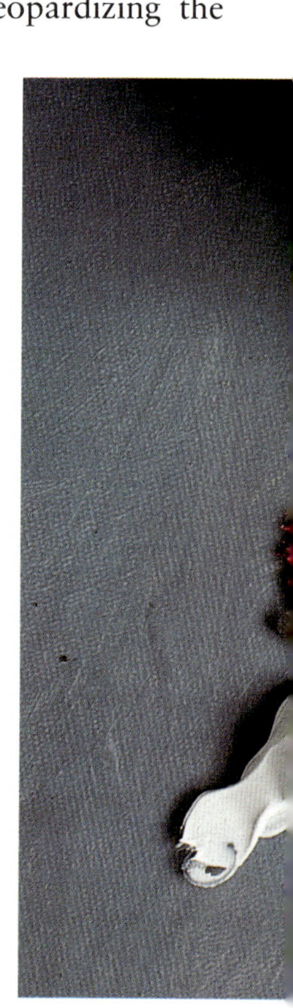

▷ *A flat palette knife is used for rapid and thorough mixing. The flexible blade enables the artist to scrape and press the red and white paints together until the two colours are completely blended.*

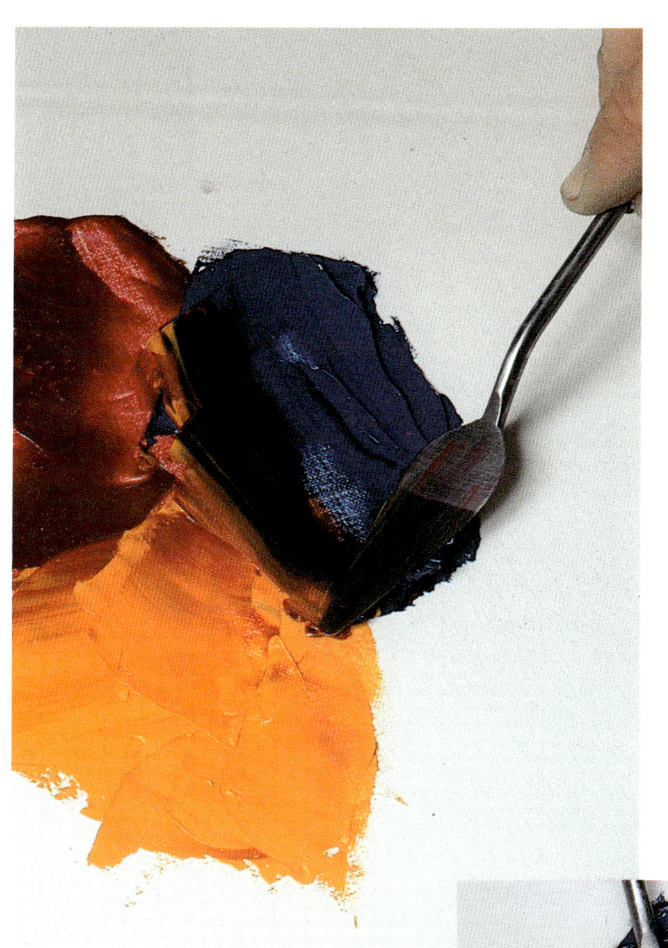

texture or spontaneity of the painting.

The shape of the knife you choose depends very much on the effect you want. As you can see from the illustrations here, an oval blade can be used to lay slightly convex ledges, while a blade with a straight edge creates a flatter effect.

Which type of knife?
Artists often 'break the rules' and use palette knives for painting. Remember, you can be flexible.

But although they come in different shapes and sizes, the painting knife and palette knife are the two basic knives used. Both have flat, flexible blades. The painting knife has a cranked handle, making it easy to apply flat colour. Palette knives are rather like the metal spatulas used in cooking, and usually have long, straight-edged blades.

Palette knives are designed for mixing colour on the palette, and for scraping off unused paint at the end of a day's work. The blades are easy to wipe, and the knives make the mixing and scraping less messy than they are when done with a brush.

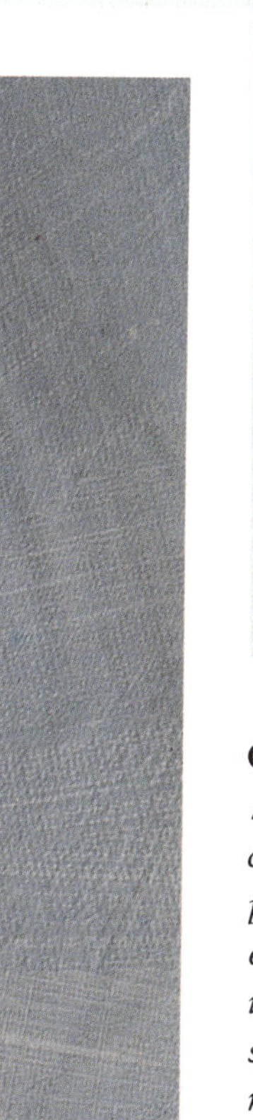

Overlaying
△△ **1** *Two or more wet colours can be used on top of each other, provided the applied paint is thick enough to cover the colour underneath. This layer of blue is too sparse to cover the colours underneath and goes muddy as it mixed with the underlying red and yellow.*

△ **2** *A subsequent, thicker layer of blue completely covers everything underneath, and the resulting colour is bright and pure.*

PROJECTS

GREEN APPLE

Chunky knife marks on coarse hessian might at first seem an unlikely way of painting this smooth, shiny cooking apple. In fact, no approach could be better. The solid wedges of colour are effectively used to simplify and describe the light and shade on the rounded fruit. And the open weave of the hessian background provides an attractive textural contrast in a painting that is otherwise built up entirely with knife strokes. The result is almost more 'apple-like' than the apple itself.

Light and planes

On a rounded object such as this apple, light and shaded areas merge into each other. There is no visible edge or outline to separate the shadows from the highlights. They have no actual shape.

When painting such objects, there are two basic approaches.

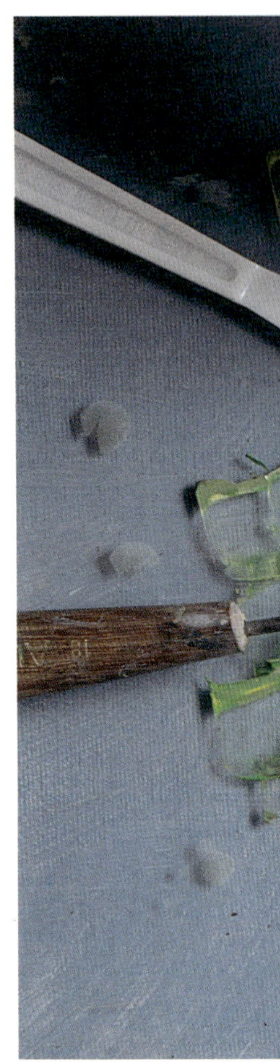

▽ **1** *Starting with the light tones, the artist begins by blocking in planes of pale green with a small, straight-edged painting knife. The pale green is mixed from viridian green, lemon and white, and the initial line drawing is painted in mid-green on a hessian-covered board primed with acrylic medium. The board measures 10 × 12 inches (25 × 30 cm).*

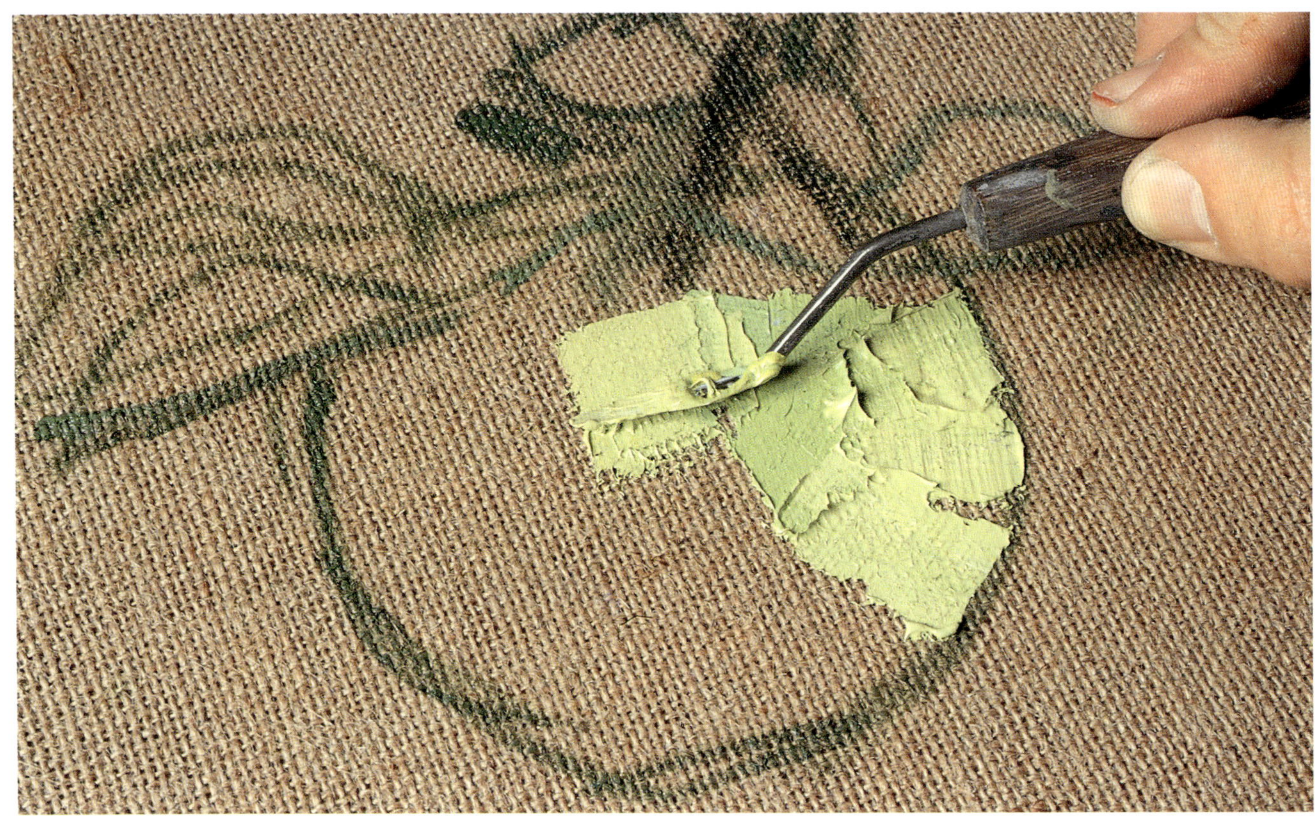

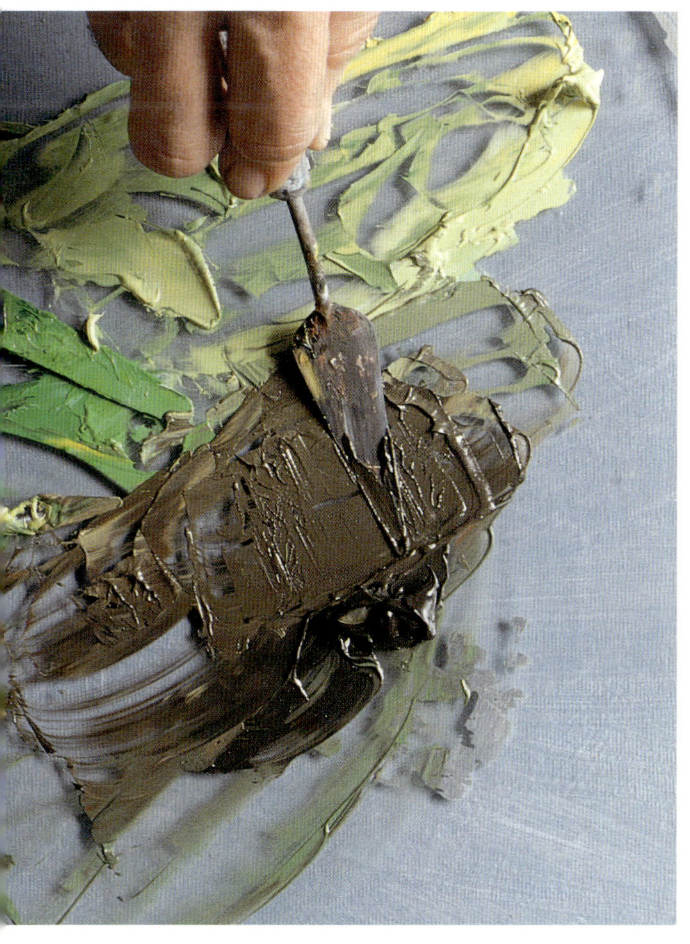

◁ **2** *All the apple tones are mixed from varying quanitites of viridian green, cadmium yellow, lemon, raw umber and white. Colours are mixed with a plastic palette knife, and applied with small and medium painting knives.*

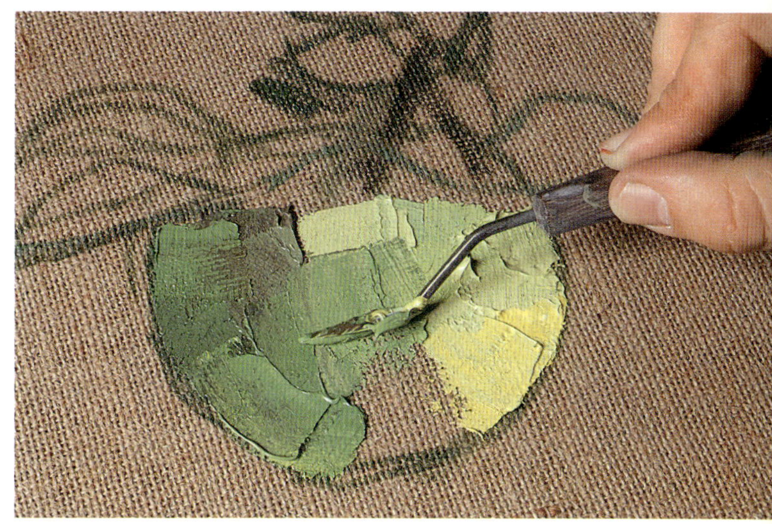

△ **3** *The medium and darker tones are laid in mid-green mixed from raw umber, viridian green, white and cadmium yellow. Paint is applied thickly, with each block overlaying the adjoining colour as the artist looks at the subject and simplifies the colours into the three main tones.*

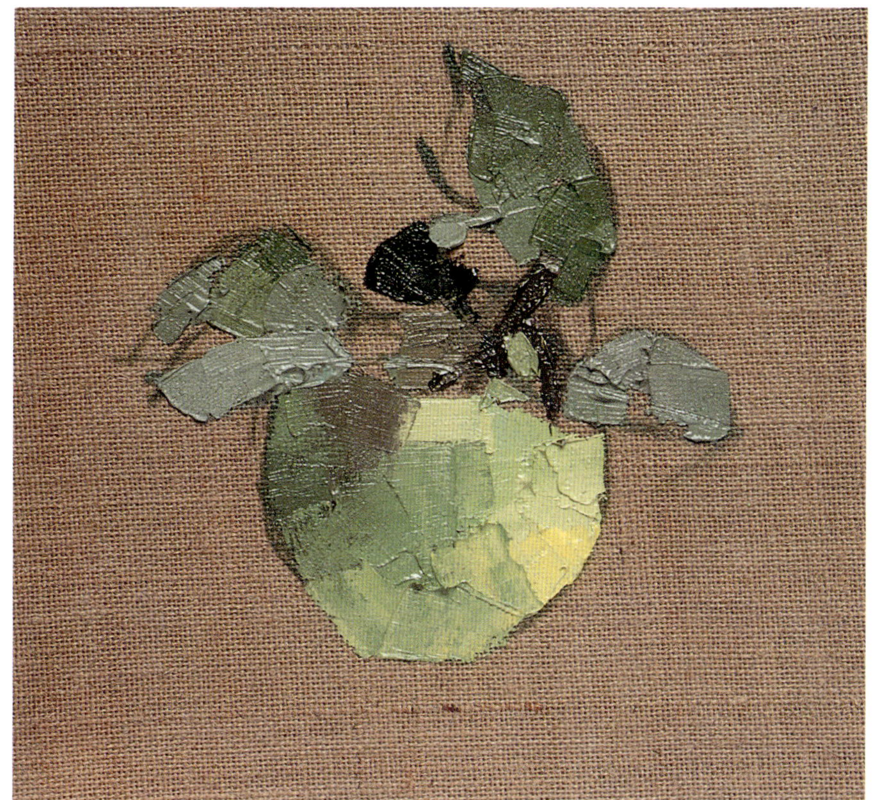

◁ **4** *Leaves are painted in a similarly simplified manner in greens mixed from raw umber, cadmium yellow, white and a little ultramarine blue.*

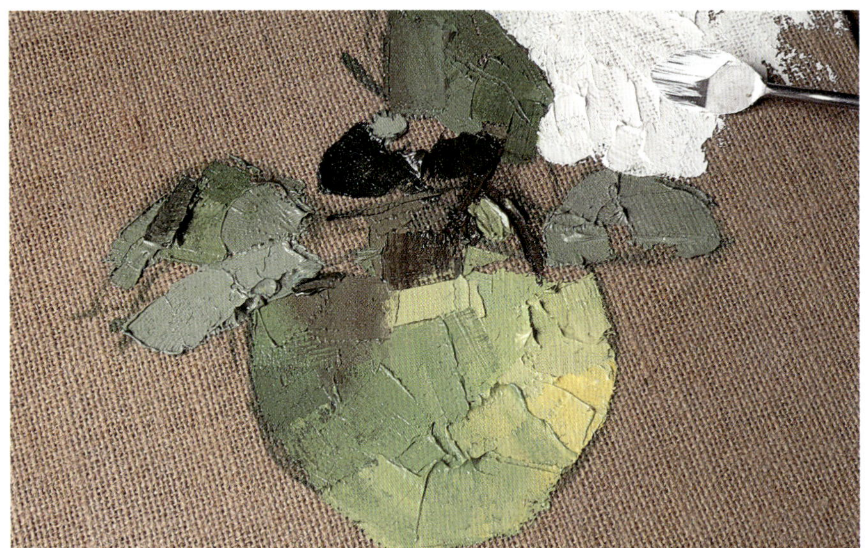

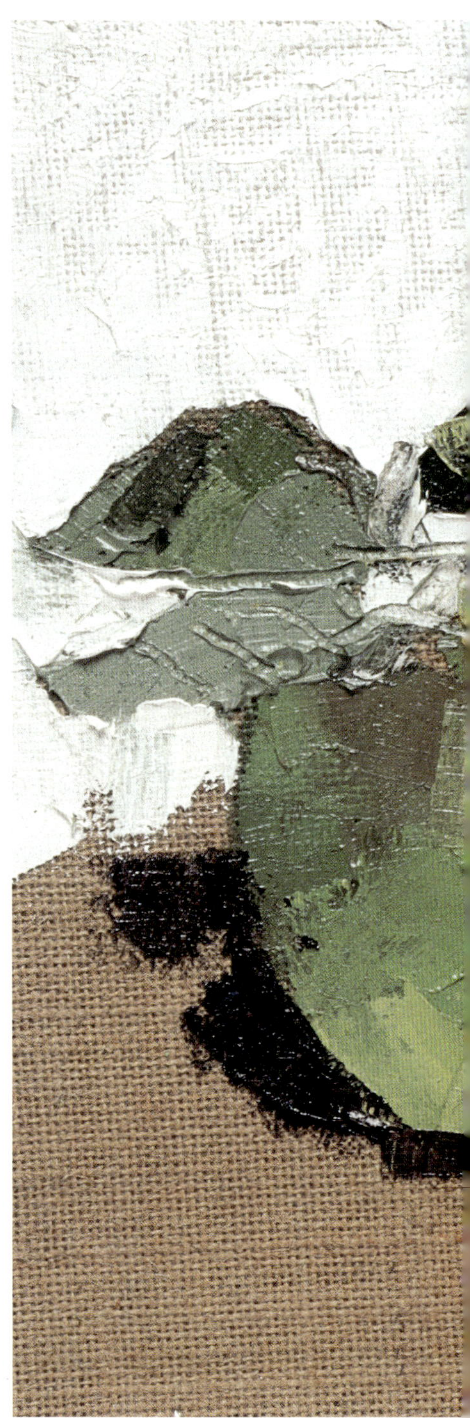

◁ 5   *The background is laid in pure white, using an oval painting knife. The ridges produced by the oval blade create a roughly textured paint surface which the artist emphasizes by using very thick paint.*

The most obvious is to blend the colours to give an imitation of the smooth surface of the actual fruit – to make the painting as superficially realistic as a photograph.

For the newcomer to the subject, this approach is not always the best one to take. Successful blending, rubbing tones and colours together to make them look smooth, works only if the tones are right in the first place. The best way to establish the tones correctly is to simplify these into approximate visible patches of light and dark, or planes.

Analysing planes

To understand the concept of planes, imagine your apple is made of folded paper – an origami apple. This apple is not a smooth, round object but a structure made of many paper planes. Each of these planes catches the light from a different angle, and its colour shows up as a light, dark or medium tone, depending on how much light it receives.

On a real, rounded apple, light also falls in different ways, with the patches blended and merging into the rounded form.

Light with a painting knife

When painting with a knife, it becomes easy and quick to block in areas of flat colour. The technique is therefore particularly good for depicting broad planes of light and shade. In this apple painting, the artist has simplified the subject and depicted each plane as a discernible patch of pale, medium or dark green, according to the source of light.

▽ **6** *A small painting knife has allowed the artist to take the paint right up to the edge of the leaves and apple, redefining and shaping these with the edge of the knife and the thick paint. Leaf tones are lightened to blend with the newly applied background, and the shadow is painted in raw umber.*

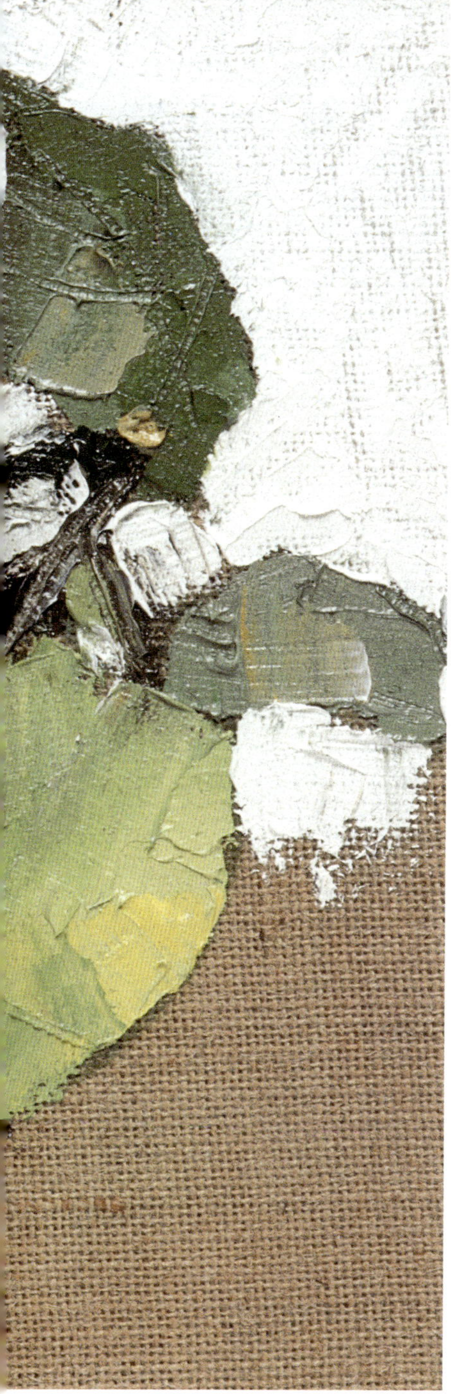

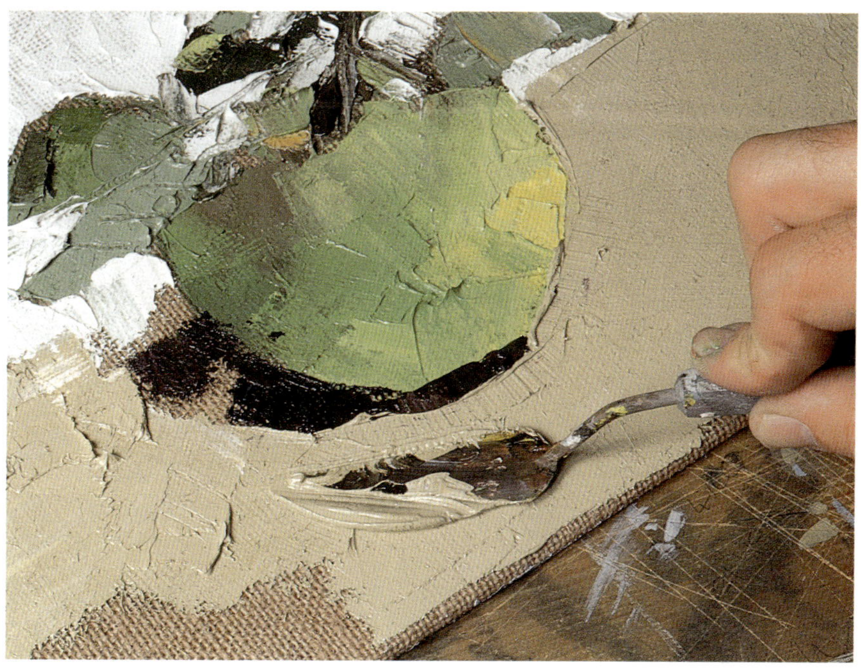

△ **7** *The table top colour is mixed from raw umber, white and a little lemon yellow, and laid in thick wedges of flat colour.*

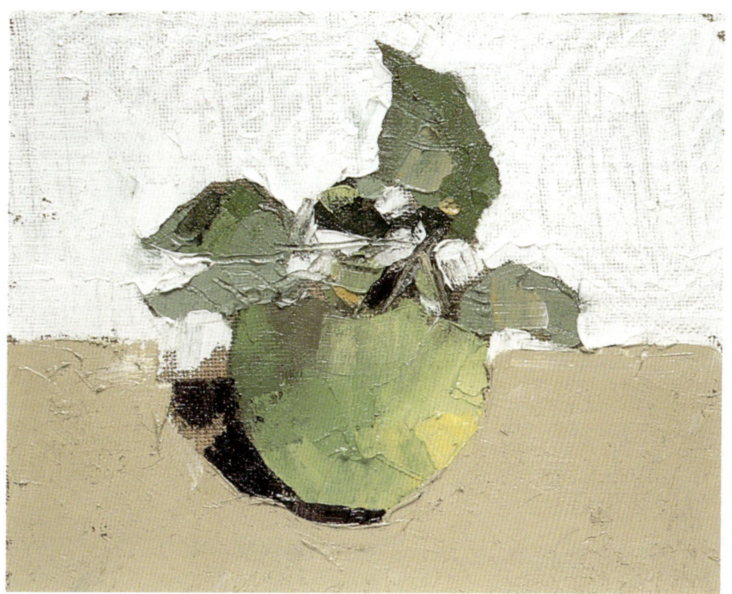

△ **8** *Patches of bare hessian are allowed to show through the paint in certain areas. Thus the completed painting combines the contrasting textures of the impasto oil paint and the coarse finish of the raw hessian canvas.*

TECHNIQUES

PAINTING OUTLINES

Your still-life painting inevitably starts with a drawn outline, which may be done in pencil, charcoal, paint or any other material. When the outline is a painted one, choice of colour is important and can be selected to blend or harmonize with other colours in the picture.

The tubes of paint shown here are predominantly grey. The artist therefore chose to paint the outline in a similar grey, so that the drawn line could eventually be blended into the painted image. The advantage here is that the initial drawing – carefully observed, with a fluid, linear quality – is not lost in the finished painting.

Pattern and line
Surprising numbers of still-life subjects contain an overall pattern which may at first seem to defy painting. Patterned fabrics and wallpapers – popular backgrounds in many still lifes – can be notoriously difficult, as can ceramic and other designs. You have to consider not only the pattern but also how the colour of that pattern changes, according to whether it is in light or shade.

Often, the best way is to treat the pattern, however complicated, as any other part of the painting – that is, to ignore the detail and paint it in broad, general terms. You aim to get a general impression rather than an exact rendering.

Pattern in context
However, sometimes a pattern is a specific and important part of the subject. The blue and white

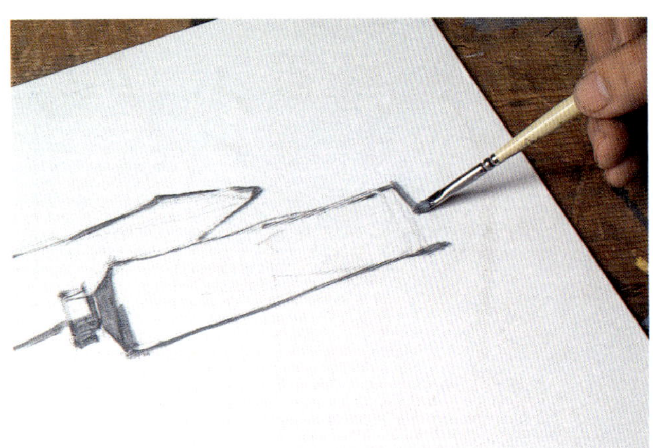

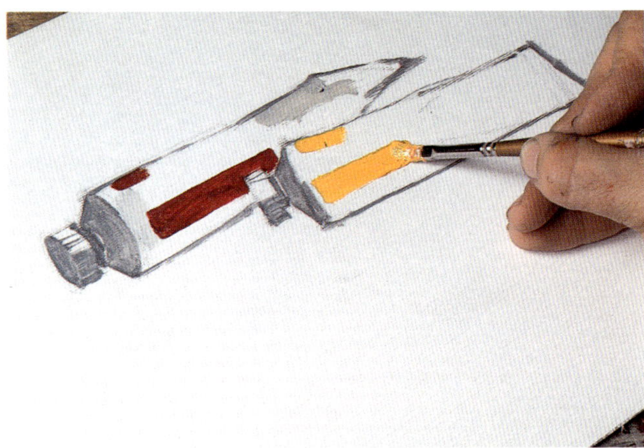

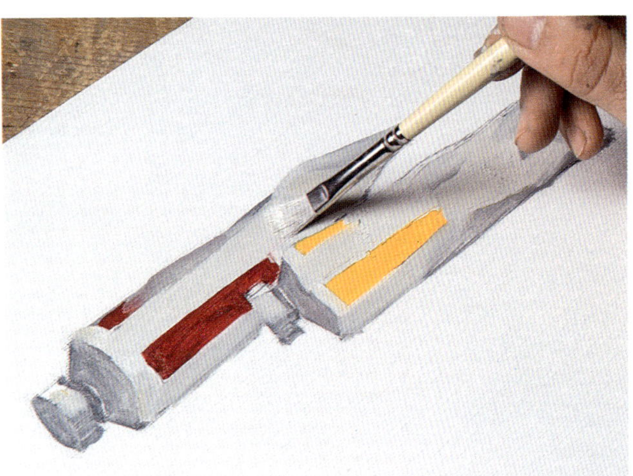

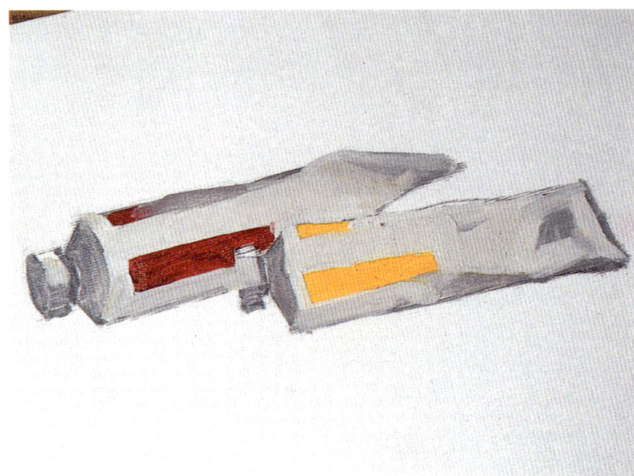

eggcups here are just such an example. They call for accuracy, yet the linear blue pattern cannot be crudely overpainted in such a way that it would stand out from everything else in a still life.

The solution here is to paint the pattern colour first. Thus each eggcup is first underpainted in blue. This is painted not as a flat, even colour, which might make the finished pattern look flat, despite the fact that it is on a rounded form. Instead, it is applied unevenly and thinly, as it appears on the actual subject.

The main white, the background colour, is then painted over the blue. This is done quite boldly, and the tones of the white – the highlight and the shadow – can be painted and changed in relation to anything else in the picture. The blue pattern is left as crisp, cut-out linear shapes.

Linear patterns
▷ **1** *Instead of painting the blue pattern on to a white background, the artist starts by first blocking in the blue. When this is dry, the white is painted around the patterned shapes.*

▷▽ **2** *By leaving the white until last, the artist has greater control over the tones, and is able to introduce grey shadows to describe the rounded forms. The blue patterns stand out as crisply defined lines.*

Blended outlines
◁◁ **1** *The predominantly grey paint tubes are drawn in diluted mid-grey mixed from black and white.*

◁△ **2** *The artist moves on, painting in the subject with red and yellow – the local colours on the tube labels.*

◁◁ **3** *Light and dark greys are used to describe the form on the rounded tubes. The paint is taken up to the grey painted outline.*

◁ **4** *The initial grey outline has been blended into the rest of the painting, giving the painted tubes a crisply defined shape.*

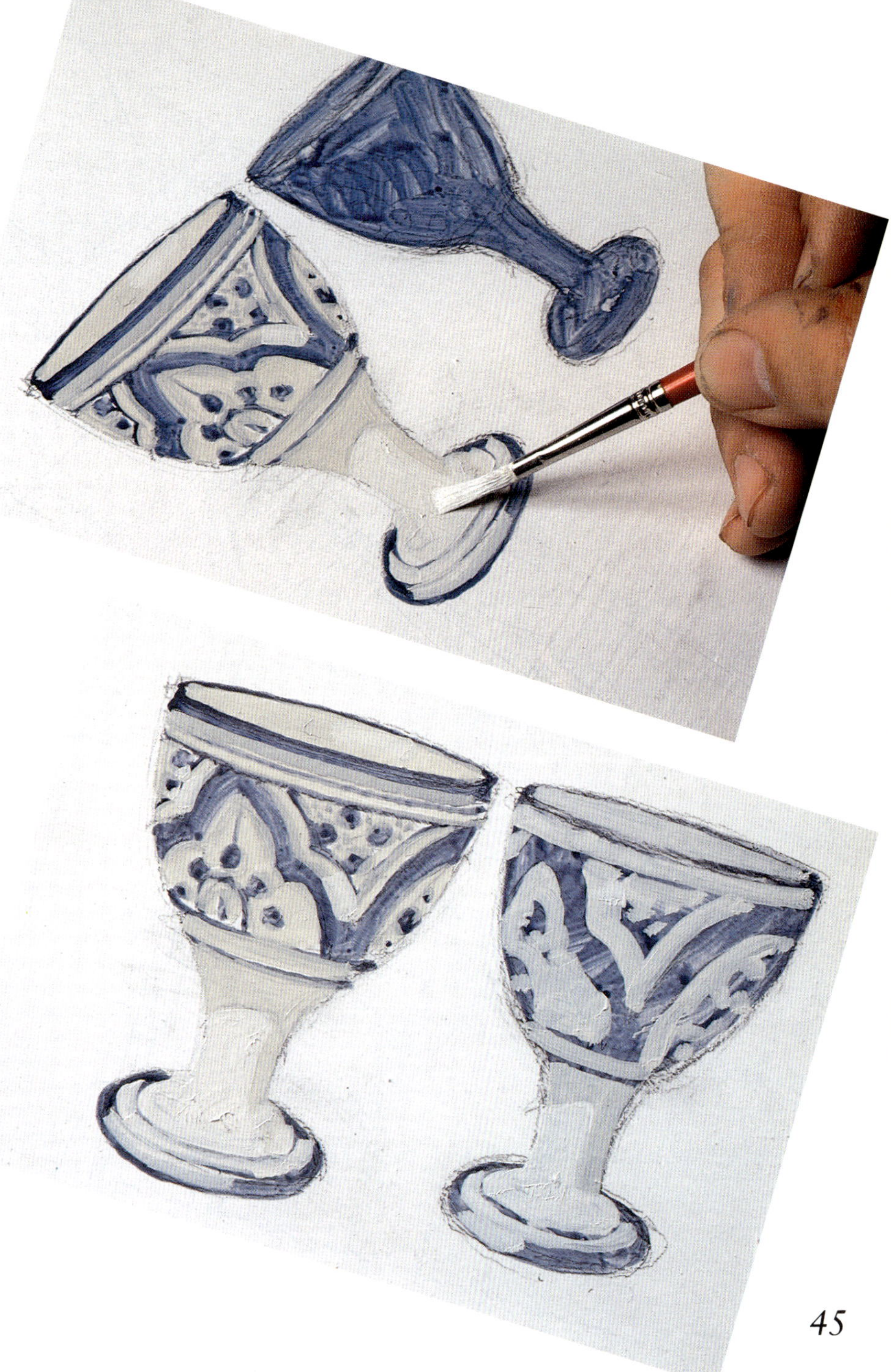

TECHNIQUES

WAYS WITH OUTLINE

Most initial drawings become integrated or covered up by the paint and are rarely visible in the finished picture. They are merely a guide for the ensuing colour. However, there are ways of using outlines that give them far greater importance and make them a feature of the painting.

Coloured outlines

A bold coloured outline will emphasize the shape of the subject, and can be used effectively to bring out the patterns and colours of a still-life arrangement. The artist has done this in the painting of a group of jugs on pages 50–55. The subject in this case is particularly rich in shape, colour and pattern, and the artist decided to emphasize these by starting with a coloured outline.

You can choose a colour that relates to the subject, using the local colour of a particular object for the outline. Thus a bright blue jug would be painted with a bright blue outline. Alternatively, you can give your subject an outline that is in complete contrast to the real colour.

When you use a contrasting colour for the drawing, the outline can affect all the other colours in the picture. For example, if you use an orange outline for a blue jug, both the orange and the blue will look brighter than if used separately. This is because orange and blue are colour 'opposites', and produce a particularly vivid optical effect.

Negative outlines

The French Fauvists often used a negative outline, or *anticerne*. Effectively, this means there is no outline at all; instead there are simply strips of bare

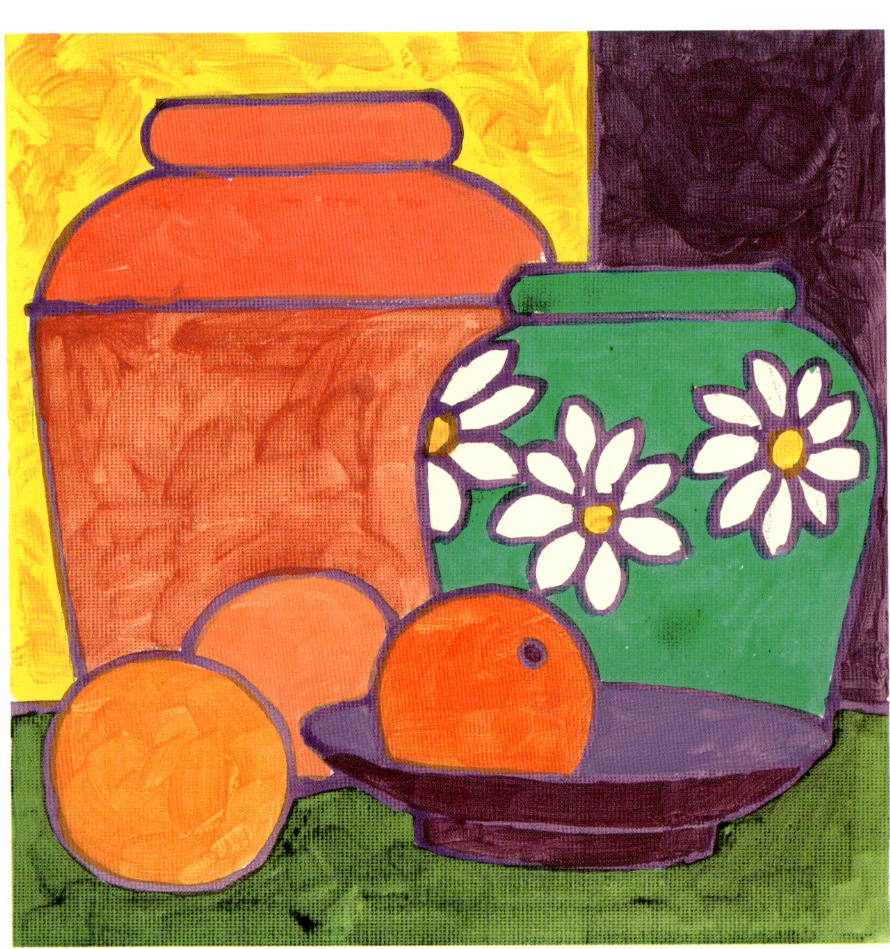

The objects here are brightly coloured, and their brilliance is further emphasized by the use of equally bright outlines in contrasting and complementary colours.

or white primed canvas showing between the patches of colour. The result is similar to that obtained with the coloured outline: it flattens the composition and isolates each shape from its neighbours.

With the *anticerne* technique, however, the dividing outline is white or neutral, so it does not directly affect the painted colours. It makes each colour look brighter merely by separating it from the adjoining colour.

Practically, you will still need a drawing before you paint. The best way is to make a light pencil sketch of the subject but not take the colour right up to the pencil line. The pencil will either not show or can be erased later, and you will be left with strips of bare canvas around each shape.

Coloured outlines
▷ **1** *Bright-red paint is used to draw the outline of the three boxes.*

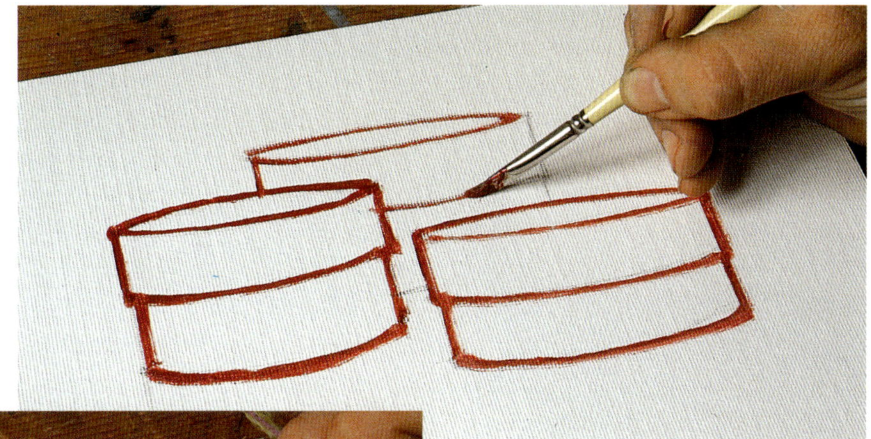

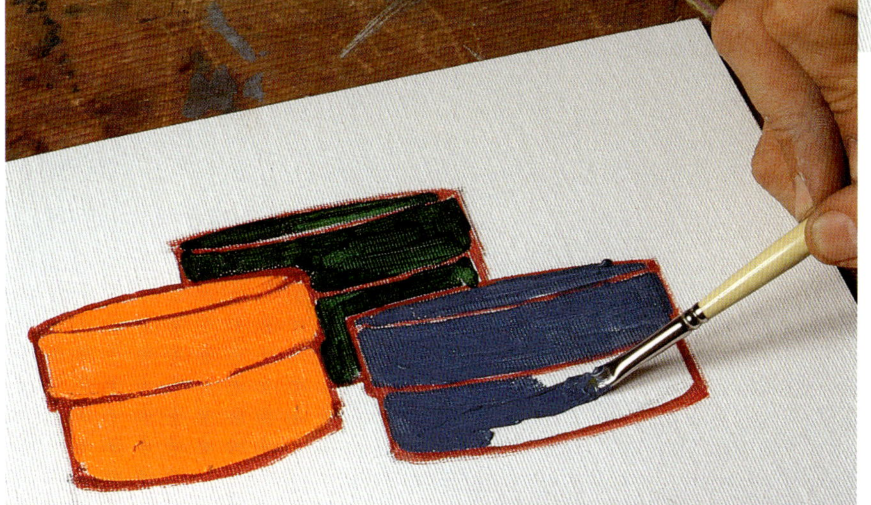

◁ **2** *The local colours – green, yellow and blue – are filled in without obliterating the initial drawing.*

▷ **3** *The artist adds a bright-mauve background. Again, the colour is taken up to the red outline without obliterating the colour. The red separates and enhances the three local colours, giving the overall image an added brightness and resonance.*

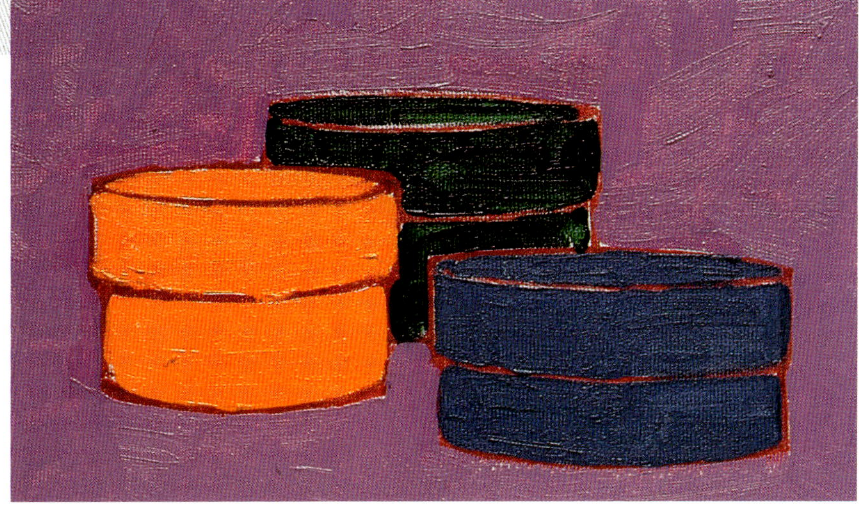

TECHNIQUES

PAINTING STICKS

Drawing with paint and brush requires practice. The very act of mixing the colour means you have to be aware of more than just drawing the subject: you have to think about the palette, whether the paint is the right consistency and whether you have enough of it. Until you are more confident and this process becomes automatic, a more direct way of using colour in your preliminary drawing is to opt for oil pastels or one of the new oil painting sticks, Oilbars.

Oil pastels and Oilbars both give an immediate and bold line which is compatible with oil paint and can be dissolved with turpentine or white spirit. They can also be used without prior colour-mixing on the palette.

Oilbars for drawing
Oilbars are especially good for drawing or sketching

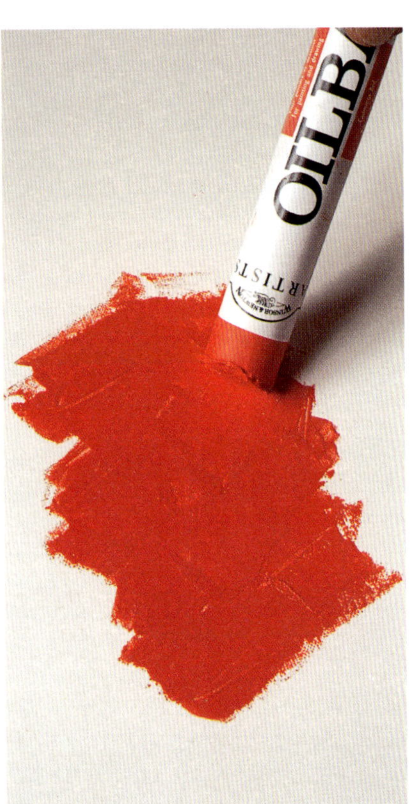

Solid colour
△ **1** *Oilbars are soft and malleable, allowing the artist to block in areas of solid, opaque colour without applying great pressure to the stick.*

▷ **2** *The same colour opacity can be achieved when drawing even or undulating lines.*

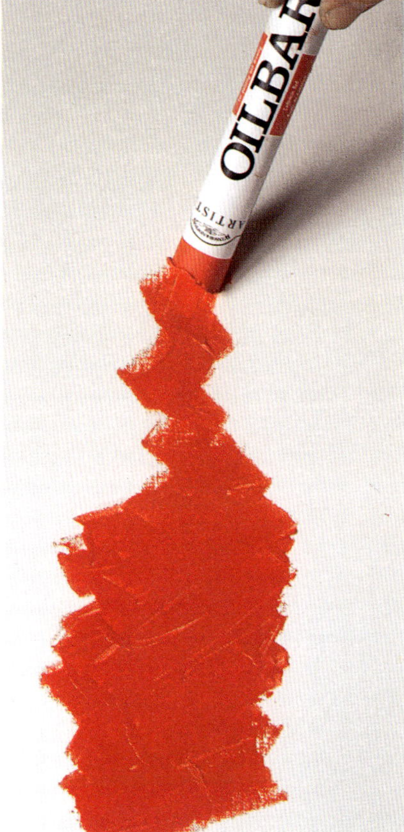

Blending
▷ *Like oil paints, the bar colours can be blended and mixed on the canvas. Here the artist uses yellow over red to get orange.*

the subject on canvas prior to applying paint with a brush. They are basically paint in stick form. These new products are made from the same materials as oil paint – pigment and linseed oil – and are bound with soft wax.

In fact, Oilbars can also be used sometimes instead of brushes if you wish to continue in a bold manner. They can be used for blocking in solid colour; they are soft enough to give a dense line and you can also dip them in turpentine to achieve a more fluid effect. This makes them an excellent drawing tool for a newcomer to oils, who is then left free to concentrate entirely on the drawing without having to think about squeezing paint out of tubes or mixing colour.

The effect is immediate, with nothing to impede or come between the artist and the still life – not even a brush.

Another positive factor from the beginner's point of view is that Oilbars are chunky and produce a similarly chunky line. They come in three sizes, but even the smallest of these discourages fiddly drawing and makes it difficult to become too concerned with detail. From the start, you are forced to concentrate on the most important elements in the subject and to draw these in a broad, minimal way.

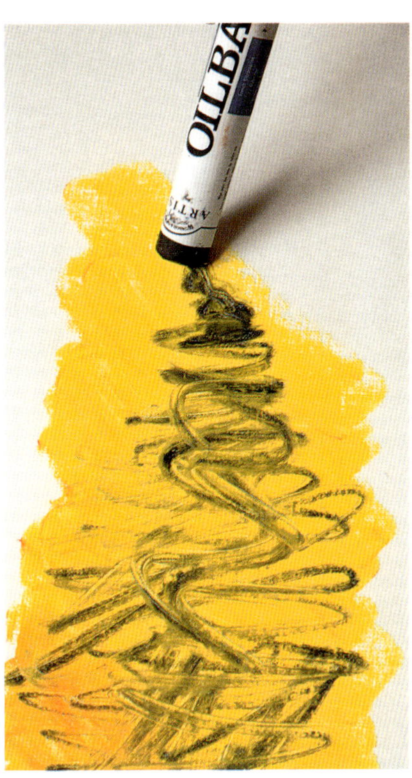

Texture
△ **1** *Overlaid colours can be applied to obtain a variety of textures and colour mixes. Here the artist uses blue over solid yellow to obtain a textured green.*

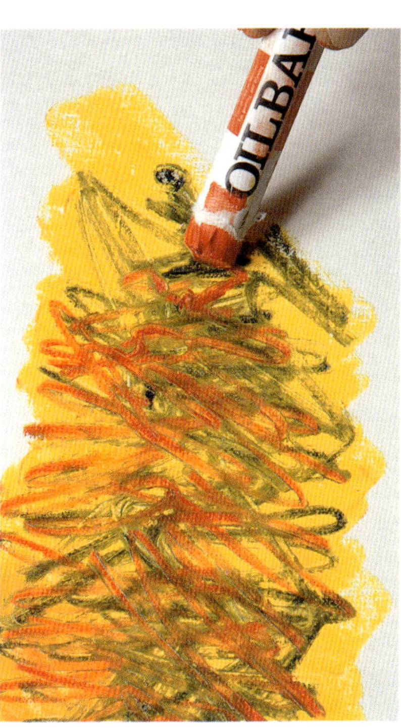

△ **2** *A third colour – or any number of subsequent ones – can be added to this. Here, the artist is scribbling red over the yellow and blue to obtain an overall area of multicoloured texture.*

49

PROJECTS

PATTERNED JUGS

No two artists see a subject in the same way. What makes a great artist stand out from others is not necessarily superb technique alone but also a special and personal way of approaching the subject. Great paintings make us look at familiar objects in a new way, encouraging us to see as the artist chose to interpret, rather than view a slavish copy of what is there.

After seeing the swirling, powerful canvases of Van Gogh, can we ever again look at a sunflower without finding in it some of the movement and colour of those remarkable paintings?

Most artists look for particular elements in a subject, and develop and isolate those things in their paintings. One might work predominantly in tones, concentrating on the lights and darks of the subject; another might choose to emphasize the patterns or textures, and so on.

For the beginner, struggling to come to terms with the medium for the first time, this may all sound rather advanced. But in fact, choosing and concentrating on a single element in a subject is an excellent learning exercise and concentrates the mind in one direction.

Shape and patterns

Colour and pattern are the most striking elements in this arrangement of jugs, and the artist decided to concentrate on these aspects of the subject.

To make the most of the decorative elements, the objects are drawn as flat shapes; there is no attempt to make them look three-dimensional. There are no shadows or highlights in the painting, so that each patch of colour looks like a flat, cut-out shape arranged on the white canvas. The table top is deliberately distorted, and that too becomes a flat shape in the overall design. There is no realistic perspective, so no illusion of space is created.

Coloured outlines

The initial drawing plays an important part in the finished painting. Bright-blue outlines establish the subject as a design – a pattern made up of a series of flat shapes – from the outset, and these same lines become part of the colour scheme of the painting.

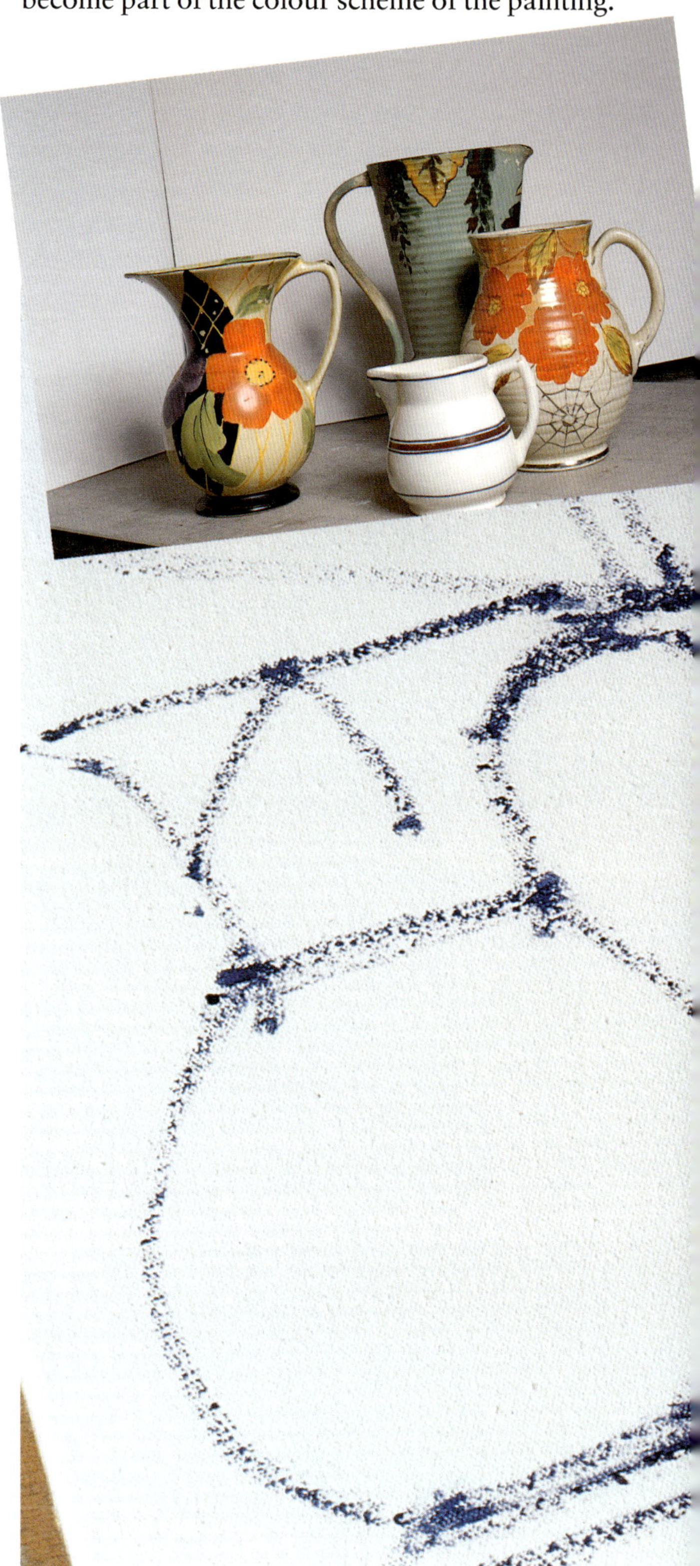

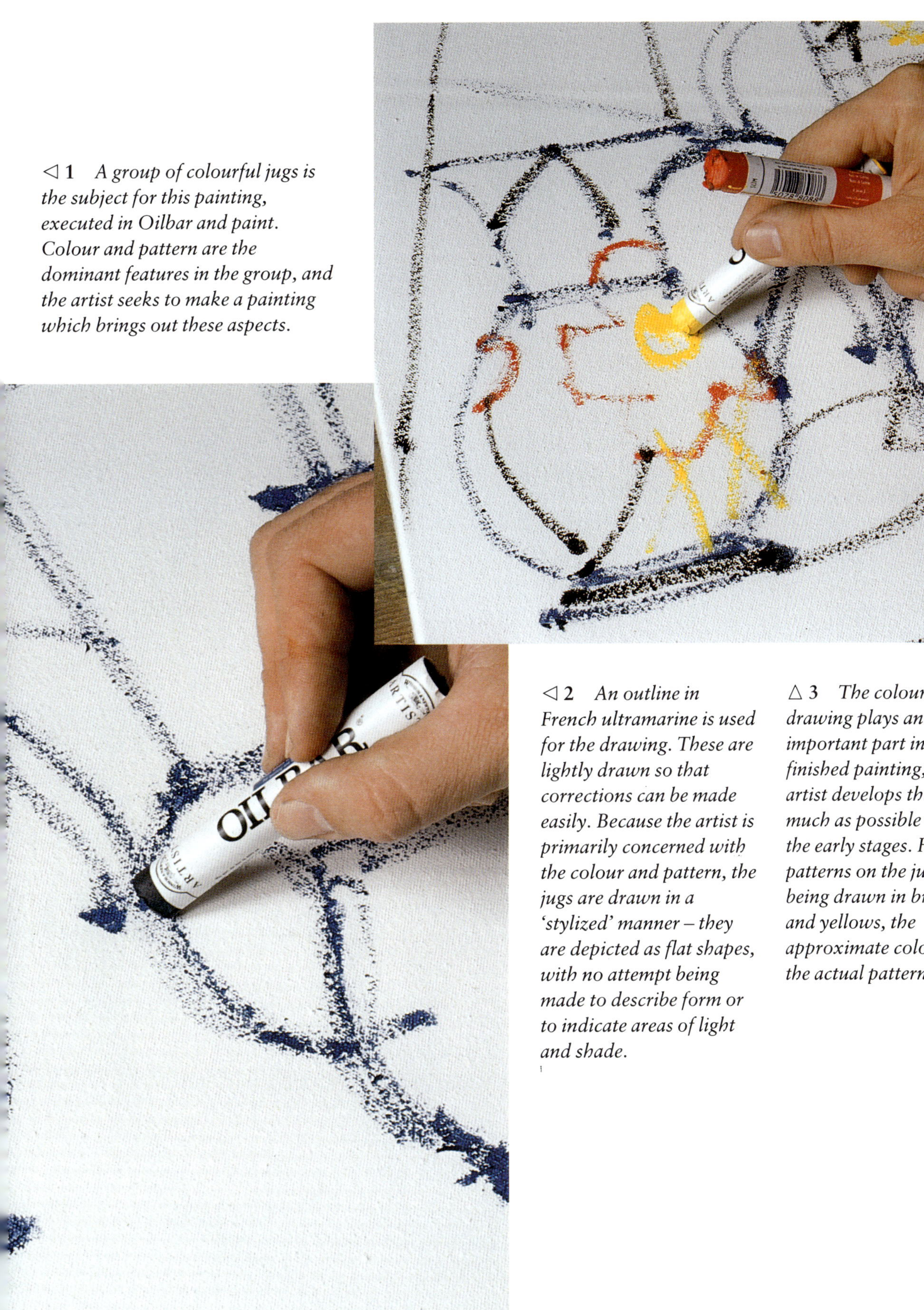

◁ **1**   *A group of colourful jugs is the subject for this painting, executed in Oilbar and paint. Colour and pattern are the dominant features in the group, and the artist seeks to make a painting which brings out these aspects.*

◁ **2**   *An outline in French ultramarine is used for the drawing. These are lightly drawn so that corrections can be made easily. Because the artist is primarily concerned with the colour and pattern, the jugs are drawn in a 'stylized' manner – they are depicted as flat shapes, with no attempt being made to describe form or to indicate areas of light and shade.*

△ **3**   *The coloured drawing plays an important part in the finished painting, and the artist develops this as much as possible during the early stages. Here, the patterns on the jugs are being drawn in bright reds and yellows, the approximate colours of the actual pattern.*

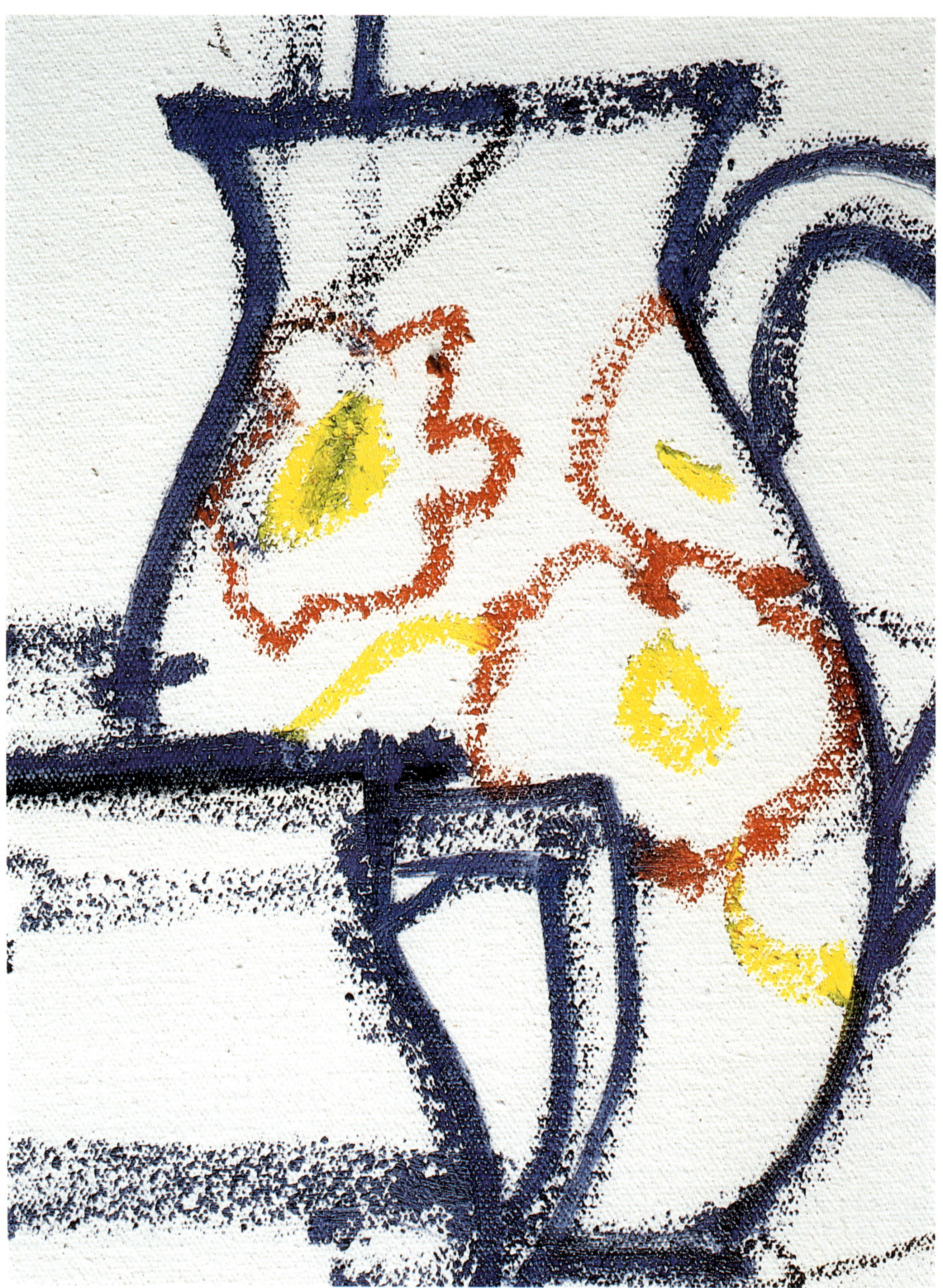

◁ **4**   *During the drawing, corrections are made by laying one light line over another, incorrect, line. Before filling in any solid colour, the artist goes over the drawing with turpentine and a brush, strengthening those lines which will appear in the finished picture.*

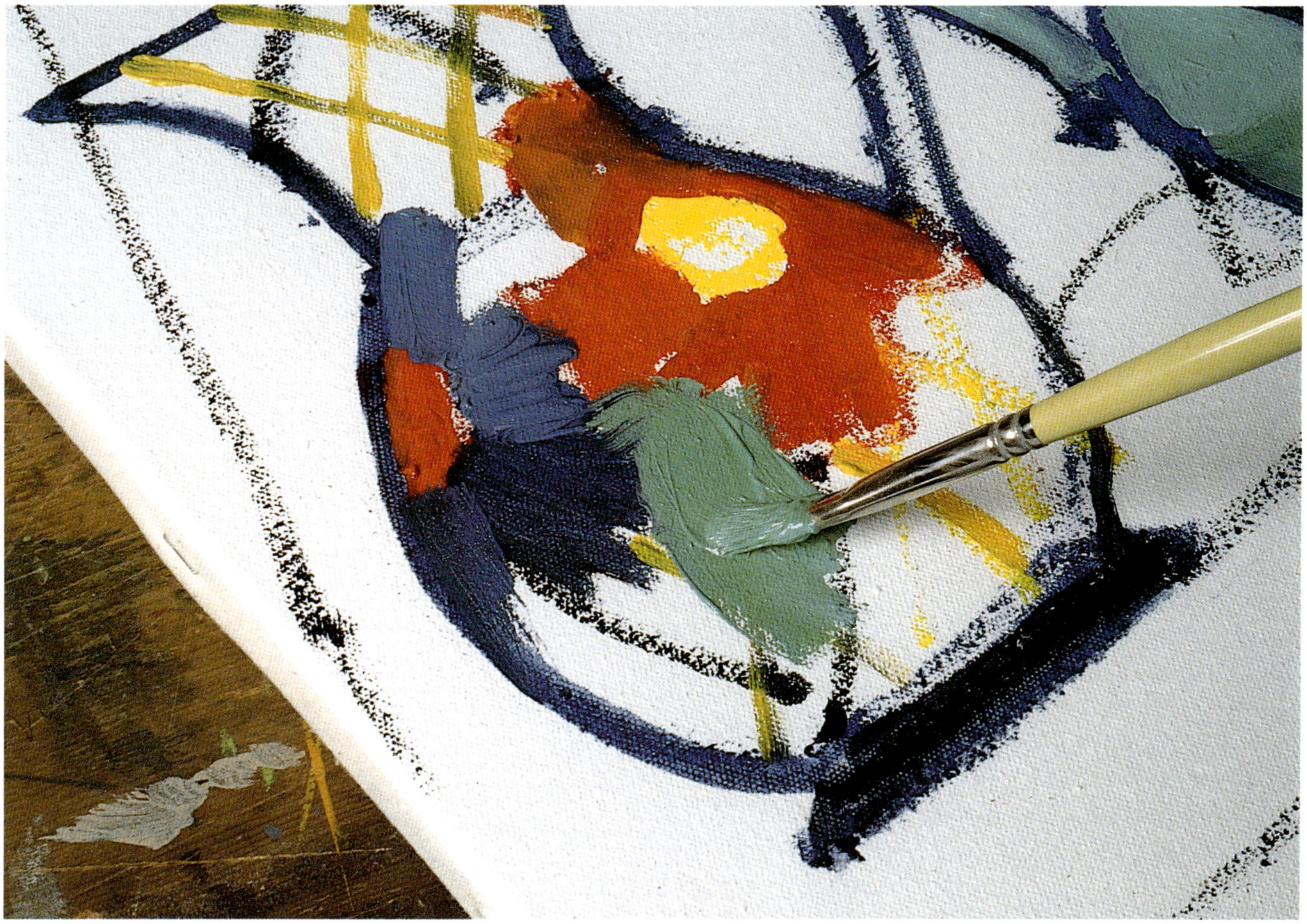

△ **5**   *The drawing is now complete, and solid colour is added in oil paint. Colours are kept flat and bright throughout. The flowers are painted in cadmium red, the leaves in a mixture of French ultramarine, cadmium yellow and white.*

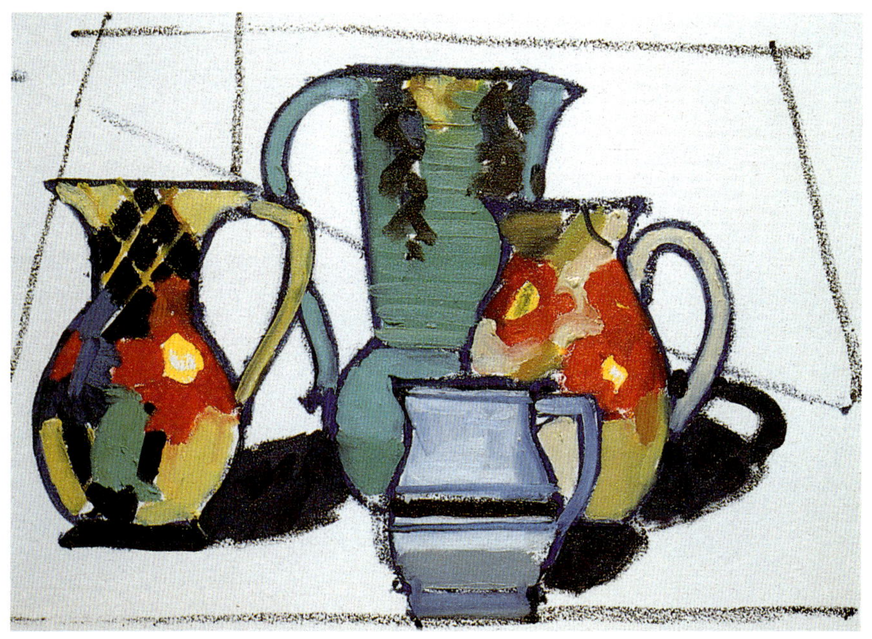

◁ **6**   *The jugs are now almost complete, with each one painted loosely in the colours present on the actual subject. Motifs and patterns are simplified to suit the flat, graphic style of the painting. Detail and fine lines have been omitted in the interests of a broad, general effect.*

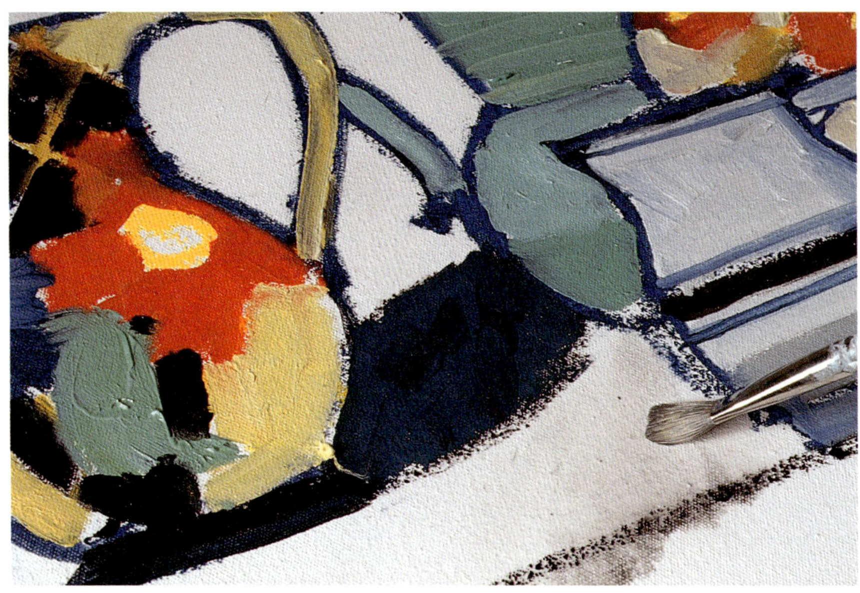

▽ **8** *The background is filled in with cadmium red. To enliven the colour, and prevent such a large area overpowering the patterned jugs, the artist uses Oilbar instead of flat red paint.*

△ **7** *Shadows are painted as flat shapes. Again, the shapes are literal and taken from the actual subject, but the colour is not. Shadows are painted in an exaggerated dark purple, mixed from black, French ultramarine and cadmium red, to fit in with the overall design of the picture. Here, the artist is removing excess black with turpentine so that it will not affect subsequent bright colours.*

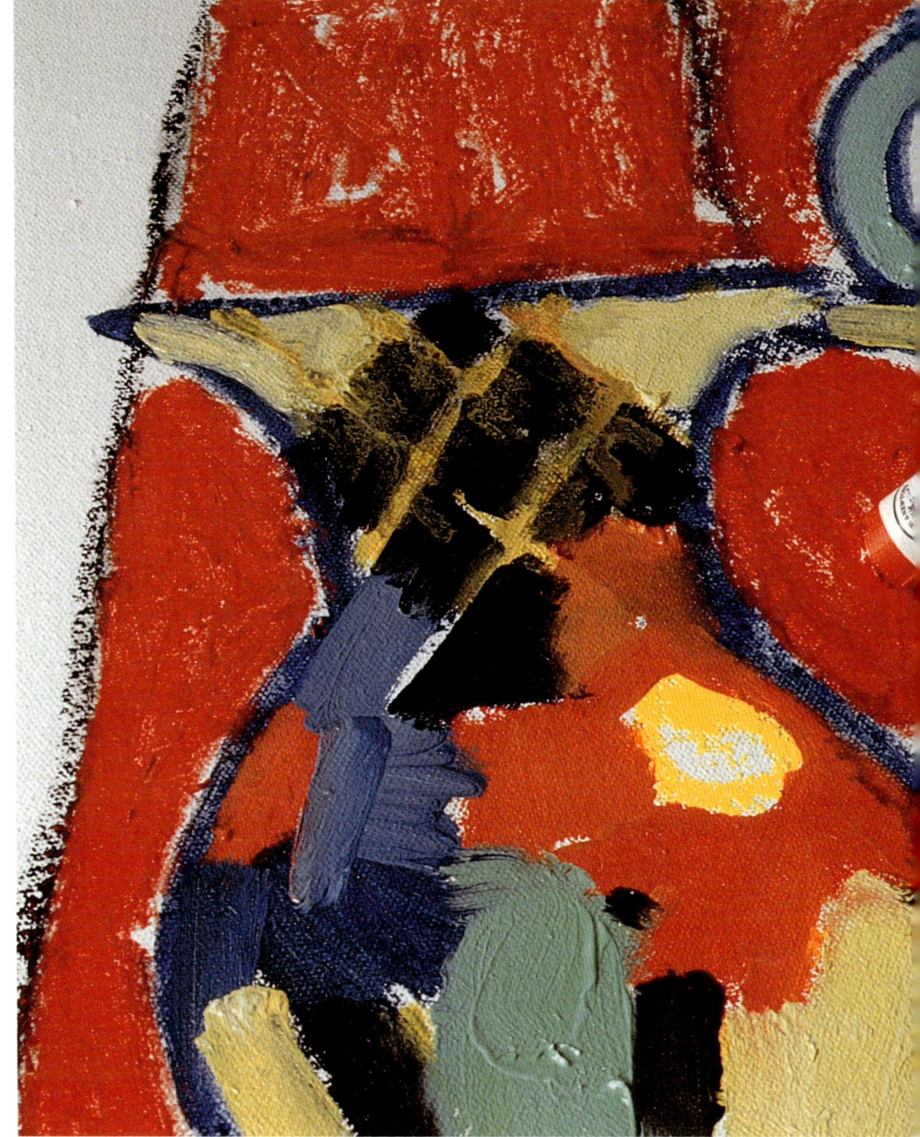

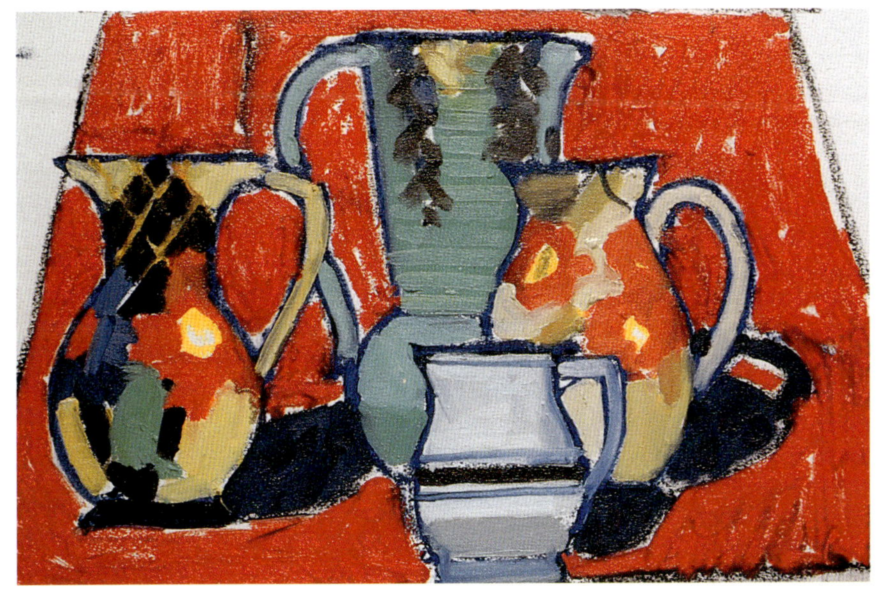

◁ **9**   *Flecks of bright white which have been allowed to show through the red break up the flat colour to produce a lively, textured background.*

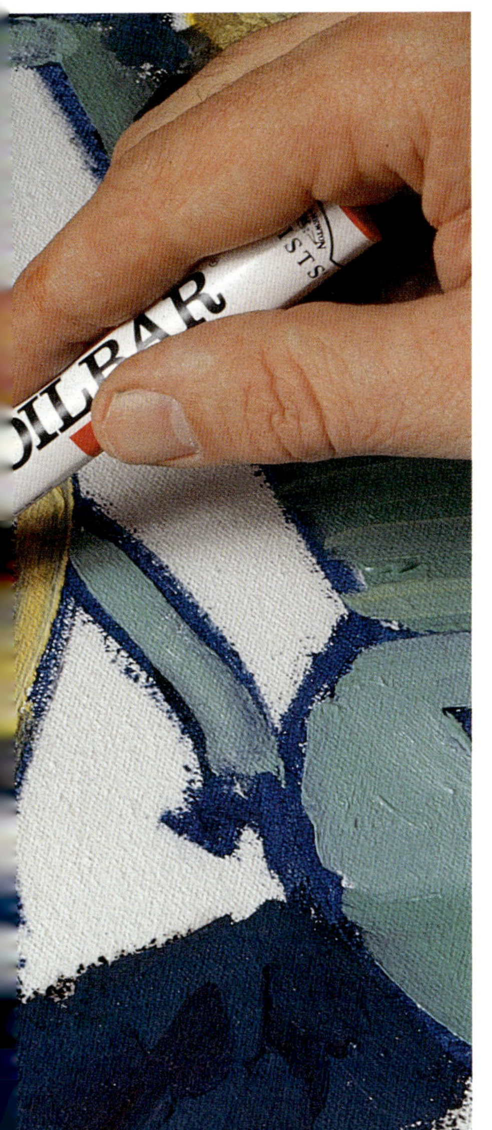

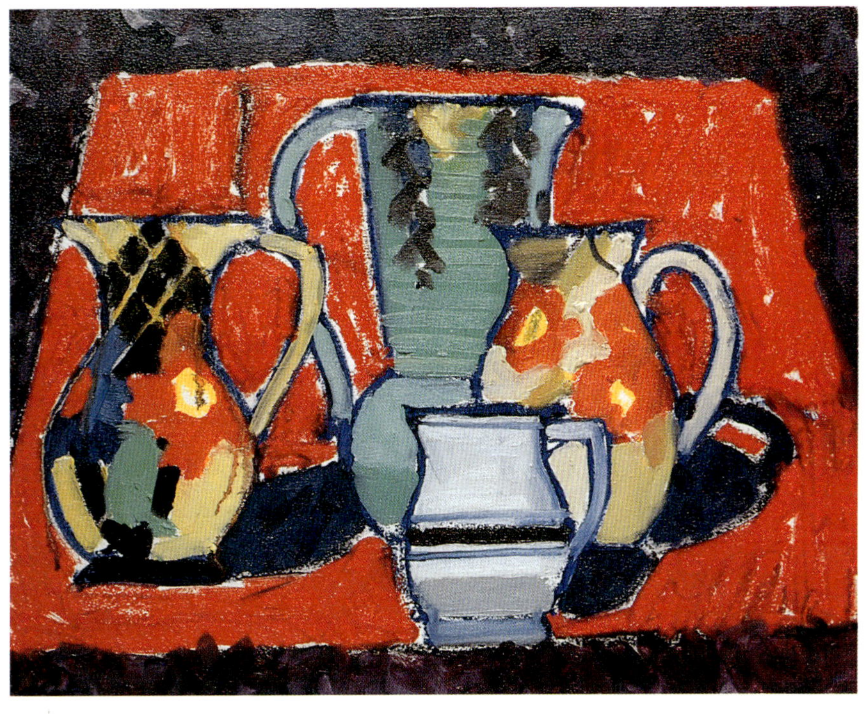

△ **10**   *The original blue drawing is a powerful element in the completed picture. Not only does it give the painting an overall unity but it also separates the shapes, making each colour look brighter than it would if used on its own.*

TECHNIQUES

NEGATIVE SHAPES

A long-established exercise for art students is to draw negative shapes. This involves drawing not the subject itself, but the shapes and spaces within the subject. So, if you were drawing a still life with a jug, teapot and cups, you would not immediately draw the shapes of those objects, but would start by drawing the spaces between them: the background shapes and the shapes made by the handles.

This is not simply a topsy-turvy way of going about a drawing; it is actually the best way of making sure the drawing is correct, and that the composition fits properly on to the paper or canvas.

If your negative shapes are not right, then the teapot and cups will be distorted. You will spot this immediately, once you begin to draw around the shapes, because you know exactly what a teapot and cups look like. However, had you started drawing the objects first, you might not have noticed if either the spaces between them or the background shapes were wrong.

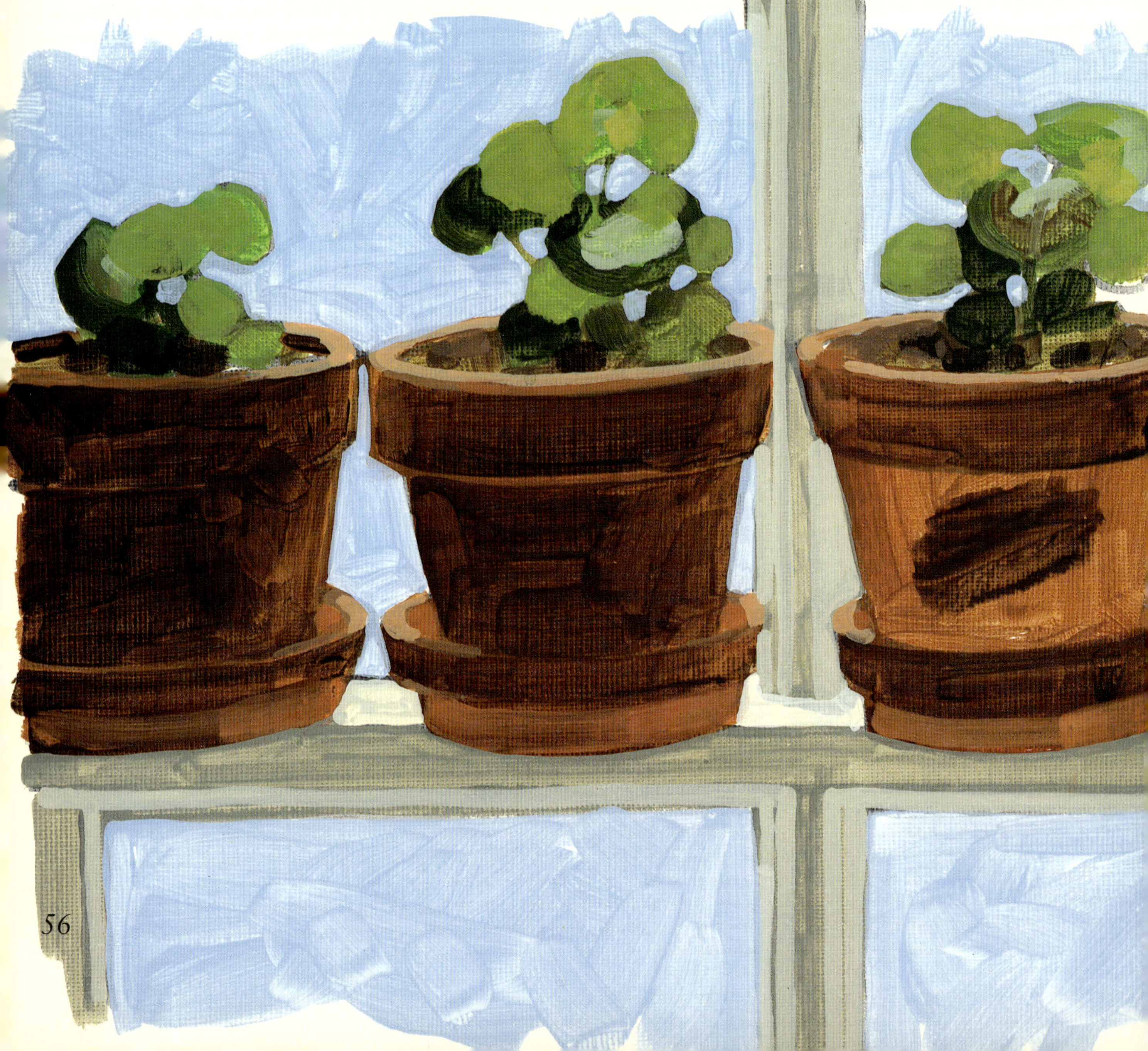

The exercise is a valuable one, because once you have made a conscious effort to see the negative shapes, you will always be aware of their existence and importance.

Background and surrounds

When starting to paint, there is a common tendency to make the subject too small in relation to the canvas. This is true of all subjects, but is particularly so with still-life ones, because they are often placed against a plain or uneventful background which tends to get overlooked. The result is lots of boring, formless background space which has to be somehow filled in, and which often fades away towards the edges of the canvas.

It is important, therefore, to treat both the background and the surface on which the objects are placed as a positive part of the composition. Backgrounds and surrounds have shapes which should be just as taut and considered as everything else in the picture. The shape and proportion of the canvas is very much part of this, because the edges of the canvas form the edges of the background shapes. They are the equivalent of a drawn line.

The illustrations here show various still-life compositions. In each case the first considerations have been the background, the surface on which the objects are placed and the spaces between the objects. The objects themselves have emerged automatically.

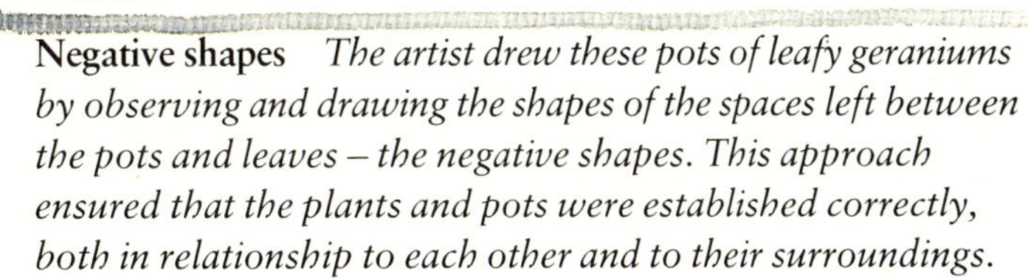

Negative shapes   *The artist drew these pots of leafy geraniums by observing and drawing the shapes of the spaces left between the pots and leaves – the negative shapes. This approach ensured that the plants and pots were established correctly, both in relationship to each other and to their surroundings.*

PROJECTS

THINGS WITH HANDLES

A cluster consisting of jug and cups makes the subject here. The cups are similar, but each is different enough to make it a tricky subject to draw.

Instead of starting with the objects themselves, the artist begins by establishing the shapes behind the group. This approach helps to improve the composition as a whole. By starting with the negative shapes, the artist ensures that these make a positive contribution to the painting and are not merely incidental.

The drawing
Negative shapes were uppermost in the artist's mind when he made the preliminary pencil drawing. The first step was to mark the positions of the vertical background division and the horizontal line of the table, dividing the canvas into three basic sections. Only when these were established was the rest of the subject considered.

A major obstacle to good drawing is an inability to forget the nature of the subject – to draw what we know to be there rather than what we can see. The artist tried to forget, therefore, that he was drawing a familiar jug and cups, and instead sought to perceive them as unknown objects.

Handles particularly can be difficult to draw. Beginners inevitably make them too small and spindly in relation to the vessel. The width of a cup or jug handle changes, usually getting a lot thicker as it joins the vessel at its base. Because we know handles are handles, and have used them all our lives, we have probably never really noticed that their bases are often three times as thick as they are elsewhere. No wonder, therefore, that we tend to understate this when it comes to drawing them.

To overcome this problem the artist decided not to draw the handles at all. Instead, they emerged as resulting shapes when he had drawn the three

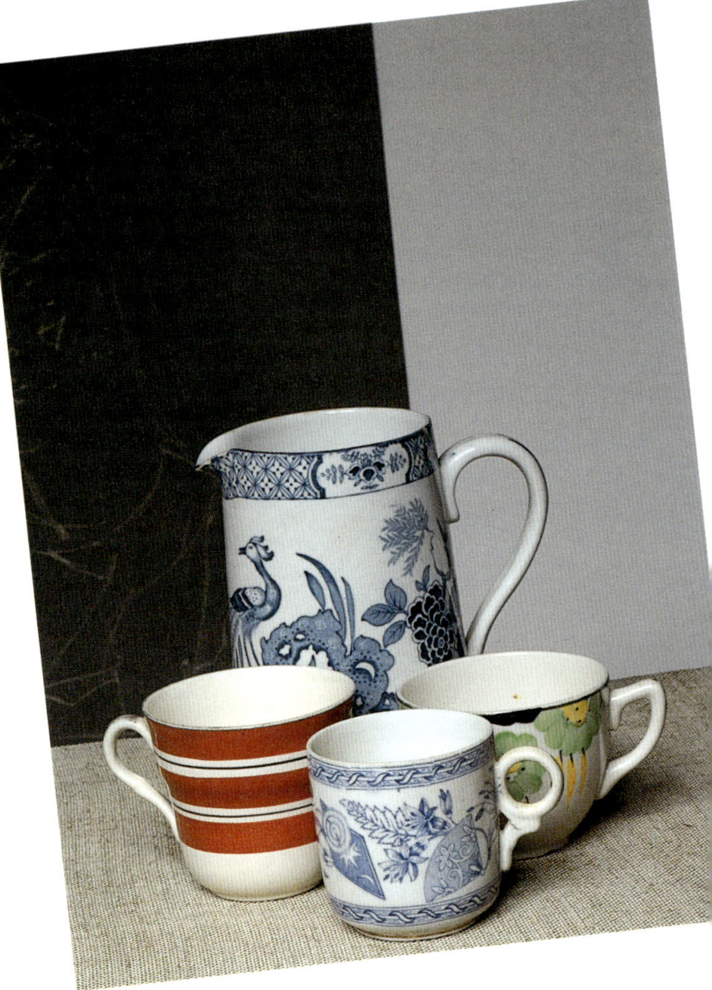

△ **1** *The subject consists of a group of cups and a jug standing on a plain table and placed against two contrasting background shapes. It is an arrangement in which the three surrounding shapes are as important to the composition as the subject itself.*

surrounding shapes – the background and table top, the basic shapes which we referred to above. The handles became evident only after the artist had drawn the background shape, taking this up to the outside contour of the handle and then drawing the shape of the space visible through the handle.

▽ **2**   In the preliminary drawing, the artist starts by dividing the canvas into three main areas – the two background shapes and the table top. The jugs and cups are then fitted into the space allocated for them, in the centre of the composition. Here, the first background is blocked in with brown, mixed from raw umber and cadmium red.

▽ **3**   The second background shape is then painted in a mixture of Payne's grey and white, with an added touch of the first colour mixture.

▽ **4**   The table colour is mixed from white, red and raw umber. As each of the three main background areas is blocked in, the subject emerges as a strong negative shape which is now ready to be developed.

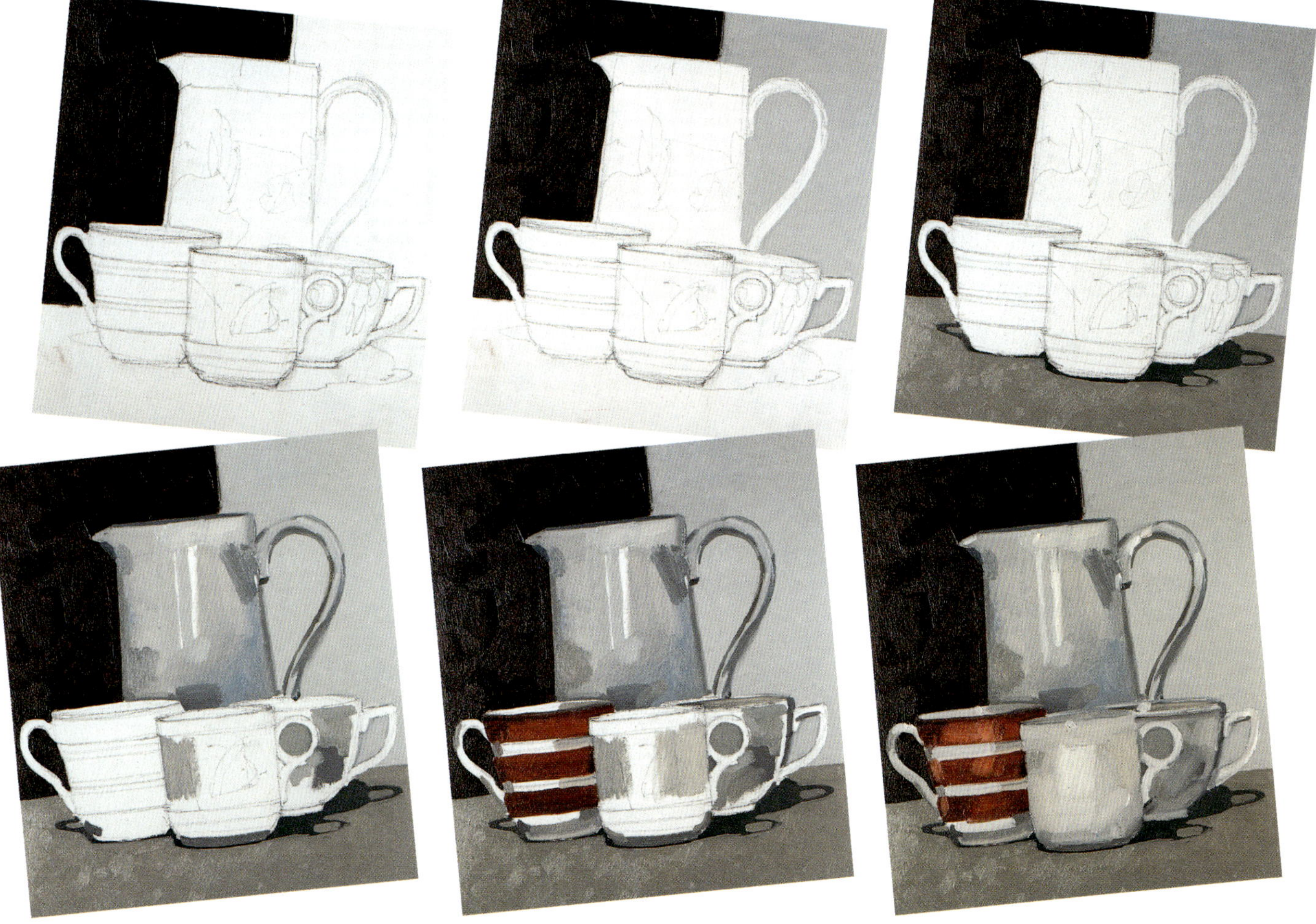

△ **5**   The jug is painted in tones of grey, and the artist then moves on to the cups and shadows. Still approaching the subject through its negative shapes, the spaces between the handles are redefined and painted before starting on the cups themselves. The handles emerge when the surrounding background is blocked in.

△ **6**   Using broad strokes, the artist works into the cups, establishing main shadow areas to describe the rounded form of the cups. The red stripes are also painted at this stage.

△ **7**   In the finished picture, the subject and background are brought together as equally important elements. By tackling the negative shapes first, the abstract elements of the composition were established before the actual subject was developed. The jug and cups are effectively 'carved' out of the surrounding background areas.

More advanced steps

THE THEME of colour is developed in this chapter in a purely practical way. Most academic introductions to the subject illustrate the 'colour wheel', showing how each of the primaries – red, yellow and blue – has its opposite, complementary colour. Thus the opposite of red is green, the opposite of blue is orange and the opposite of yellow is violet.

Instead of reproducing the colour wheel, we put the complementaries immediately to practical use, with paintings designed to introduce basic colour-use as part of the development of specific pictures. Following the steps of the professionals, the examples in this chapter cover such related techniques as masking and glazing.

A natural extension of colour is tone, which recognizes and uses the light and dark properties of particular colours. Everybody knows what colour is, but tone is often overlooked, even though it is just as important.

This chapter also illustrates underpainting, in which the first stage of a painting is to lay monochrome tones. Colours are developed from this, leading to a harmonious whole.

(top row, left to right)
Cobalt blue + cadmium yellow deep
Cobalt blue + lemon yellow
Cerulean blue + cadmium yellow medium
Prussian blue + cadmium yellow pale
Prussian blue + yellow ochre

(centre row, left to right)
Alizarin crimson + lemon yellow
Indian red + yellow ochre
Cadmium red + cadmium yellow medium
Cadmium red + lemon yellow

(bottom row, left to right)
Cadmium red + cobalt blue
Prussian blue + alizarin crimson

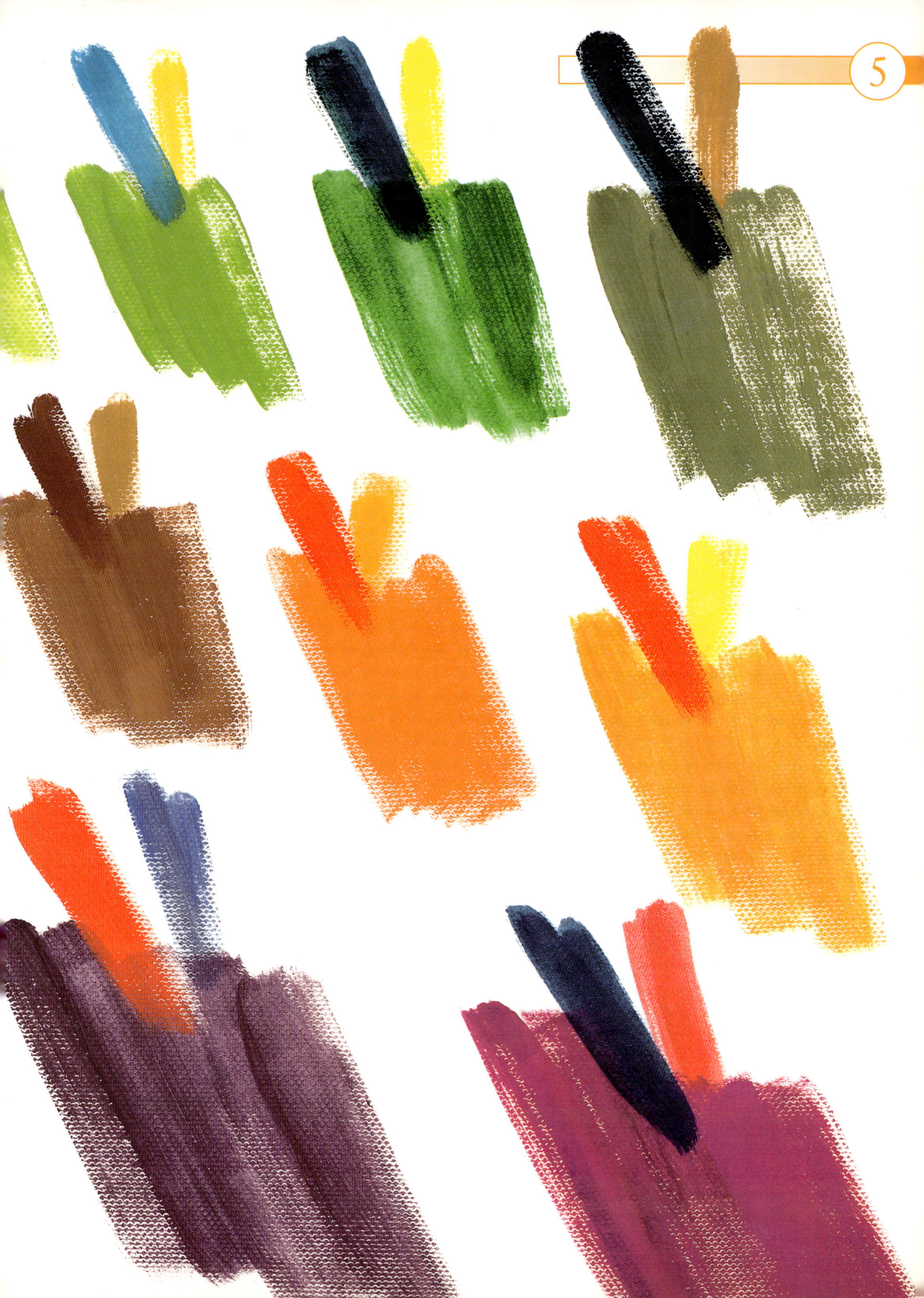

TECHNIQUES

PRACTICAL MIXING

Your basic palette already contains a fair number of colours – more than enough easily to mix any colour you are likely to need. The combinations are endless, and discoveries will be made in the course of your painting. However, a few informed experiments will familiarize you with the colour range and help you to become aware of the possibilities.

Primaries and secondaries

The primaries – red, yellow and blue – are the most flexible of all colours, and from these you can in theory mix any other colour you need, including the secondary colours – violet, orange and green. A little practice, using just the primary colours, will greatly increase your colour vocabulary and make colour-mixing a much less daunting prospect.

Strictly speaking, primaries and secondaries are pure colours that do not vary. But in practice there is no such thing as objective colour-mixing, and you will greatly increase the range of your palette if you start with two reds, cadmium and alizarin; two blues, French ultramarine and cerulean; and two yellows, cadmium and lemon.

The chart on the previous page shows how different the secondary colours can be when they

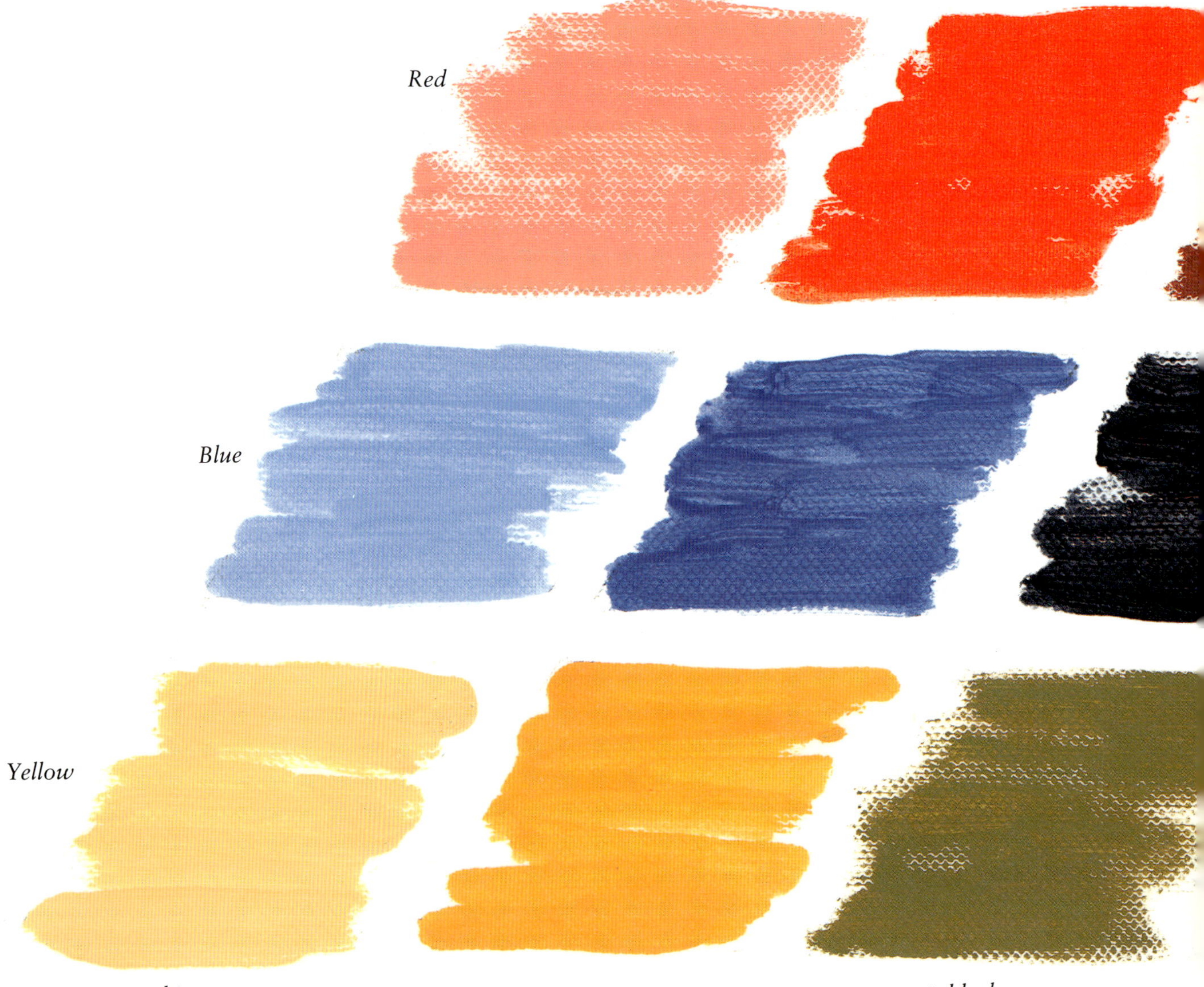

come from different reds, yellows and blues. You should also try varying the quantities of each primary colour, thus making yellow-greens, blue-greens and so on.

Tones

Some colours are pale; others are dark. The light or dark content of a colour is referred to as its 'tone', or tonal quality. Occasionally pale tones are referred to as 'tints'. To lighten the tone of a colour, you add white; to make a colour darker, it can be mixed with black.

In practice, however, the use of too much black in a painting can produce a grey, muddy appearance, and there are practical alternatives to darkening a colour simply by adding black. The three examples opposite show the results when the primaries are darkened by mixing with black, raw umber and Payne's grey.

Neutrals

A true neutral is mixed from the primaries but has no recognizable colour of its own. Strictly speaking, there is no such thing as a neutral colour, but in painting language a 'neutral' blue is one that contains a little red and yellow; a neutral red, one that contains some blue and yellow; and a neutral yellow, one that has a little blue and red mixed with it.

This sounds complicated, but all it means is that you can neutralize a colour simply by mixing it with a little of its opposite colour. Thus, if a red is too bright, you can tone it down with a touch of green, dulling the colour without changing it.

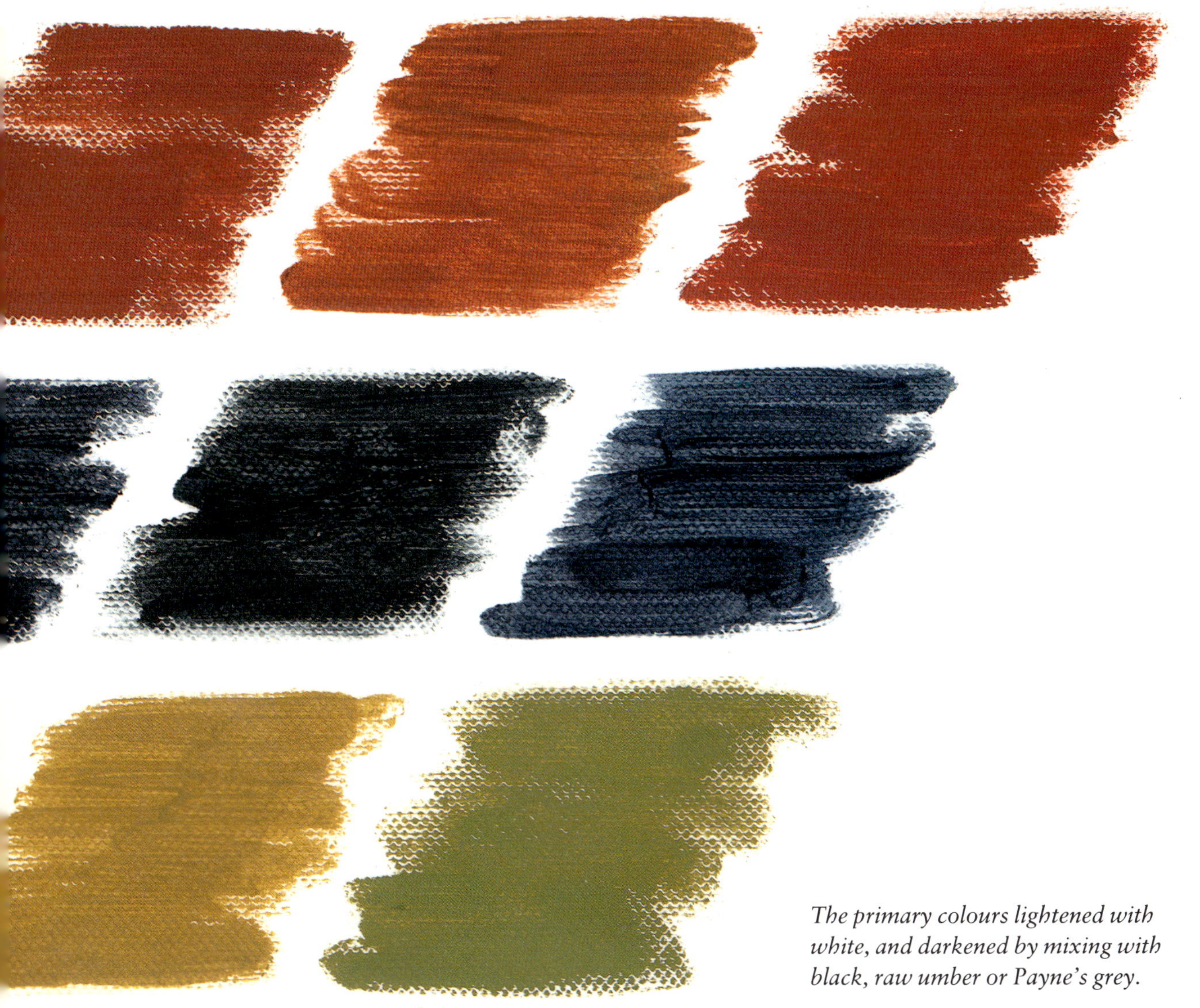

raw umber   *+ Payne's grey*

The primary colours lightened with white, and darkened by mixing with black, raw umber or Payne's grey.

TECHNIQUES

UNDERSTAND COLOUR

For the painter, colour is not so much a technical subject that can be worked out scientifically; rather, it is what makes painting fun and what inspires so many to take it up. The only way to get to know about colour is to have a go. Explore the possibilities and do not be afraid to experiment. The paints laid out on your palette are just the beginning – the basic ingredients for many recipes – and you can use them as you like. There is nothing sacred about the paints themselves; they are produced by a manufacturer. It is you, the artist, who decides how to mix and use the colours.

Local colour
When we talk of a green apple, a yellow lemon and so on, we are speaking of the actual colour of the object – the colour it is when not affected by light, shade or reflections. 'Yellow' and 'green' are useful labels for describing objects, but they are best forgotten when painting, because the colour of every subject is affected by other factors. An apple cannot be painted just green, or a lemon simply yellow.

Looking for colour
Take your lemon or apple, place it on any surface and look carefully to see how many other colours you can see in a single piece of fruit. You will find

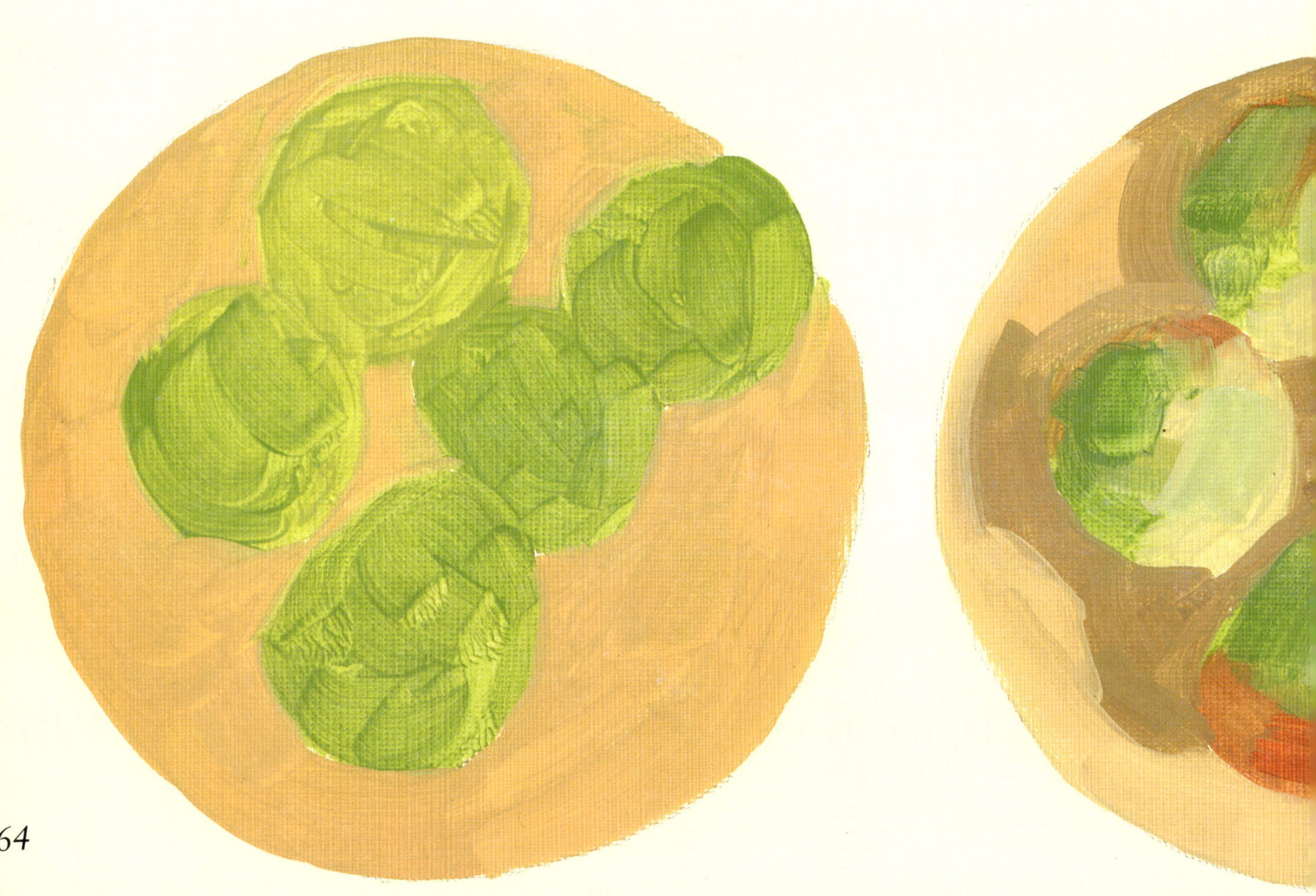

that the shadow areas are not just grey, or even a darker tone of the local colour; and the light areas are not merely a paler tone. You will also see traces of many other colours, particularly those reflected from the surrounds and background.

The still-life paintings of Cézanne and the Impressionists are obvious and excellent examples of colour observed in this way. These artists not only saw colour but also manipulated their findings in a creative and imaginative way. Cézanne captured the 'appleness' of apples by selecting and exaggerating the colours he observed within them.

(left to right)
Local colour
'Found' colour
Coloured shadows

Colourful shadows
The shadow thrown by an object is never totally isolated from the object itself. Obviously the colour of the table or surface on which it is placed affects the colour of the shadow to a large extent. The table may be brown, but the shadow is never merely a darker tone of the same brown. It is inevitably affected by the colour of the subject.

Look at the shadow of the painted orange on page 71. The fruit is placed on a sheet of blue paper, but the shadow is deep purple – a mixture of the blue with added tones of orange.

Frequently, when painting a simple, brightly coloured subject, you will find the thrown shadow contains traces of an opposite or complementary colour. Thus a lemon might throw a purple shadow; a green apple, a reddish shadow; and so on. By slightly exaggerating these colours, the shadows will become a lively and interesting part of the whole subject.

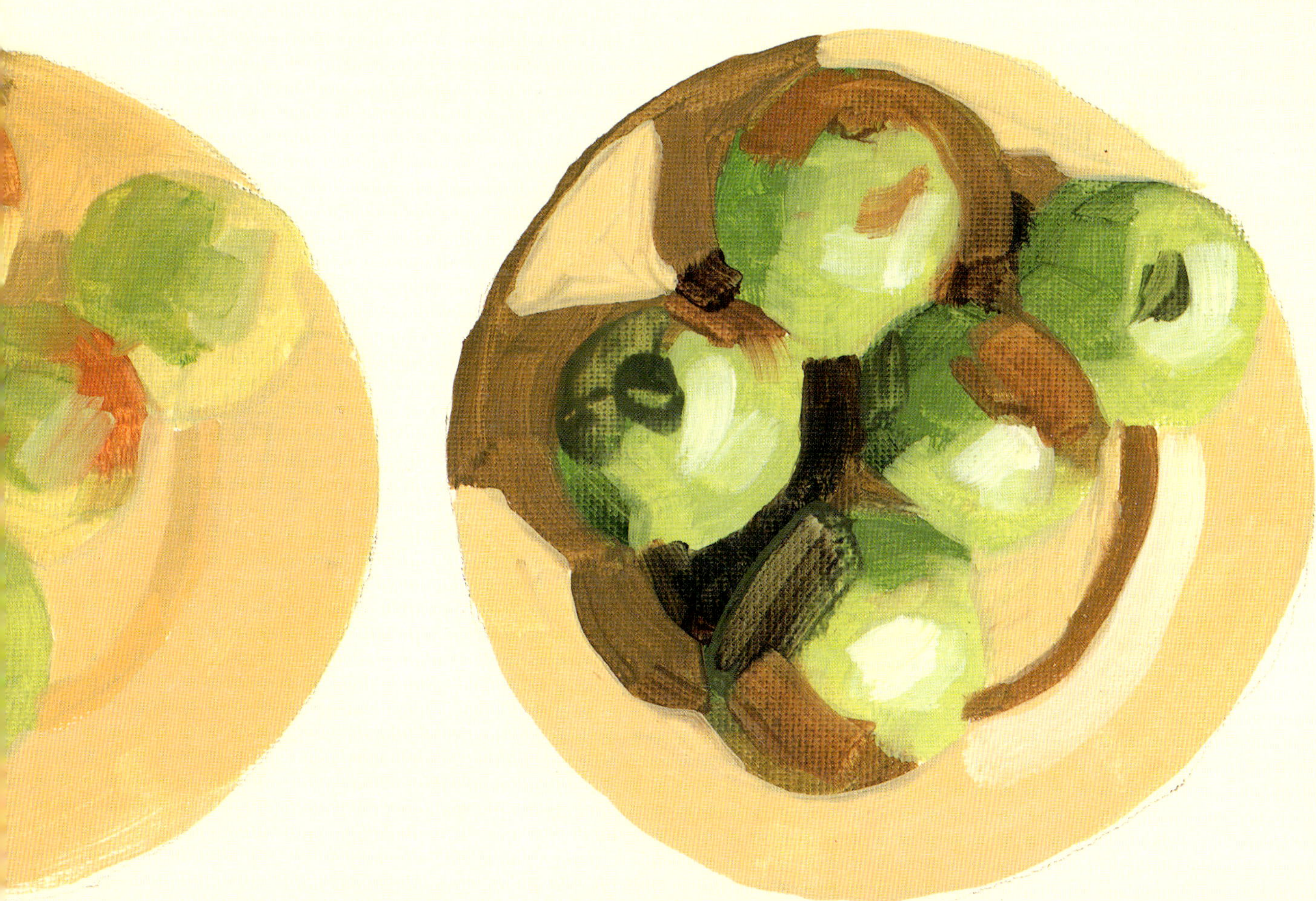

TECHNIQUES

EASY COLOUR

A primitive or naïve painting is one in which the colour is used literally rather than visually – painted from knowledge rather than from looking at the subject. Children's pictures are often painted in this way, with the grass bright green because they 'know' it's green, a blue sky and so on.

These preconceived ideas about colour, often with us since childhood, are not easy to overcome in later life. This is why, when it comes to painting, we fall back on knowledge rather than observation. Yet in our everyday lives, most of us have a sophis-ticated and highly developed sense of colour. This is usually manifested in the way we appreciate our surroundings, the way we dress or the way in which we decorate our homes.

So why can colour cause such problems when it comes to painting? And what is the best method of getting away from the crude colours of childhood and using colour in a creative and personal way?

A simple exercise

One very simple way to achieve a harmonious colour scheme in a painting is to mix a little of a selected colour with all the other colours you use.

Obviously, if the chosen colour is too strong, you will end up with a tinted painting – a picture which looks as if the subject has been viewed through a sheet of coloured glass. But if you choose a fairly neutral colour, one that corresponds with the

(inset)
Colour harmony   *The colours used in this still life are predominantly warm earth pigments including the siennas and umbers. These were applied to a warm, neutral support of a similar tone, thus giving an overall unity to the finished picture.*

Colour perspective   *A sense of space is achieved here by contrasting strong, warm foreground colours with a cooler, paler background.*

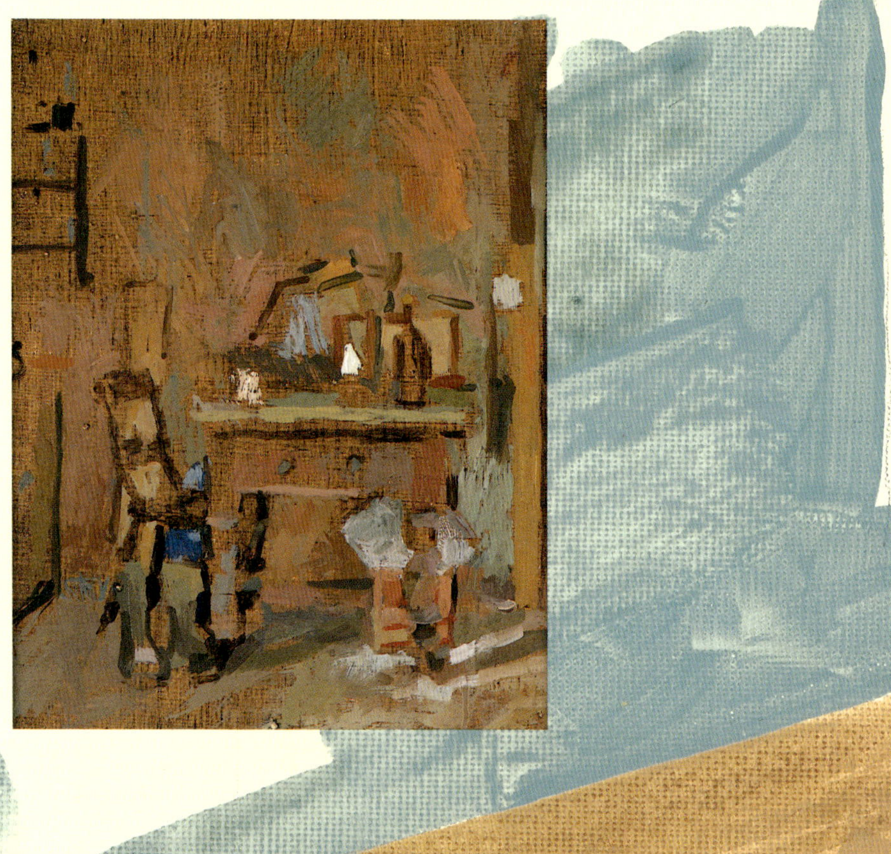

subject, it can act as a sort of visual binder to the painting and 'tone down' the colours without greatly changing them.

This is an elementary exercise, and a device that you will not necessarily want to use once you are more accustomed to mixing tones and colours. But it does demonstrate what a little 'toning' can achieve, and it gets you into the habit of mixing colour rather than using it literally or directly from the tube.

Colour perspective

Pursuing this idea a little further, you can create a sense of space in a painting by using a predominance of one colour in the foreground and another in the background. By separating distant objects from nearer ones in this way, you effectively create distance or colour perspective in the picture.

Colour perspective is common in landscapes, when the far distance is paler and usually contains more blue than the foreground. But the theory applies equally to still-life subjects, particularly those in which there is an obvious space between the foreground and background or, like the illustration here, there is a window or other extension of space behind the subject.

Cold colours tend to recede, while warm or hot colours stand out. So, if the furthest objects contain traces of cool grey, blue or green, they will fall back in the picture, especially if the near objects are painted in warmer tones.

Again, this is an exercise in colour behaviour and you will doubtless want to modify and develop it. But it is a useful way of tackling colour in painting, and one which is used by many artists.

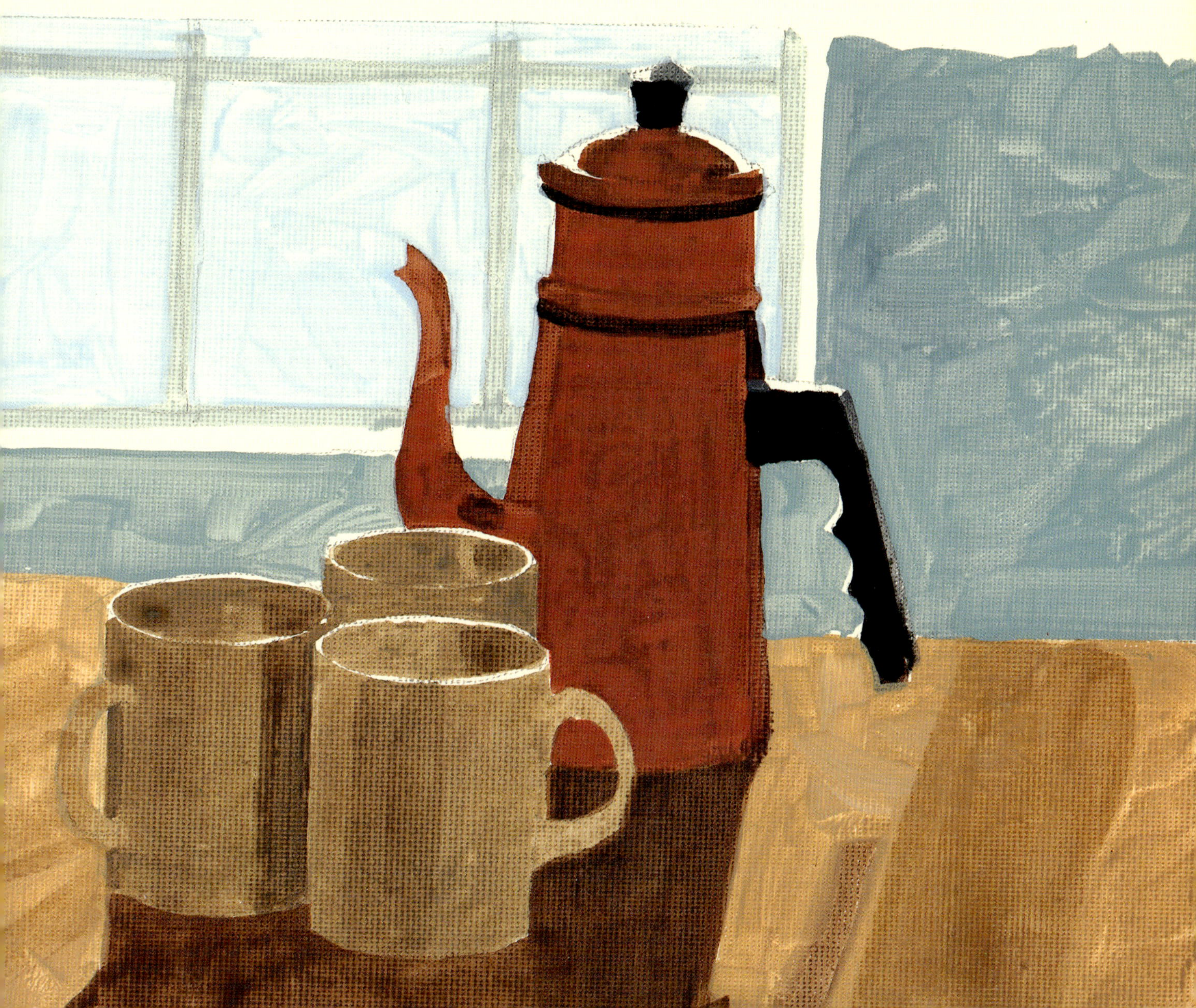

PROJECTS

ORANGE ON BLUE

Here is a straightforward example of the use of complementary colours – oranges against a blue surround. Orange and blue are opposites on the colour wheel and are therefore complementary. When used next to each other in a painting, complementary colours create an optical effect which brings out the brightness in each colour. As a warm colour, orange tends to jump forward from the picture surface, while the cooler blue recedes.

This characteristic of opposite colours can be useful when the intention is to create a sense of space in the picture. It works here because the receding blue is the background to the oranges. Even so, the subject and its surroundings cannot be completely separate, and the artist must find ways to harmonize the composition, to bring the two together.

Cool shadows

To unite the subject with its surroundings, the artist has mixed cooler blue tones with the orange, and vice versa. The fruit is painted predominantly in warm oranges mixed from cadmium yellow, cadmium red and white – the local colours. In some shaded places, however, the artist has added alizarin crimson – a cooler, purplish red – to the orange mix, while the very dark areas are heavily tinged with the blue of the background.

The shadow is a mixture of blue, alizarin and touches of red and yellow.

Background shapes

The purpose of this painting is to demonstrate the use of complementary colours. Everything else, including the composition, is therefore kept deliberately simple and minimal, so as not to distract from the main theme of the picture.

A simple composition, however, requires as

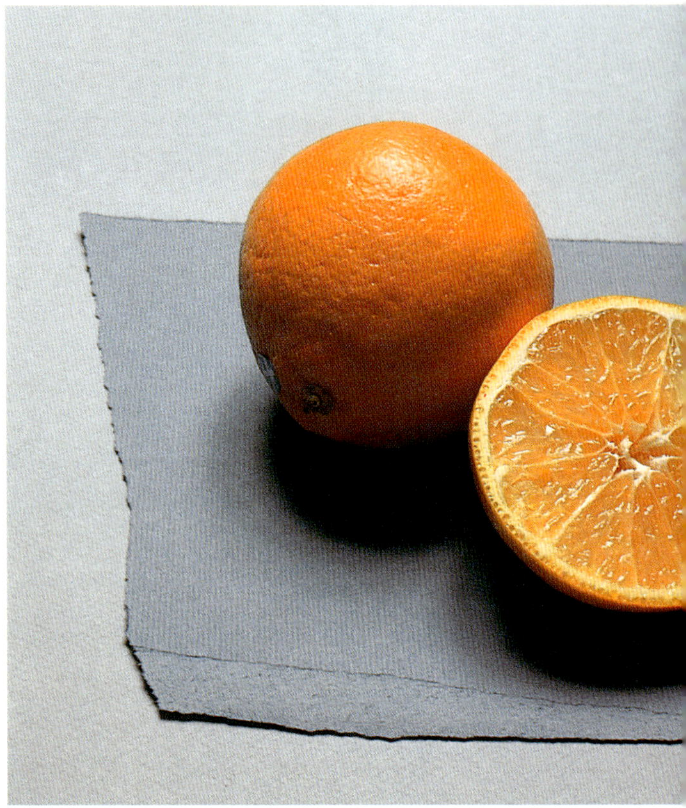

△ **1**　*A simple subject is made interesting by being placed on a two-tone blue surface. The angular blue shapes, one of which juts in from the side of the composition, provide an interesting and contrasting background to the rounded oranges.*

much consideration as a complex one – sometimes more. When the elements are few and simple, each one attracts more attention than it would in a more complicated arrangement.

The artist is standing above the table top, looking down at the still life. No background is visible, but the oranges are standing on two sheets of blue paper. These shapes are as important to the composition as the oranges, formally dividing the canvas into two flat, angular pieces and so emphasizing the solid roundness of the fruit.

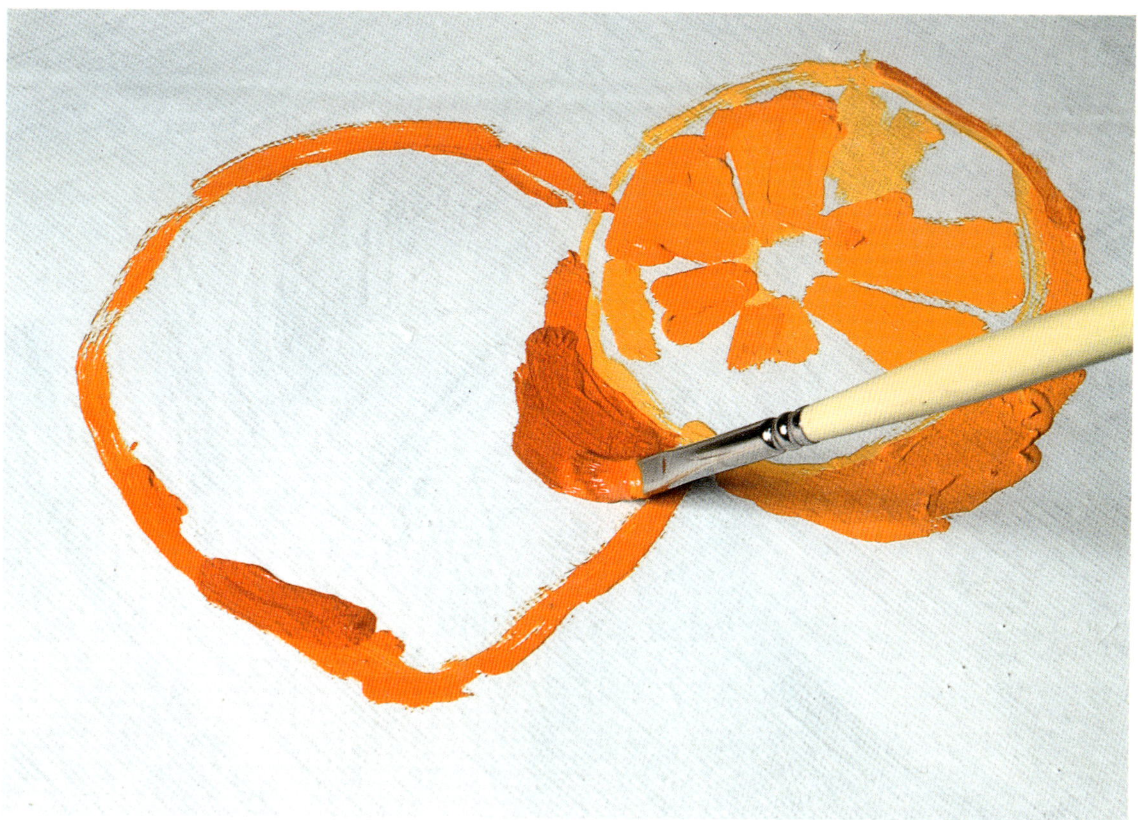

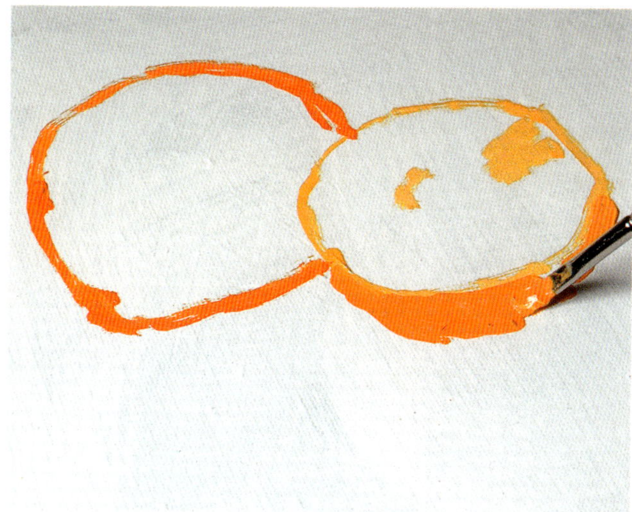

△ 3   For the darker, shaded areas, a little alizarin crimson is added to the orange. In order to keep the colours as bright as possible, black and other darkening tones are generally avoided in this painting.

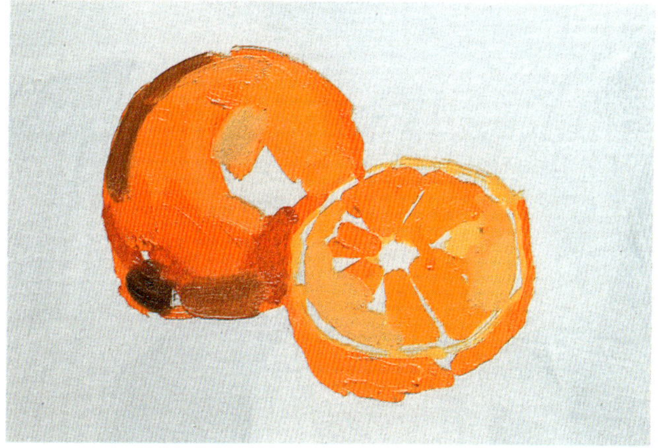

△ 2   The use of complementary colours is central to this still-life arrangement, and the artist starts by 'drawing' the fruit in paint, using various shades of bright orange mixed from cadmium yellow and cadmium red.

△ 4   The fruit is now blocked in with a range of orange tones, mixed from varying quantities of cadmium red and yellow. For deeper tones, the artist adds a touch of alizarin crimson and French ultramarine; for the lighter areas, a little white.

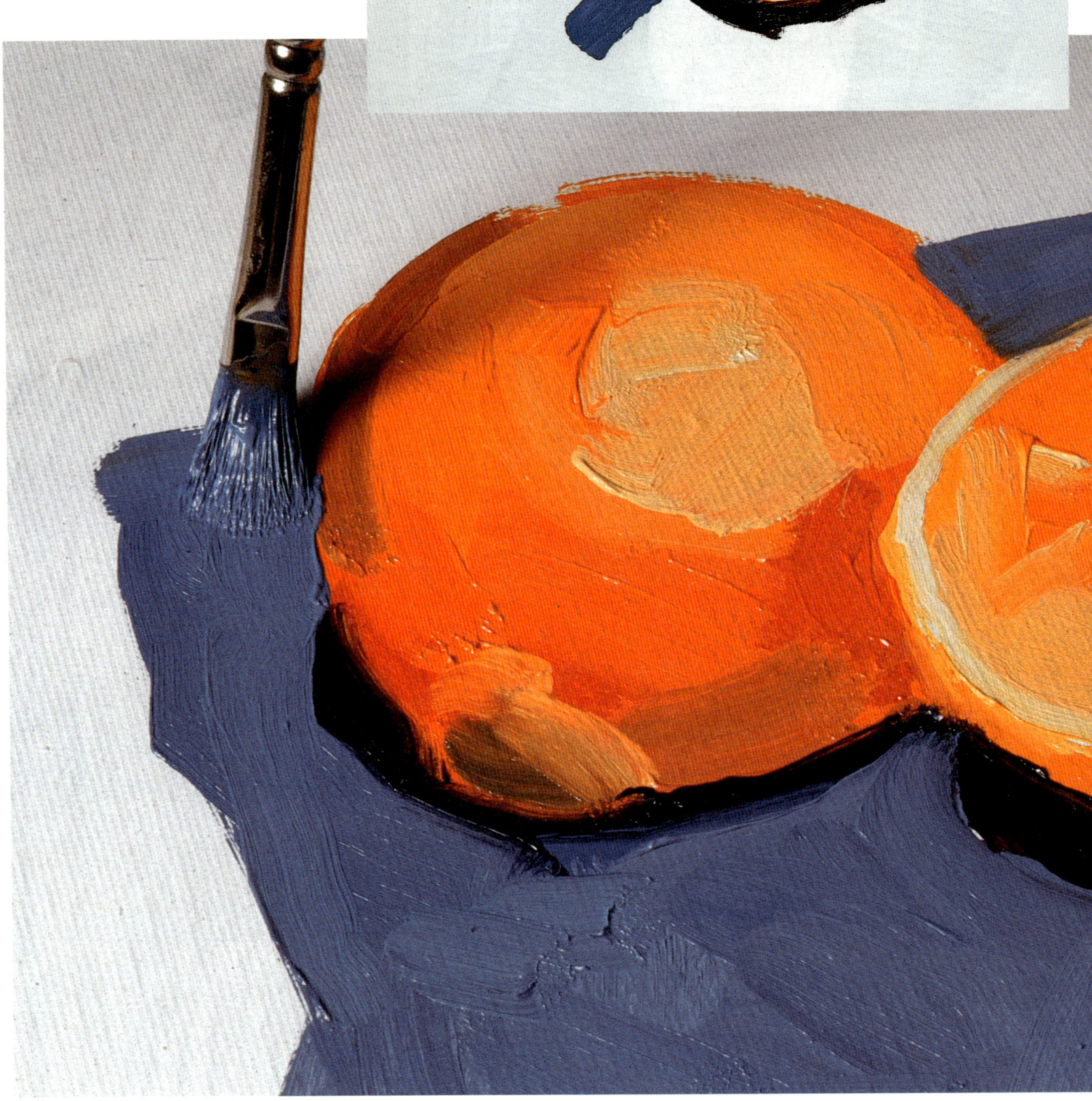

▷ 5　*Dark shadows cast by the fruit are painted with a mixture of French ultramarine and alizarin.*

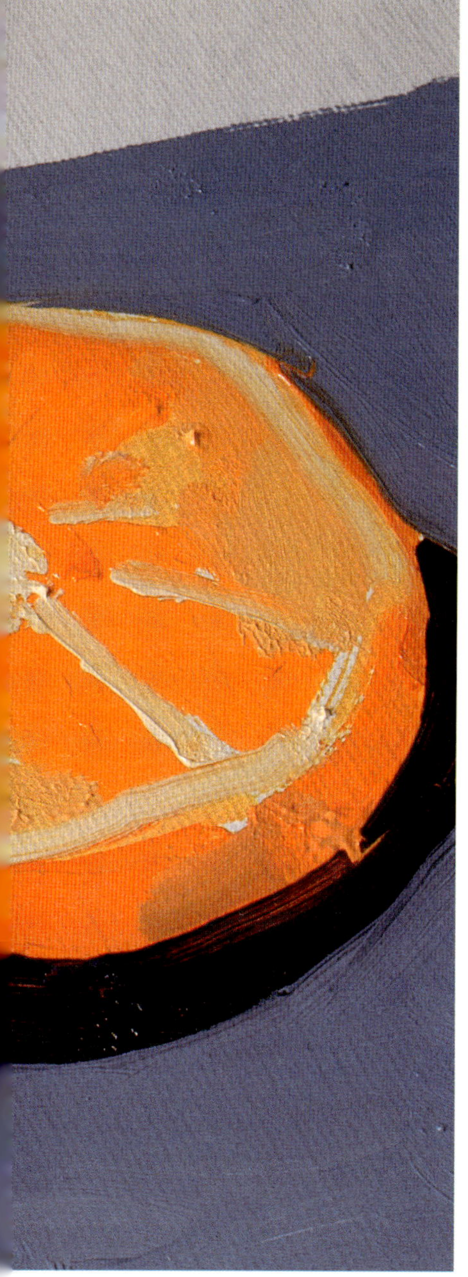

▽ **6** *The sheet of blue paper is French ultramarine mixed with white. This is applied boldly with a large brush, and the artist takes the colour up to and over the shadows and the fruit, cutting into the contours in order to redefine the shapes.*

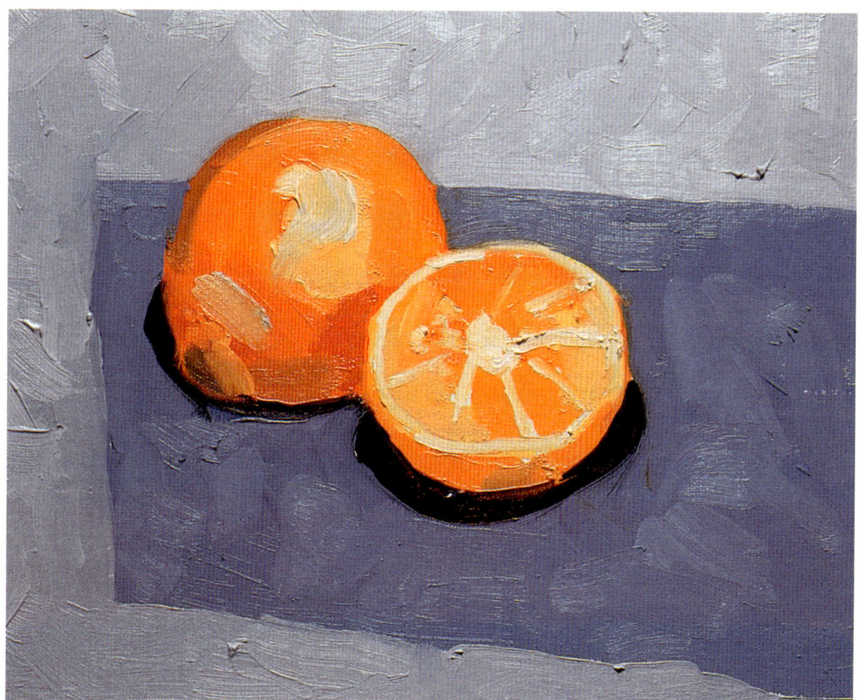

△ **7** *Finally, the blue table top is painted in French ultramarine blue and white mixed with a little raw umber. The painting is completed using a limited palette of just five colours – cadmium yellow, cadmium red, alizarin, French ultramarine and raw umber – with white. The relative purity of the colours allows the complementary orange and blue to work together, making the most of this very simple still-life arrangement.*

PROJECTS

SEASHELLS

These shells are more colourful than you might think, even though there is no strong colour among them. If you were asked what colour they were, you would have to say beige or grey. Yet the shells are actually much more varied than that – it is just that the colours are muted and neutralized. The artist sees and recognizes the potential in this subject and wants to convey a sense of colour in the painting. With this in mind, he selects a palette of cadmium red, Indian red, yellow ochre, cadmium yellow, French ultramarine, raw umber and white.

Black and white?

A mixture of black and white produces a strong, colourless grey which can look cold or warm, depending on the surrounding colours. One painter who uses a palette of warm earth colours finds he never needs blue because when surrounded by warm colours, grey mixed from black and white takes on the appearance of blue.

However, black and white are by no means the only way of making grey, as you can see from this painting. The greys are colourful, yet the artist had no black on his palette.

Coloured greys

If you look at the shells in this painting, you will notice that each grey and beige is different. Apart from the tonal variations – the lights and darks – you will find that every grey or beige has a 'colour': a pink, yellow, purple or other coloured tinge. Seen in isolation, each shell is either grey or beige, but when these 'coloured' greys are painted next to each other, the colours are bright and resonant.

Grey or neutral does not therefore mean dull. But as with all colour mixtures, they will become so if you overdo the number of pigments. The secret is to treat each mixed colour as if it were a pure, bright colour, straight from the tube. In other words, once you have mixed it, keep it separate on the palette.

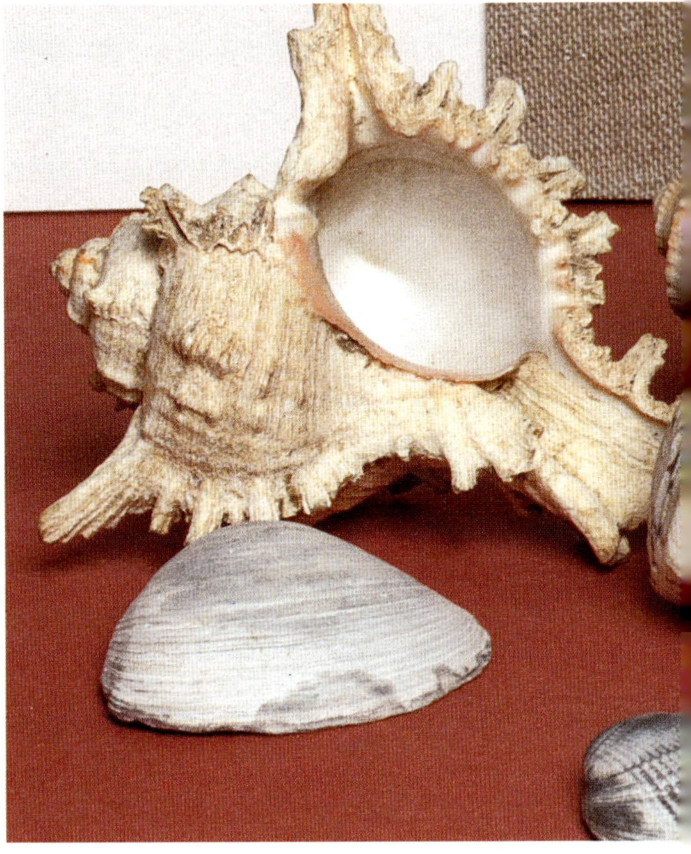

△ 1   *An assortment of shells is laid out ready to paint. Most of the colour in this subject lies in the red tablecloth, but the shells themselves contain hidden colour. For this reason, the artist lays out a varied palette of cadmium red, Indian red, yellow ochre, cadmium yellow, French ultramarine, raw umber and white.*

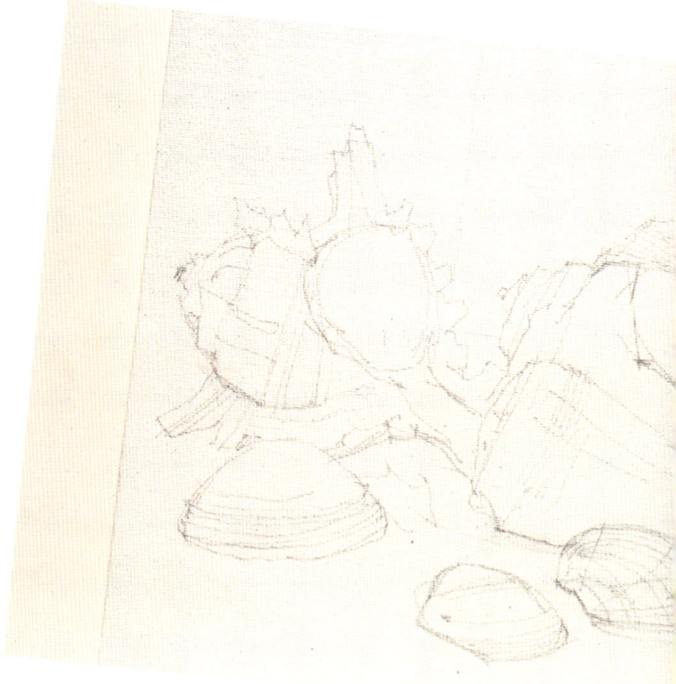

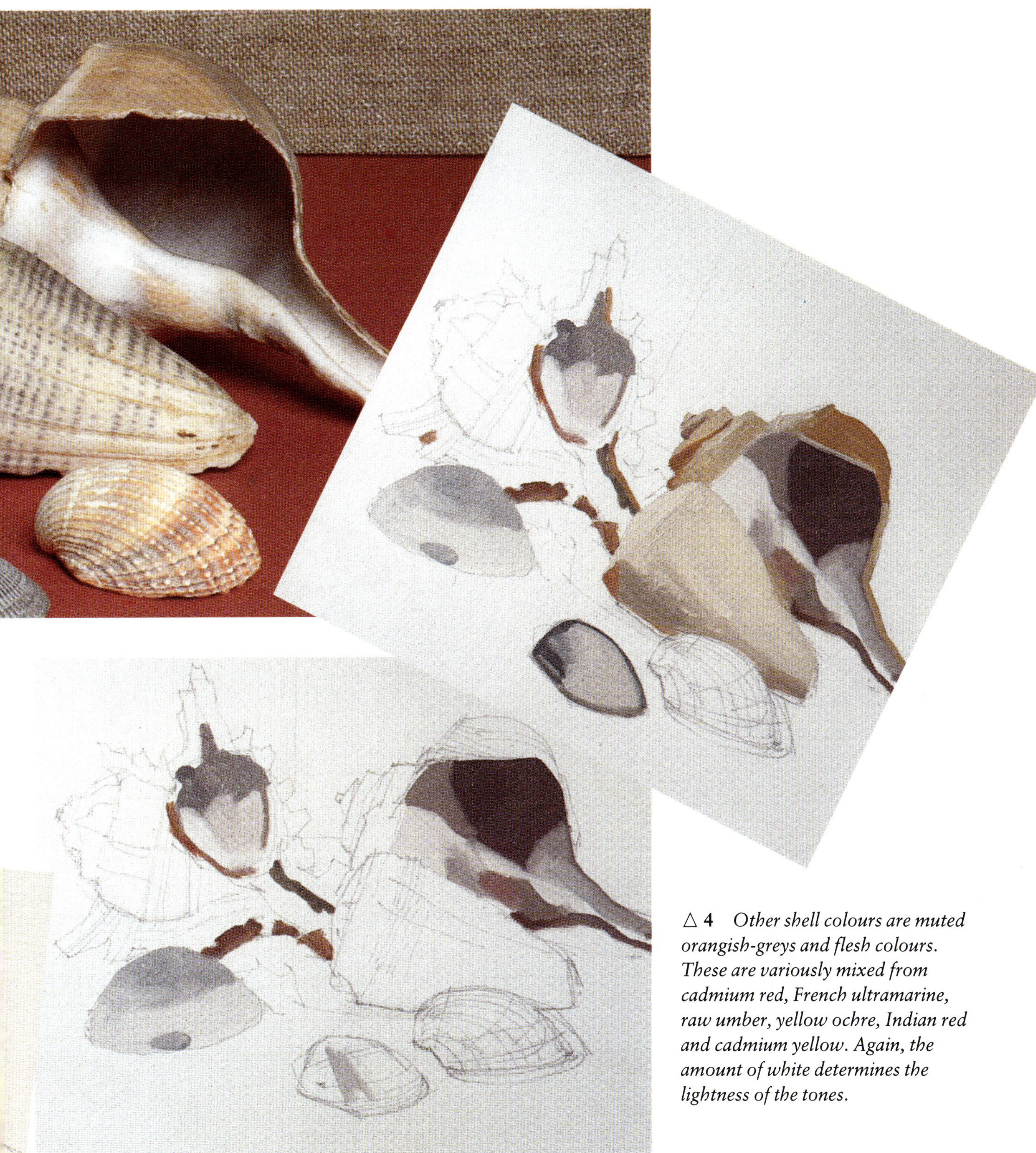

△ **4** Other shell colours are muted orangish-greys and flesh colours. These are variously mixed from cadmium red, French ultramarine, raw umber, yellow ochre, Indian red and cadmium yellow. Again, the amount of white determines the lightness of the tones.

◁ **2** The artist starts with a pencil drawing – a light outline of the shells and the background shapes.

△ **3** On close observation, many of the greys visible in the shells have a pronounced purple or pink tinge. These are mixed from raw umber, French ultramarine and cadmium red. Varying amounts of white are added to obtain the medium and light tones.

▷ **5** *Working with the same colour mixtures, the artist continues to develop the shells. Each colour and tone is carefully related to its neighbours, so that the shells begin to stand out as three-dimensional objects. The very darkest colours represent the shadows and interiors of the shells.*

▽ **6** *The addition of a dark background – raw umber mixed with a little white – also helps to establish the shells as solid three-dimensional forms. This umber background brings out and emphasizes similar colours in the shell arrangement.*

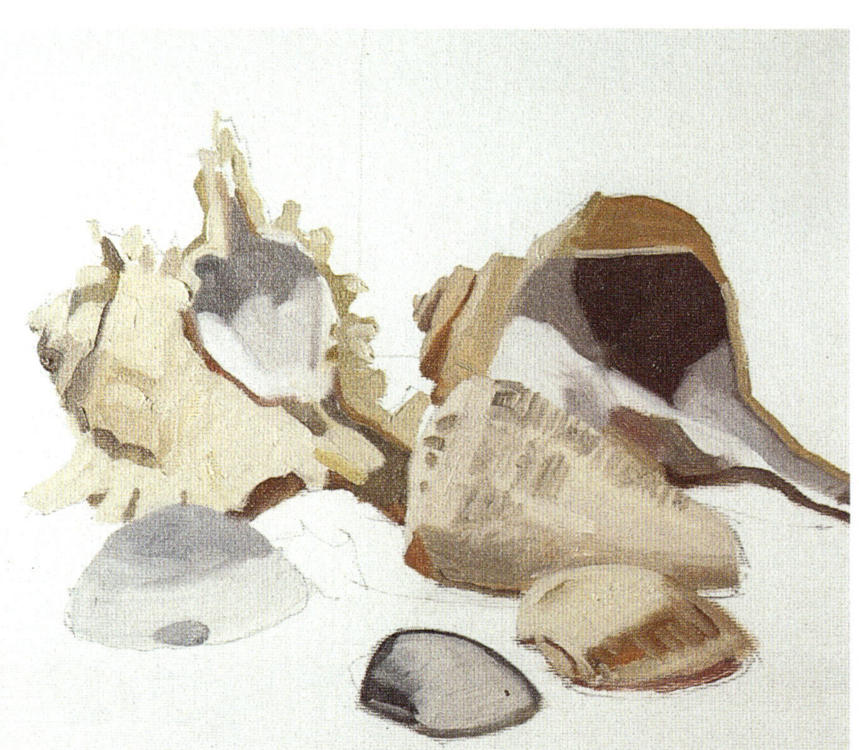

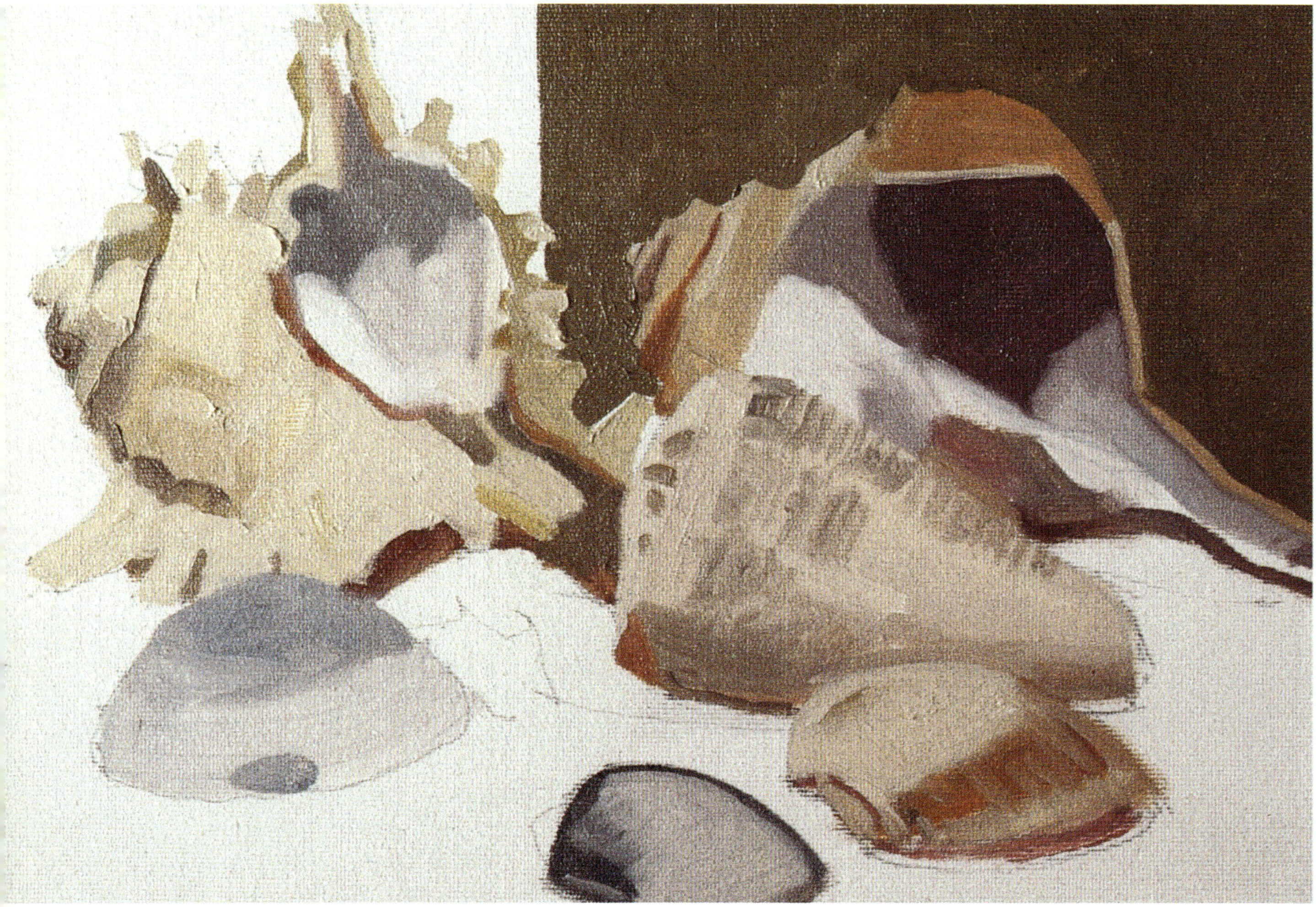

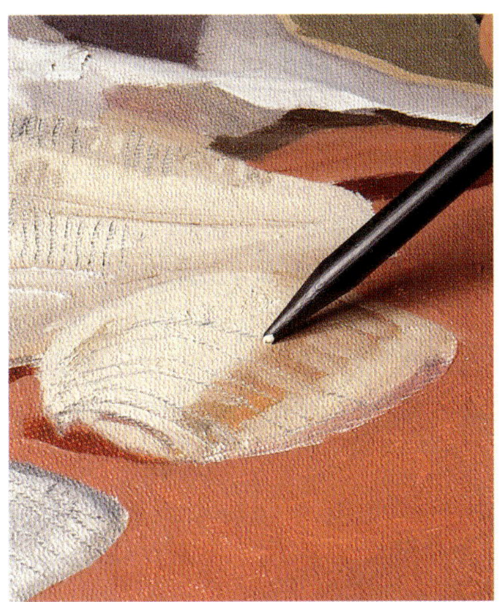

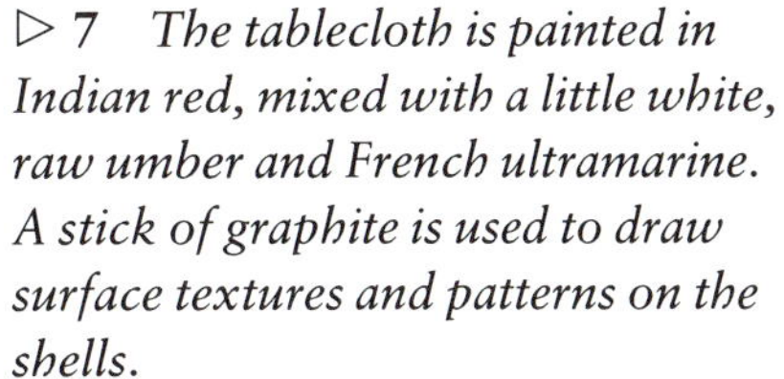

▷ 7   *The tablecloth is painted in Indian red, mixed with a little white, raw umber and French ultramarine. A stick of graphite is used to draw surface textures and patterns on the shells.*

▽ 8   *In the finished painting, the addition of the tablecloth and background affects the colours present in the painted shells. The red cloth and umber background pick out and emphasize similar colours in the shells; at the same time, the blue and purple tones in the shells also appear stronger because they contrast with the background and cloth colours.*

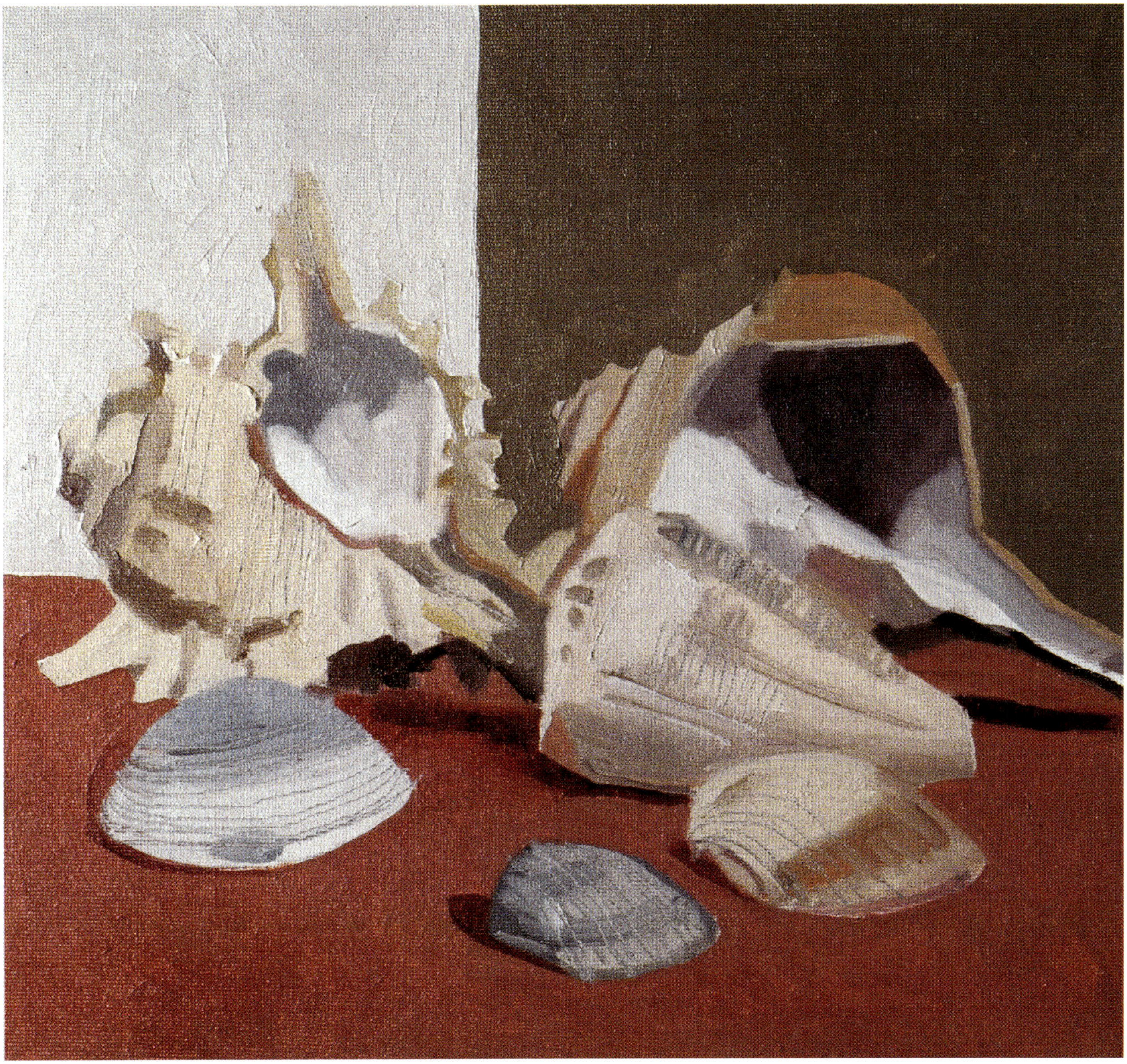

TECHNIQUES

TEXTURE WITH PAINT

Painting with a knife is only one way of creating texture in painting. The thick consistency of oil paints gives you the choice of applying the colour heavily, to create an impasto effect, or diluting the colour to apply it as a thin wash.

Glazes

Depending on the pigment, some paints are naturally transparent when diluted with turpentine; others remain opaque, however much you dilute them.

Traditionally, the use of transparent colour is known as glazing. By laying a thin transparent colour over another colour, the underlying colour will show through the glaze. The result is a shimmering combination of the two colours, quite unlike the effect you would get by mixing the two in a conventional manner. It is important to allow the first colour to dry before attempting to glaze over it.

Many painters, from the Renaissance onwards, used glazing to capture the transparency of flesh tones and the effect of light on folds of fabric. The technique is still widely used today.

Contemporary artists have the advantage of the new glazing media – viscous substances available in tubes – that can be mixed with any colour to give it a lustrous transparency. In the past, painters were limited to those colours that were naturally transparent. Even then, it was often difficult to dilute them with oil and turpentine without losing some of the strength of the colour.

Glazing with turpentine alone is never recommended. Colours tend to dry with a dull, lacklustre finish that defeats the purpose of the glaze because it deadens the colours.

Impasto

Oil paint lends itself to thickly impastoed textures that can be applied with either a brush or a knife. The only restriction to the thickness of paint you use is the amount of time it takes for very thick paint to dry. Even here, technology has an answer: you can buy effective drying media to mix with the colour, and this speeds up the drying time considerably.

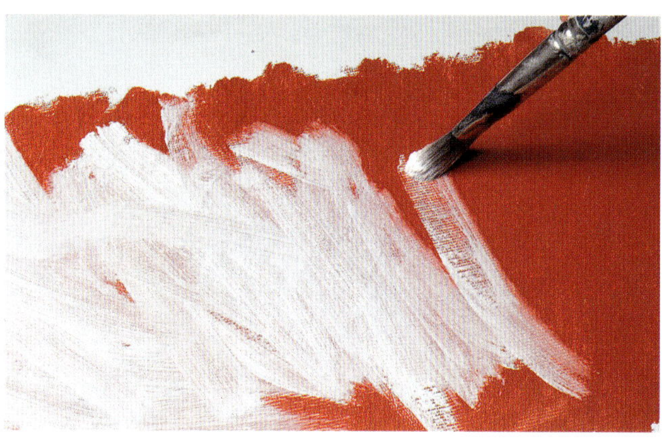

Sgraffiti

△ **1** *White paint is applied over a red base which has been allowed to dry completely.*

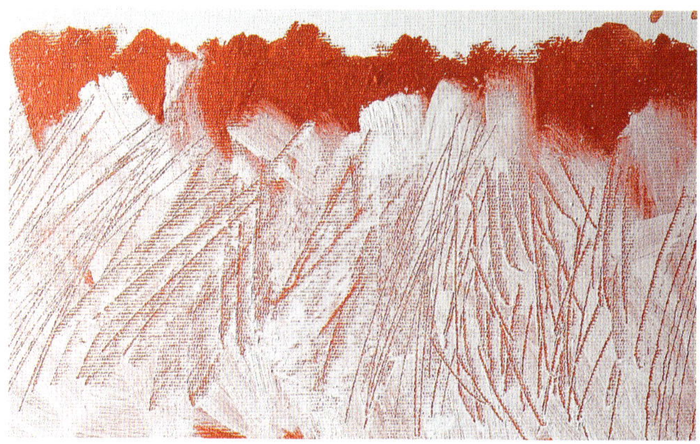

△ **2** *Here the artist has used the edge of a palette knife to scratch into the wet white, revealing the red underneath.*

On their own, oil paints are naturally slow-drying. Although your picture may be dry enough to work on if you leave it standing overnight, it can take weeks for the paint to dry properly – longer if it is very thick. Until it is completely dry, the paint is unstable, which is why manufacturers usually recommend leaving the finished painting for some weeks before applying varnish.

Other texture techniques

Oil paints may be a long-established and classical medium, but there is no reason why your own approach should not be entirely creative and personal. Sgraffiti, for instance, is the term used to describe any scratched texture on the painted surface – usually applied while the colour is wet.

In fact, any technique that gives you the effect you want is fine – provided, of course, that you do not introduce materials that are incompatible with oil paint. It is important to remember that water-based paints such as acrylic and gouache cannot be mixed with oils.

Possibly the most versatile texture-making tool you possess, however, is a paintbrush. With it, not only can you produce the dry-brush and broken-colour effects shown on this page, but you can also develop your own brushstrokes and ways of applying paint to create equally effective textures.

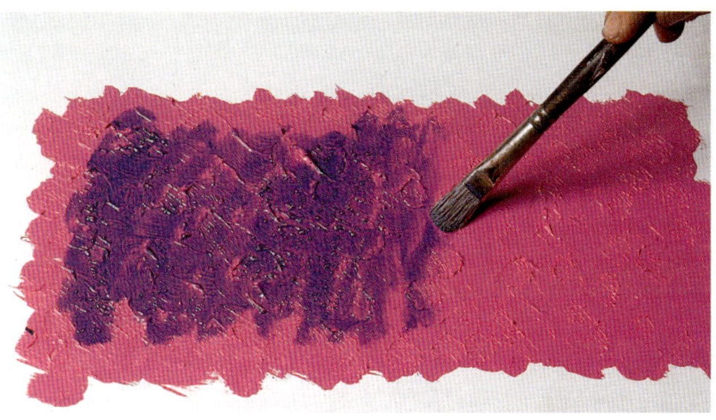

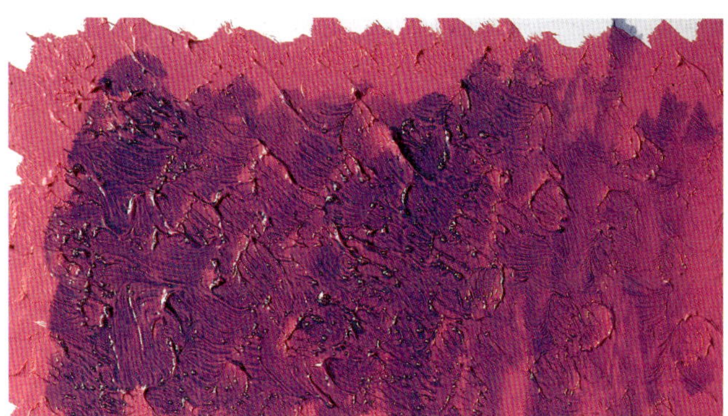

Glazing over impasto

△ **1**   *An impastoed pink undercolour is allowed to dry completely before a thin blue glaze is applied. The blue is mixed with a little glazing medium to increase its transparency.*

△ **2**   *The result is a textured, translucent violet – a combination of the blue and pink in which both of these colours are discernible.*

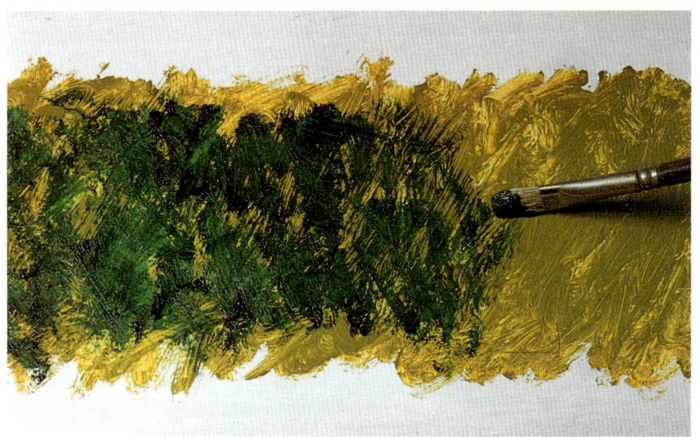

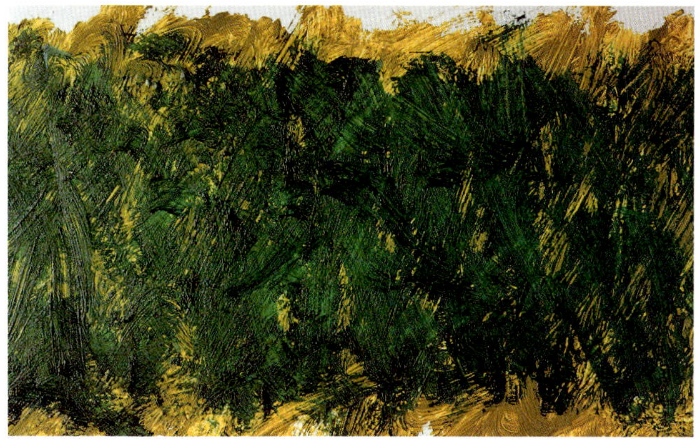

Broken colour

△ **1**   *Short strokes of viridian green are painted over a dry, yellowish undercolour. To achieve this broken, scratchy effect – sometimes called 'scumbling' – the artist uses a semi-dry brush and applies the colour in light, feathery strokes.*

△ **2**   *The result is a textured area of broken colour in which patches of yellow show through the darker top colour.*

PROJECTS

ROSES IN A GLASS VASE

Flowers and foliage can be dauntingly difficult. Each bloom is a mass of folded petals; each leaf, a complicated structure of planes and delicate veins. Yet this vase of roses was painted at one sitting, and the artist has succeeded in capturing the essence of the subject without analysing every botanical detail.

Working 'alla prima'

This rapid, spontaneous way of working is sometimes known as 'alla prima' – literally, 'at the first' or 'at one go'. Such paintings are often done with a minimal preliminary drawing, sometimes with no drawing at all. Here, the artist has started with a light sketch in oil pastel – a quick but accurate guide for the paint.

As with all alla-prima work, the sketchy effect belies the care with which the painting has been planned. It is an approach which calls for accuracy and great powers of observation. The paint itself may be laid at speed, but you can do this effectively only if you know exactly where you are going to put the colour. Colour and rendering on the roses are simple in the extreme, but every dab of paint has been mixed and placed with deft accuracy.

The leaves are simplified into three tones of green; the roses are painted almost as flat shapes in a limited range of yellows, reds and pinks. There is no detail in either the flowers or the leaves. Apart from the single stroke of thick colour that represents each furled petal, the artist has not attempted to describe the three-dimensional form of the roses.

Dynamic impasto

Cut flowers in a vase have an explosive composition which is often lost in more finished paintings. This is simply because it is difficult, in the same painting, to retain a sense of movement while also depicting detail. Here, the thick brushstrokes capture exactly

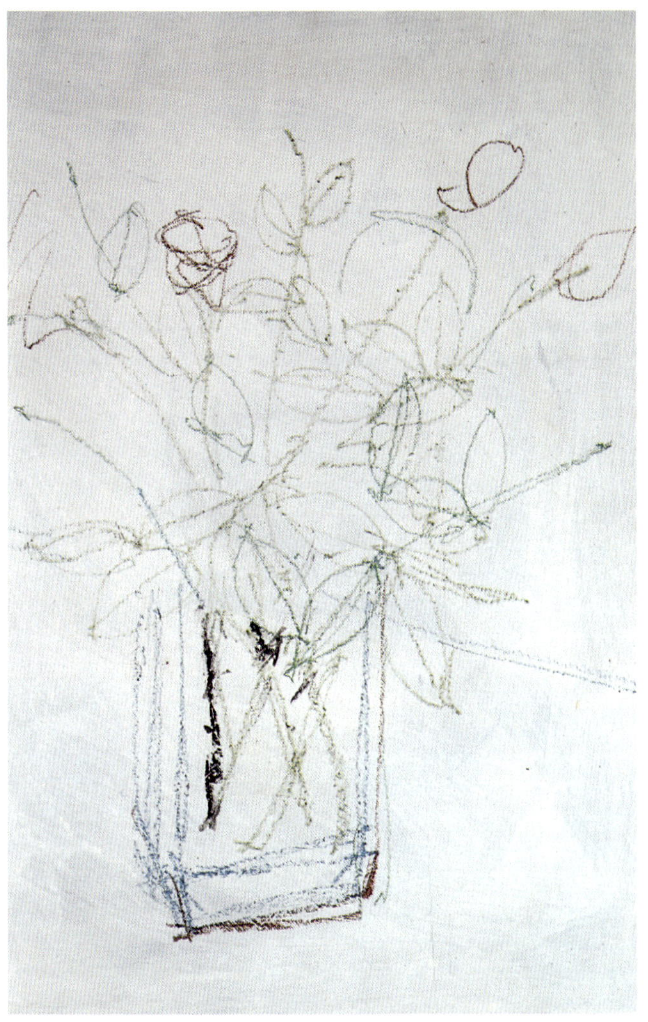

△ **1** *The initial drawing is a lively, minimal sketch done in oil pastel. It indicates the position of the vase and roses, and contains just enough information to act as a guide for the paint.*

the explosive growth in the arrangement of flowers, leaves and stalks.

An important aspect of this painting is the flat blue background. This is taken up to the edge of the subject, but the artist applies the colour in swift, decisive strokes, using the thick paint to define and sharpen the shapes of the flowers and leaves.

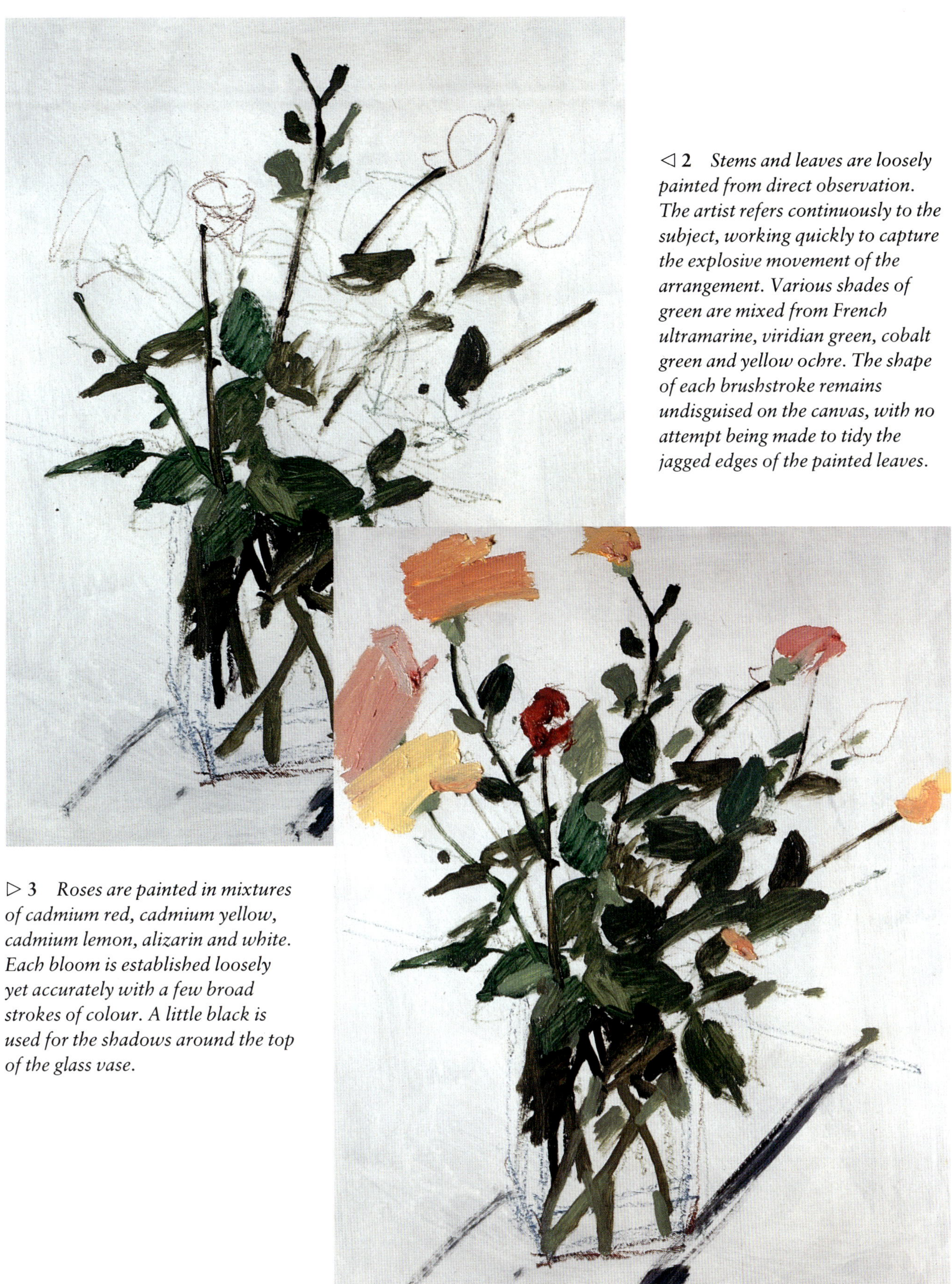

◁ 2 *Stems and leaves are loosely painted from direct observation. The artist refers continuously to the subject, working quickly to capture the explosive movement of the arrangement. Various shades of green are mixed from French ultramarine, viridian green, cobalt green and yellow ochre. The shape of each brushstroke remains undisguised on the canvas, with no attempt being made to tidy the jagged edges of the painted leaves.*

▷ 3 *Roses are painted in mixtures of cadmium red, cadmium yellow, cadmium lemon, alizarin and white. Each bloom is established loosely yet accurately with a few broad strokes of colour. A little black is used for the shadows around the top of the glass vase.*

▷ **4** A close-up of the flowers shows how each bloom has been established in a few seconds, using thick paint and partially mixed colour. Yet, because the artist works closely from the subject, the strokes are sufficiently accurate to create a convincing impression of roses.

▽ **5** The background is mixed from cerulean blue and white. The artist takes this opportunity to redefine and sharpen some of the flowers and foliage by cutting into the shapes with the blue paint.

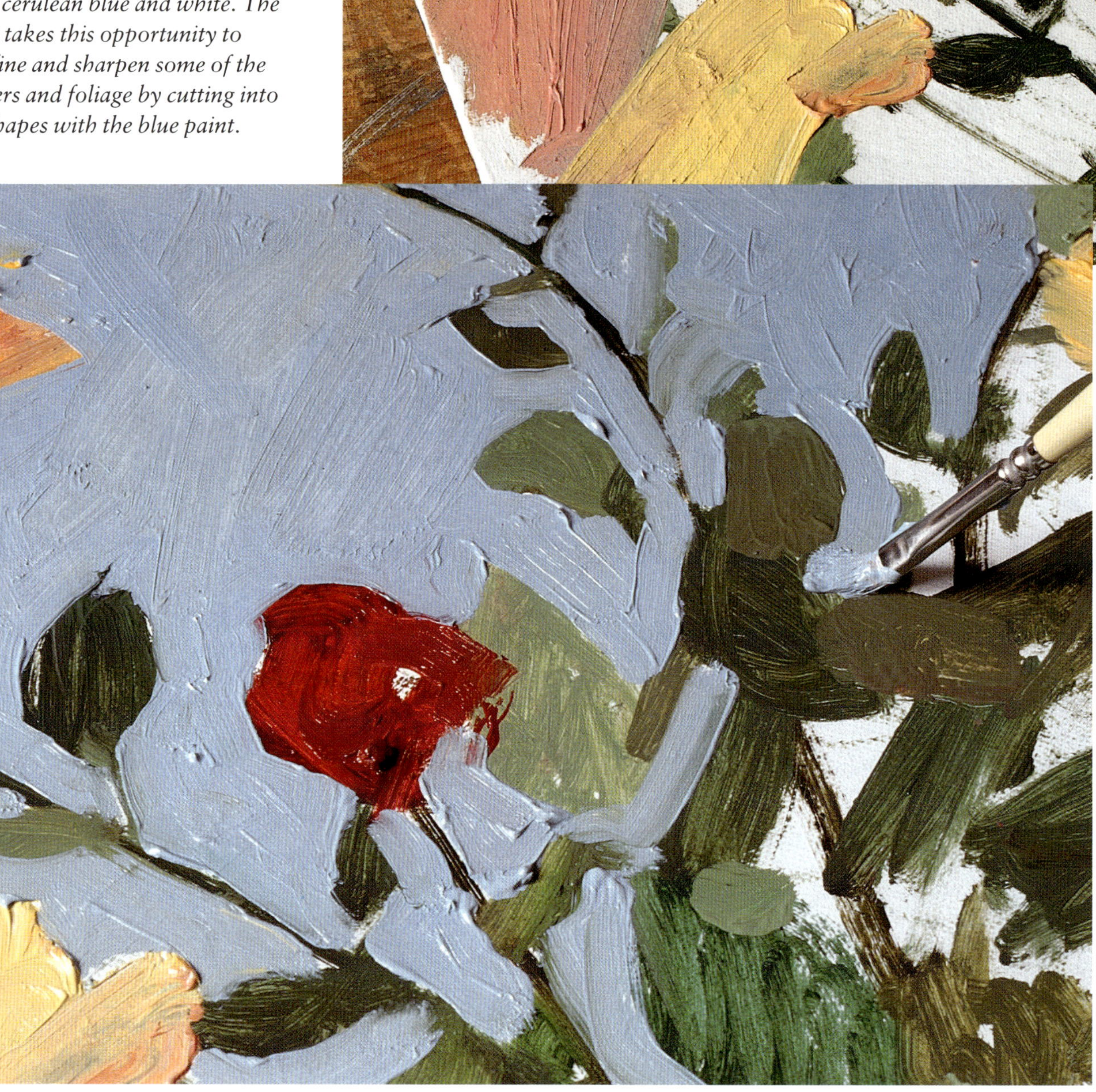

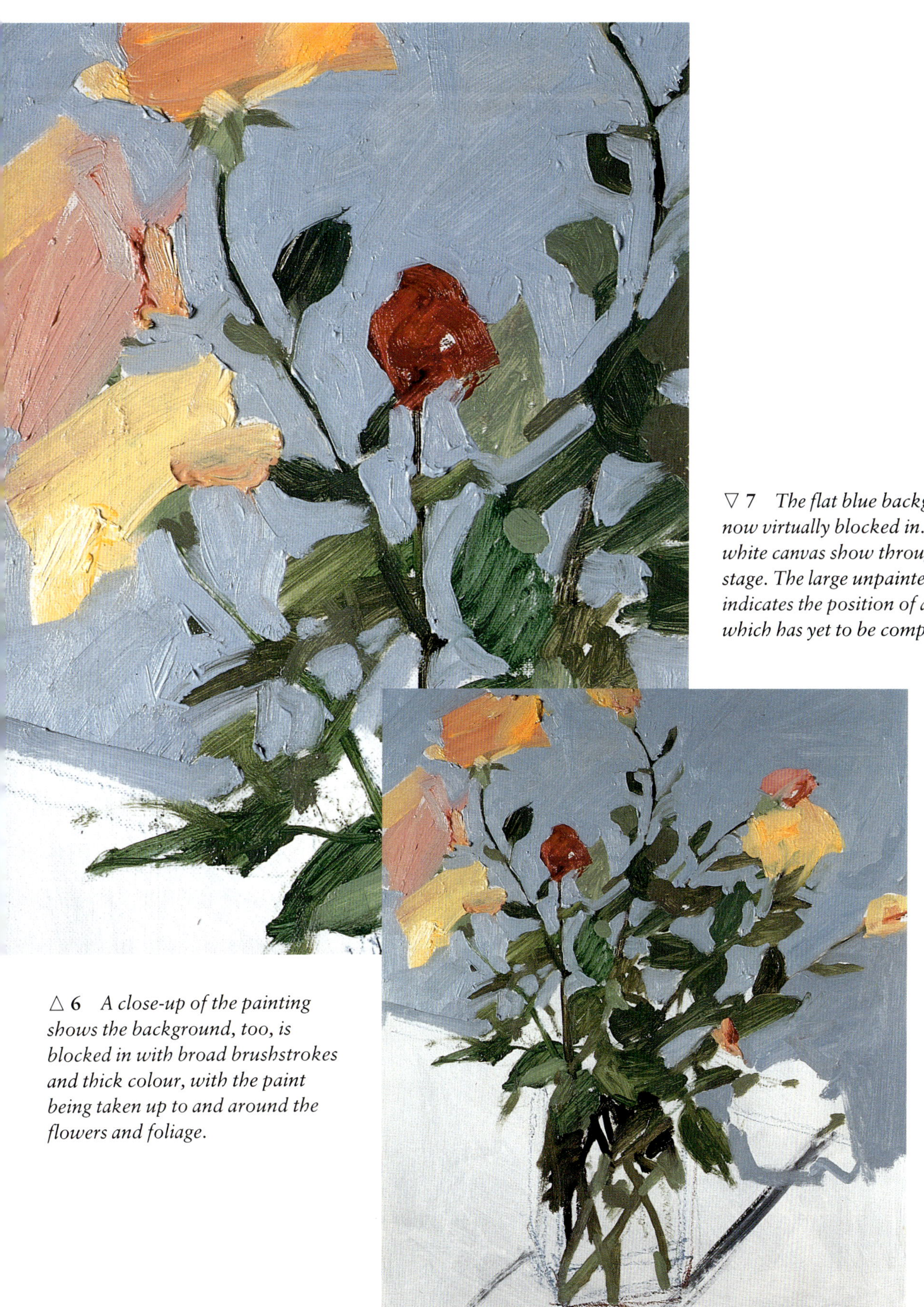

▽ 7   The flat blue background is now virtually blocked in. Flecks of white canvas show through at this stage. The large unpainted shape indicates the position of a white rose which has yet to be completed.

△ 6   A close-up of the painting shows the background, too, is blocked in with broad brushstrokes and thick colour, with the paint being taken up to and around the flowers and foliage.

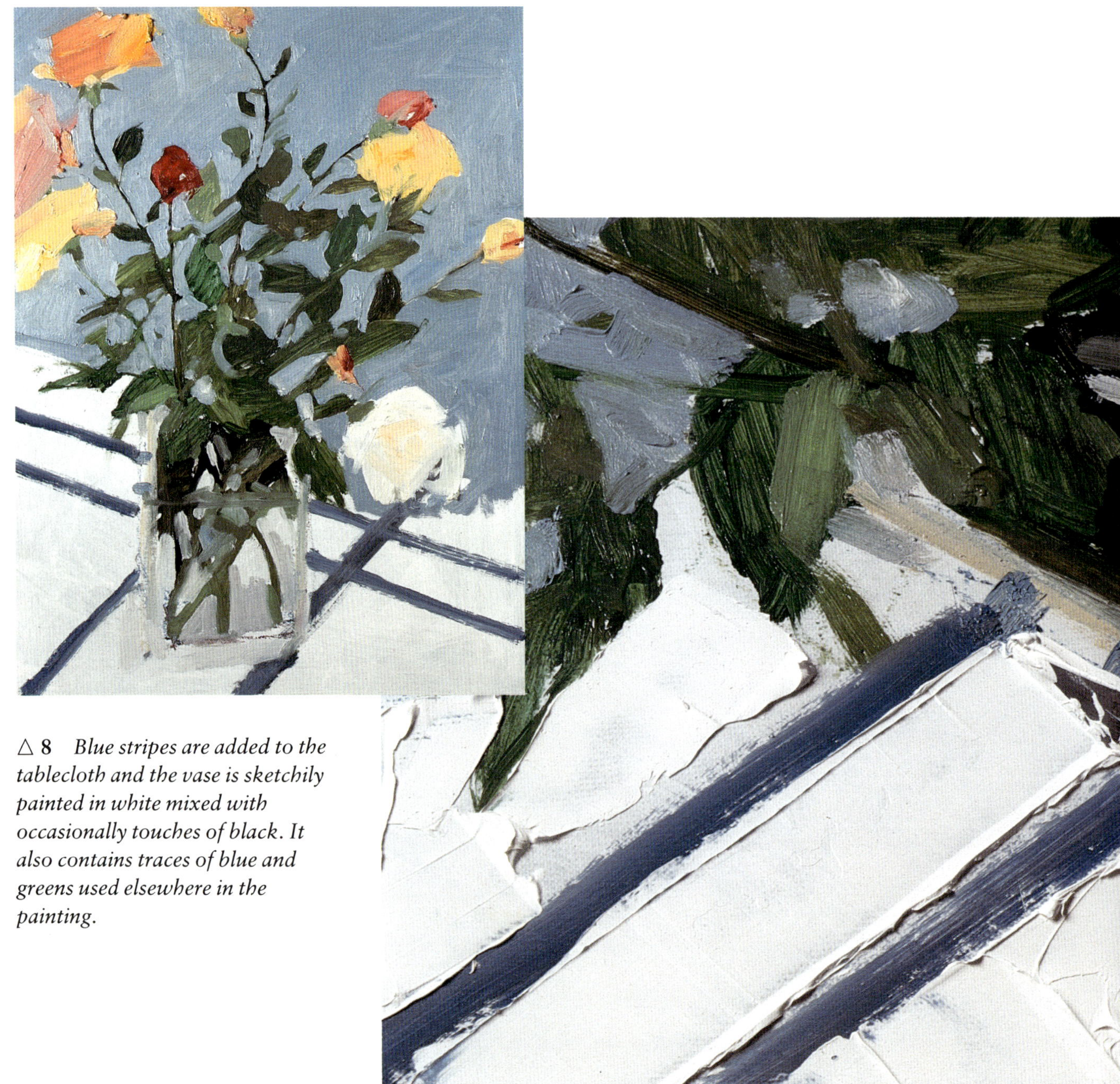

△ **8**   *Blue stripes are added to the tablecloth and the vase is sketchily painted in white mixed with occasionally touches of black. It also contains traces of blue and greens used elsewhere in the painting.*

△ **9**   *The tablecloth is laid thickly in pure white, applied with a small painting knife. Once laid, each impastoed stroke is left untouched; the textured knife strokes and ridges of paint become part of the finished painting.*

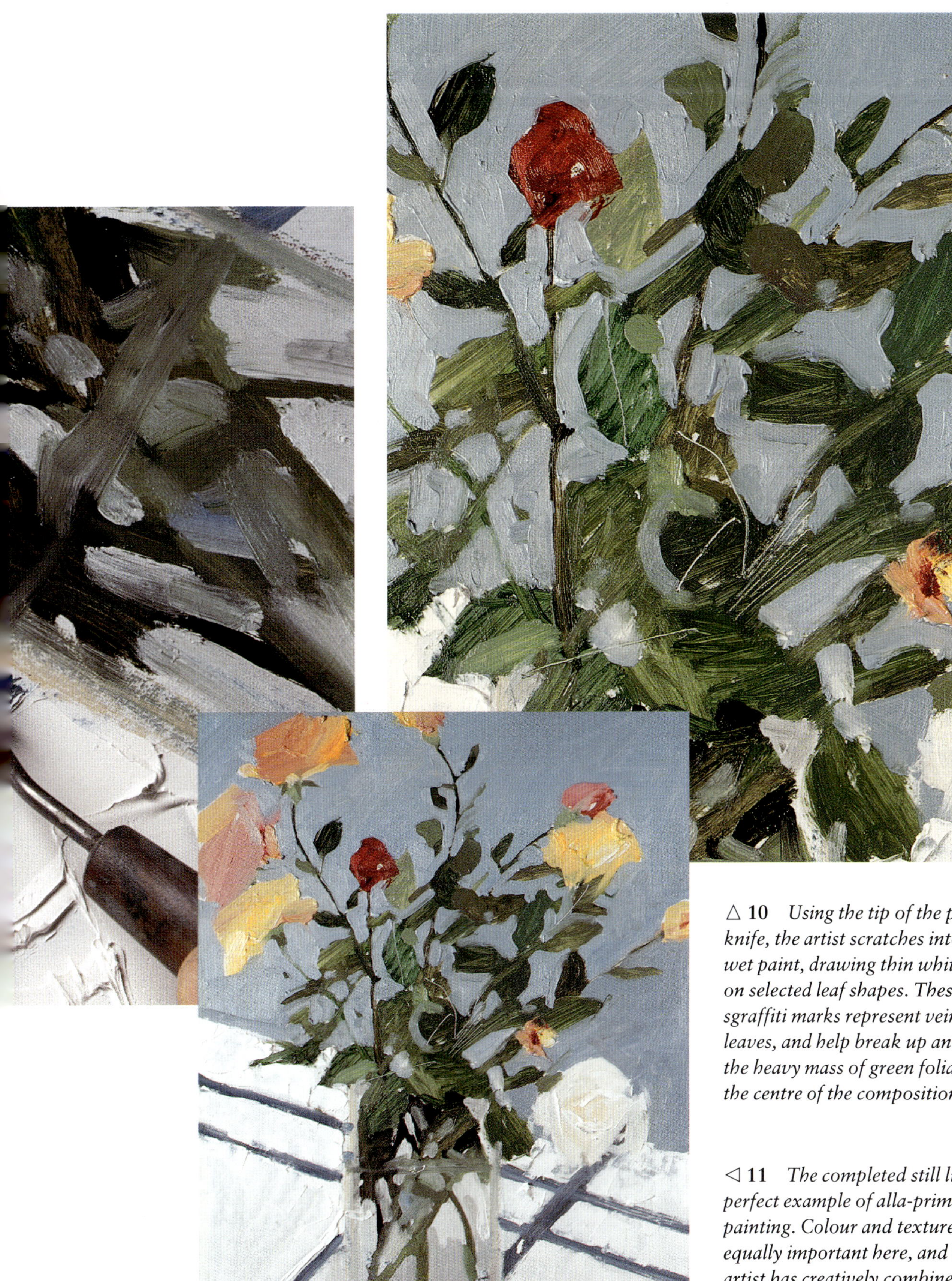

△ **10**   *Using the tip of the painting knife, the artist scratches into the wet paint, drawing thin white lines on selected leaf shapes. These sgraffiti marks represent veins in the leaves, and help break up and 'lift' the heavy mass of green foliage at the centre of the composition.*

◁ **11**   *The completed still life is a perfect example of alla-prima painting. Colour and texture are equally important here, and the artist has creatively combined these elements to capture the life and freshness of the subject.*

TECHNIQUES

UNDER-PAINTING

A useful and very common way of starting any painting is with a monochrome underpainting. The underpainted colour should be diluted with turpentine to an extremely thin consistency. This is partly because thin colour dries quickly, allowing you to carry on with the painting almost immediately, and partly because a thin wash will not affect subsequent texture or colour.

Overall tone

A primed canvas is not necessarily the best starting point for an oil painting. Apart from distorting each colour and tone as you paint it – the white prime makes everything else look much darker in comparison – the prime is generally too bright even to represent the palest tones of most subjects. A sensible first step, therefore, is to give the whole support a coat of thin, medium-toned colour.

The colour for this thin underpainting depends on the subject. Usually, a neutral colour is best because it does not interfere too much with subsequent colours. But if your subject contains a lot of one colour, you may want a contrasting underpainting to counterbalance this. For instance, if you are painting an arrangement of red earthenware pots, a green underpainting which is allowed to show through in places will enhance the reds and can add zest to the picture.

One of the most natural ways of starting a painting is to block in some of the main colours and tones. Once these are established, it then becomes

Underpainting

▽ **1**   *Mix the oil colour with turpentine to a thin, runny consistency. Underpainting can be done with either a large brush or a cloth. A cloth will generally produce a lighter, more even colour. Here the artist applies a pool of diluted paint to the centre of the support and starts to spread this with a clean cloth.*

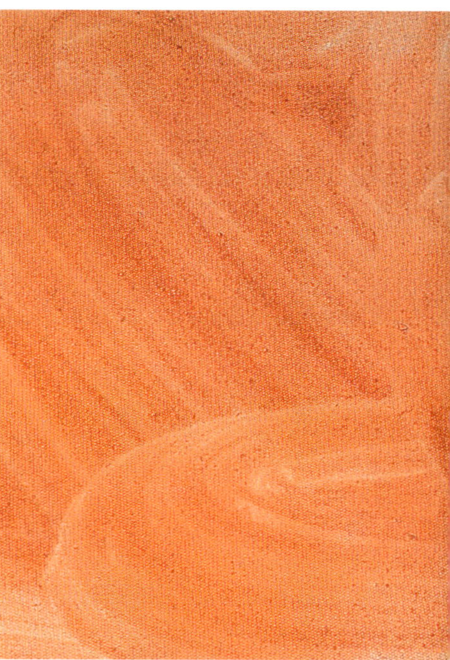

△ **2**   *Continue spreading the paint, using the rag to smooth the colour out towards the edges of the canvas.*

easier to add and develop later colour. The initial tones – the lights, mediums and darks – must be correct in relation to each other, and it is far easier to establish these relationships if you start off with a medium-toned canvas. Against this mid-tone, you can then begin to establish the lights and darks of the composition.

Underpainting is very flexible, and can be used to suit your particular way of working.

Tonal underpainting

An alternative start to a painting is to skip the overall underpainting and begin immediately by blocking in the main tones with thin washes of one colour. If you do this fairly loosely, using a large brush, the intimidating whiteness of the primed canvas will soon bcome broken up into manageable areas of tone, and you can take the painting from there. The approach is similar to the overall colour underpainting, but you accomplish two stages in one. The oil sketch on pages 86–9 was started in this way.

Acrylic paint

Thick oil paint can take some time to dry, so if you particularly want an opaque or thick colour, you can do the underpainting in acrylics. The quick-drying colour enables you to start work in oils almost immediately.

An acrylic underpainting can be taken to any stage. You may simply want to tint the canvas with a flat coat of colour. Or you may decide to do much of the initial painting in acrylics, changing to oils for the final stages when the slower-drying, more malleable oil paint is better for blending and detail.

Incompatible paints

It is important to remember that oils and acrylics are not usually compatible, and should certainly never be mixed together when painting. Although it is possible to use oil on top of an acrylic base, it is not wise to reverse this order, because the oily base will eventually repel the acrylics.

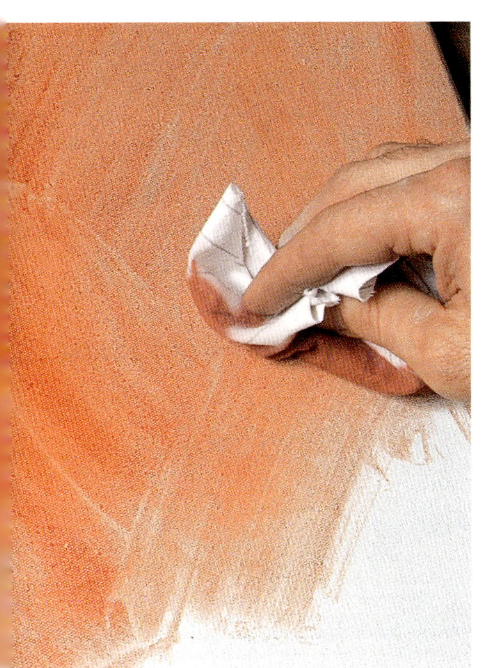

▽ **3**   *When the underpainting is dry, the canvas is ready to work on. The drying process will be considerably speeded up if you use a hair-dryer.*

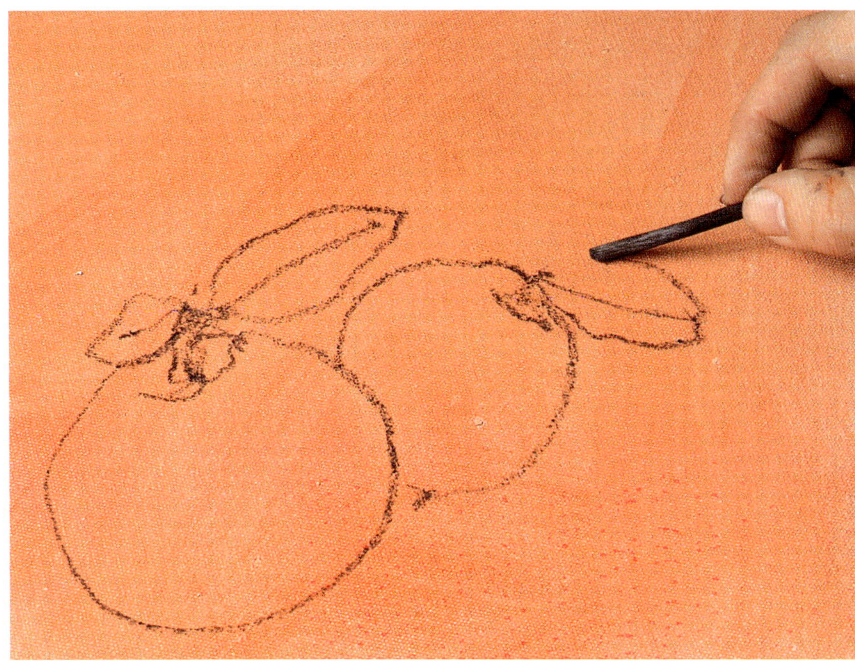

PROJECTS

GARDEN TOOLS: SKETCH

This is a colour sketch for an anticipated, later oil painting. Its purpose is to enable the artist to work out the main tones and colours in the composition before being committed to the finished picture.

Because this is an exploratory sketch, the artist starts with a light charcoal drawing. There is nothing final about charcoal – mistakes can easily be corrected and the lines rubbed back by flicking the surface of the canvas with a dry cloth to remove excess charcoal dust. This initial drawing was rubbed back and redone several times before the artist was happy with the composition.

Tonal underpainting

A tonal underpainting in diluted raw umber is mixed to block in the light, medium and dark areas. The same colour is also used to strengthen and define the charcoal drawing. For both the redrawing and the tonal underpainting, the colour is mixed with a lot of turpentine to give a thin, washy consistency. Slightly more paint is added for the darker tones. The umber wash is laid lightly and loosely, and the diluted colour is easily removed with lots of turpentine and a large brush or rag. This enables the artist to move the paint around until the lights and darks of the subject have been broadly, yet accurately, established.

Raw umber is a useful and popular colour both for underpainting and for painting the initial drawing. The greenish-brown earth pigment is more transparent than many paints, and can provide a lively and light start to a painting. It is a clear, cool colour that is sufficiently subdued to harmonize with subsequent colours, yet dark enough to represent the deep tones of most subjects.

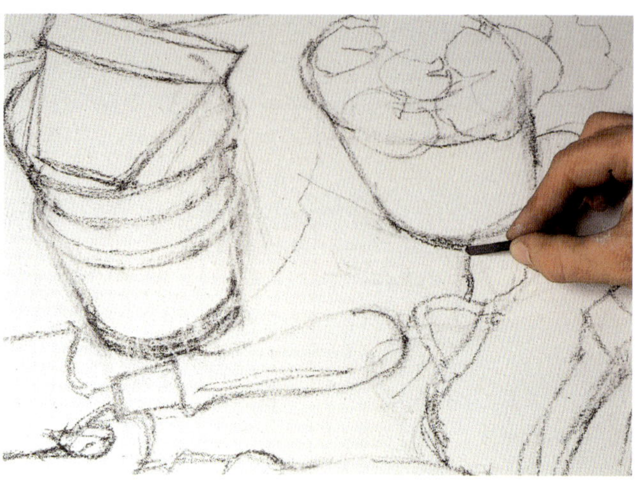

△ **1** *For this preliminary colour sketch, the artist makes a light outline drawing on the canvas in charcoal. Charcoal is easily erased, allowing the artist plenty of scope for trial and error in the early stages of the sketch.*

▽ **2** *When the drawing is complete, excess charcoal dust is flicked off the canvas with a clean, dry cloth. The result is a light outline that is clear enough to follow, but not so heavy that the charcoal will mix with subsequent painted colour and cause this to go muddy.*

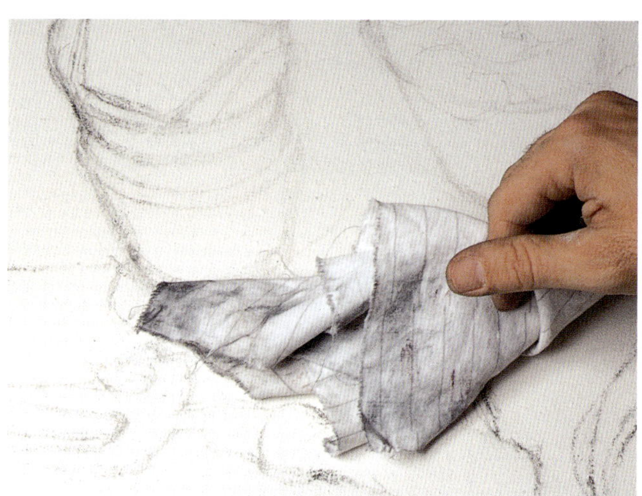

Local colour

Once the tonal composition is complete and dry, the artist is able to move on to develop the rest of the sketch. Using the tonal underpainting as a guide, local colours are blocked in and adjusted until the overall arrangement works as a whole. At this stage, nothing is brought to a conclusion. Detail and last-minute adjustments are left to the final painting.

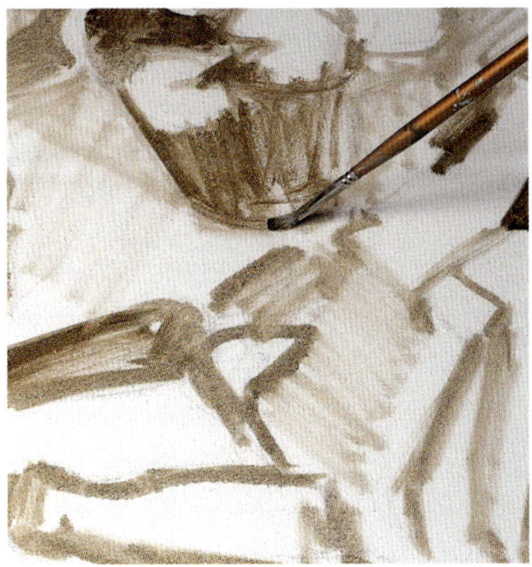

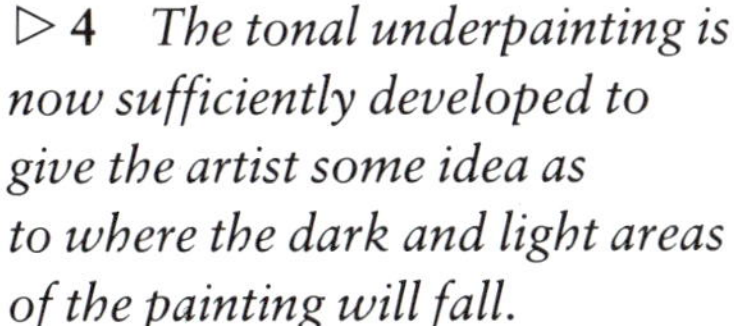

△ **3**   *Using the charcoal outline as a guide, the artist starts to block in the main areas of tone with raw umber diluted with turpentine. The paint is applied loosely, enabling the artist to manipulate and change the tones until each is correct in relationship to its neighbours.*

▷ **4**   *The tonal underpainting is now sufficiently developed to give the artist some idea as to where the dark and light areas of the painting will fall.*

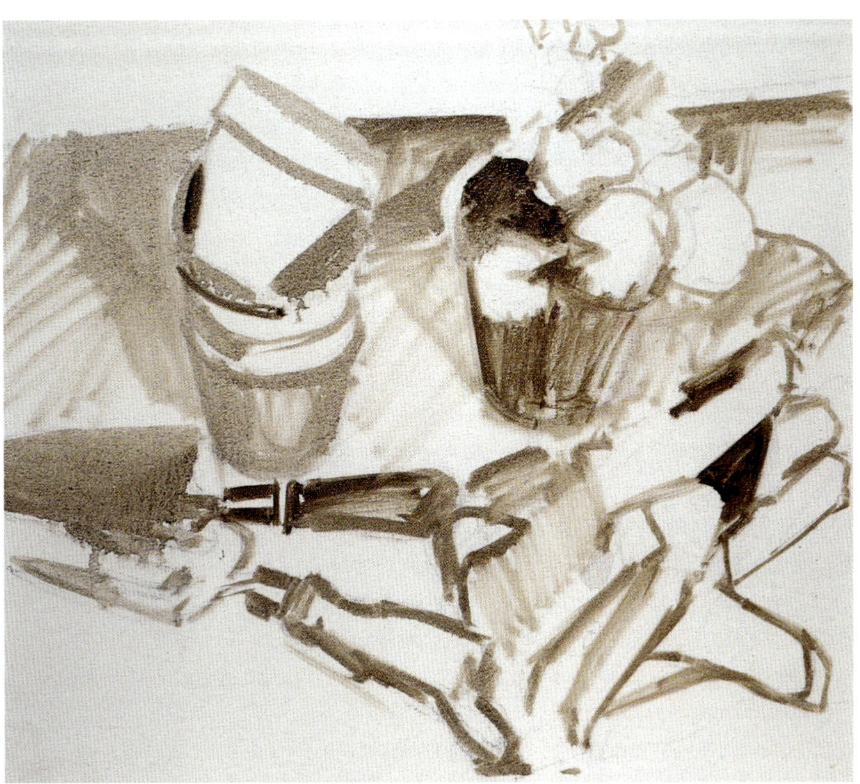

▷ **5**   *The underpainting is now dry and the artist takes this opportunity to develop the colour sketch, trying out various colours and colour combinations. Depending on their success in this sketch, the trial colours will be either adopted, rejected or modified in the final painting.*

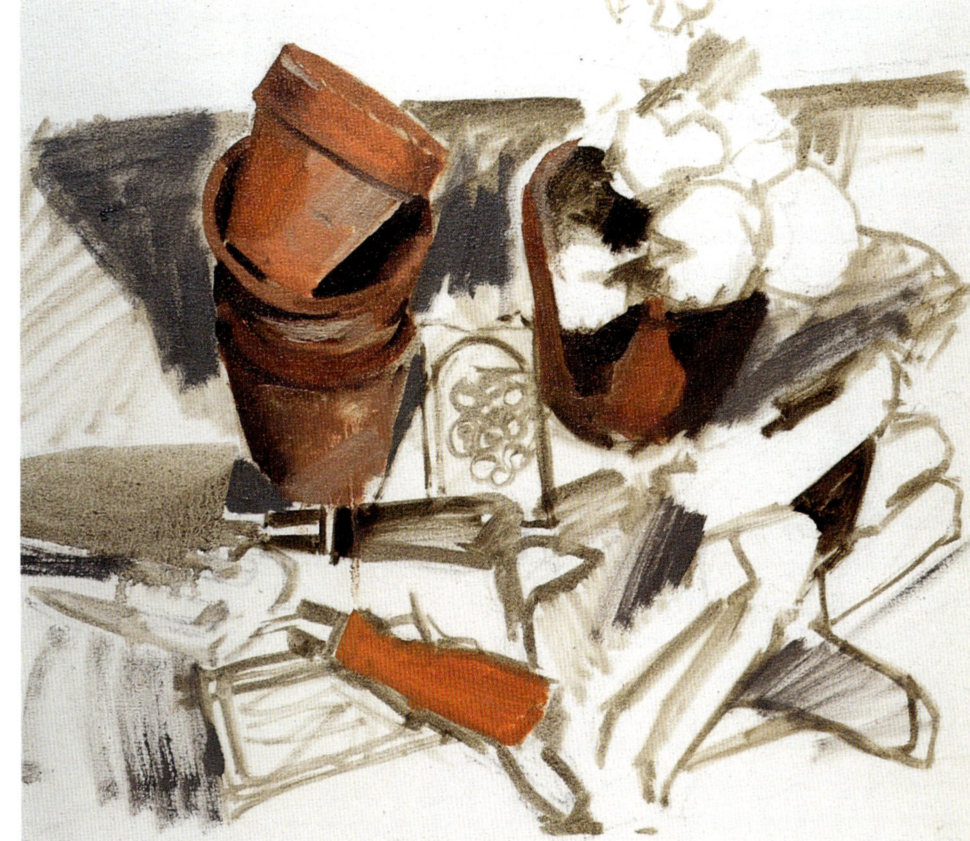

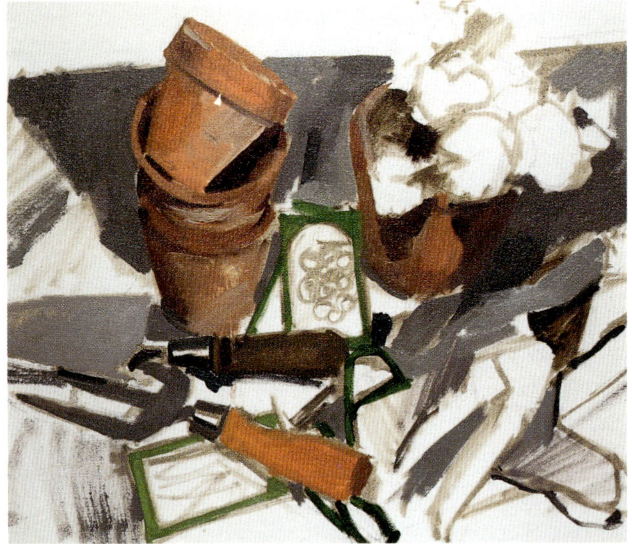

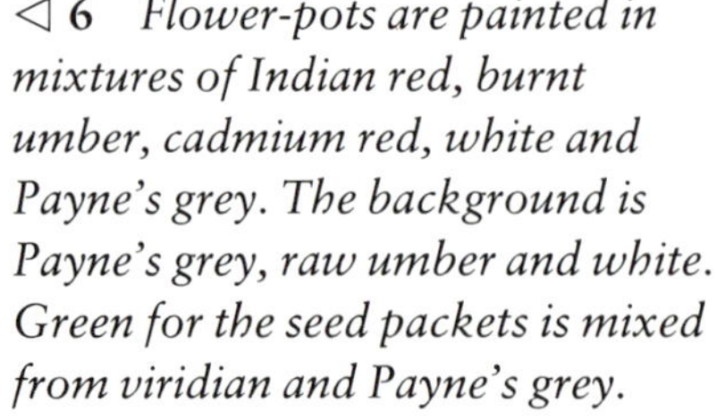

◁ **6** *Flower-pots are painted in mixtures of Indian red, burnt umber, cadmium red, white and Payne's grey. The background is Payne's grey, raw umber and white. Green for the seed packets is mixed from viridian and Payne's grey.*

◁▽ **7** *Much of the canvas surface is now blocked in. The object of this sketch is to work out relating tones and colours, rather than produce a finished work. Brushstrokes are, therefore, left deliberately rough and approximate; no attempt is made to render detail.*

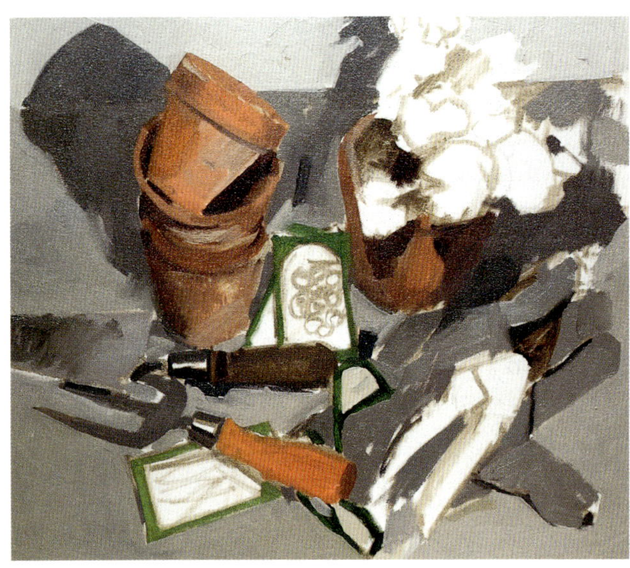

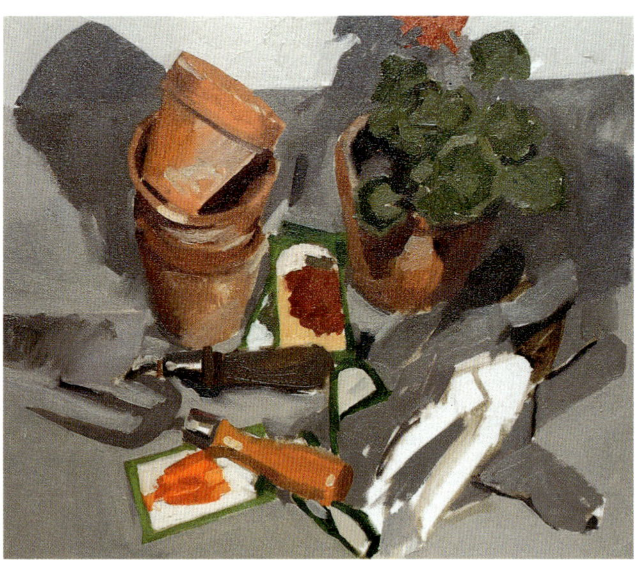

△ **8** *Most of the tones are now blocked in and the artist feels these work well, with one or two minor corrections.*

◁ **9** *The shadows directly behind the pots are too light in relation to dark areas elsewhere in the painting. To darken the shadows without making them too dense, the artist uses a stick of graphite.*

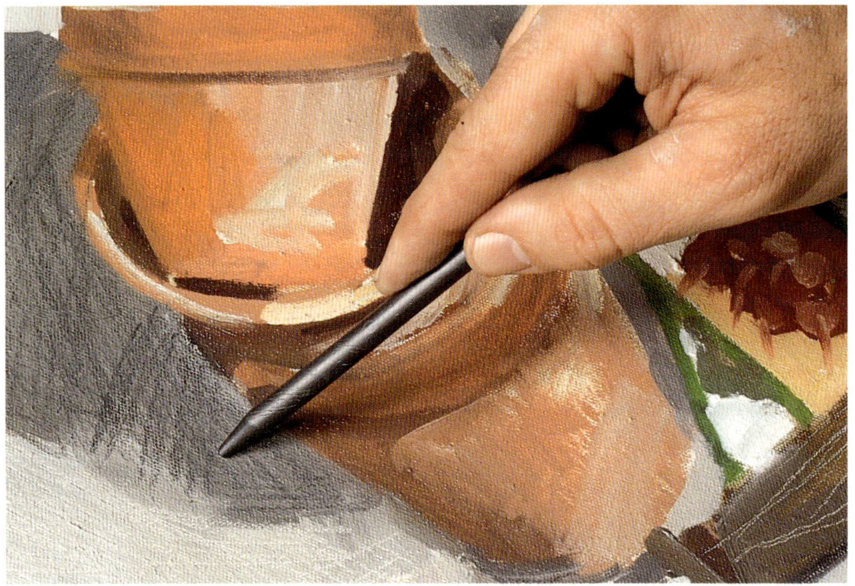

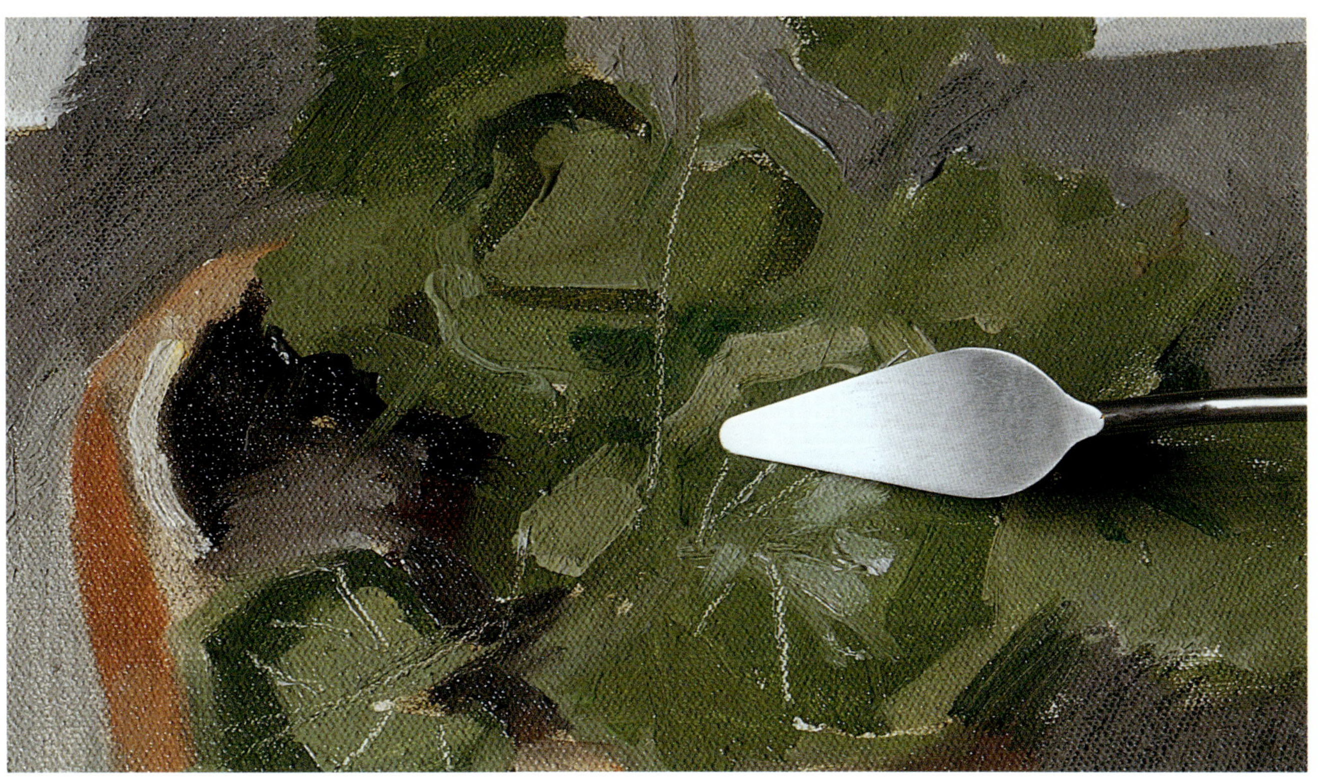

△ **10**   *The geranium leaves look dense and heavy, and the artist lightens them with sgraffiti lines made with the edge of a painting knife. This effectively lightens the solid colour without altering the overall tones.*

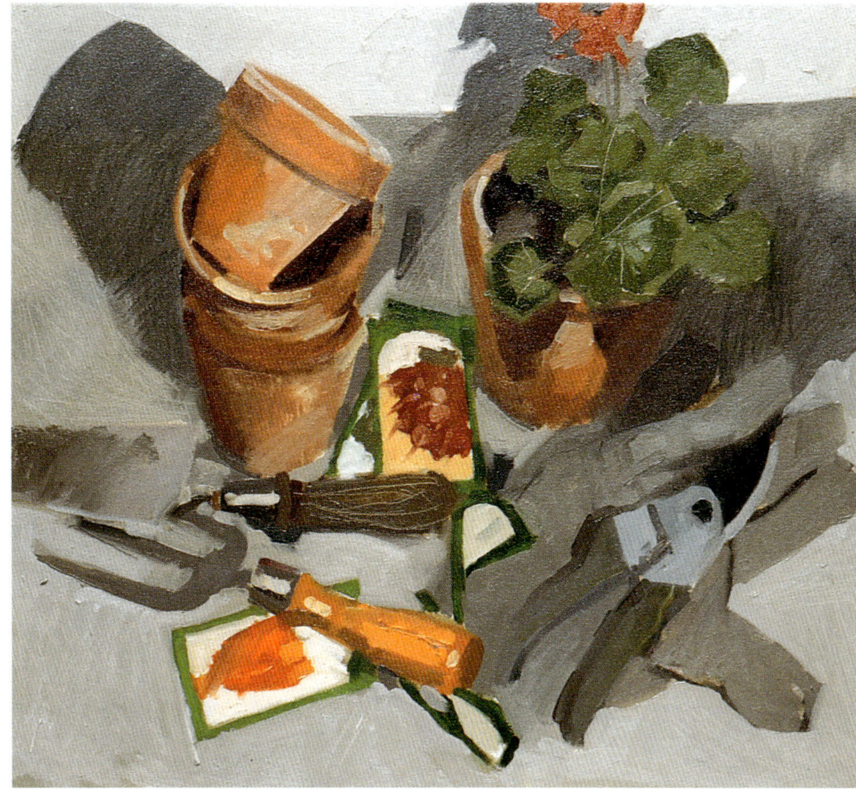

▷ **11**   *In the finished colour sketch, the main colours and tones have been worked out and broadly established. The artist is now able to use this sketch as a starting point for a more finished painting.*

TECHNIQUES

MASKING

Masking is used to help you make crisp shapes and sharply defined edges. This, however, seems to be a contradiction when it comes to using oils.

Oil paint is a malleable medium, used mainly by artists who appreciate the textural qualities of brushstrokes and knife marks or the controlled tones and subtle blending made possible with oils. The medium, therefore, is best suited to brushwork, to freehand painting.

Not all painters wish to be totally committed to the spirit of the medium, however. Some artists are attracted to the graphic aspects of a subject, and find hard edges and sharp shapes suit their style of painting. There may also be times when you want a crisp edge or a straight line in an otherwise freehand painting, and find a brush or knife too clumsy to achieve this. You may want occasional

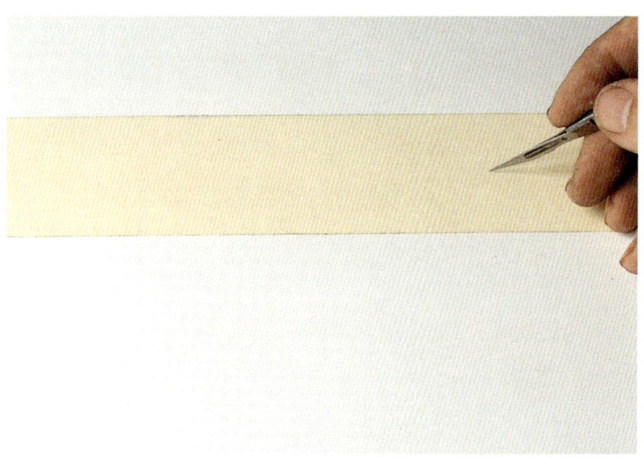

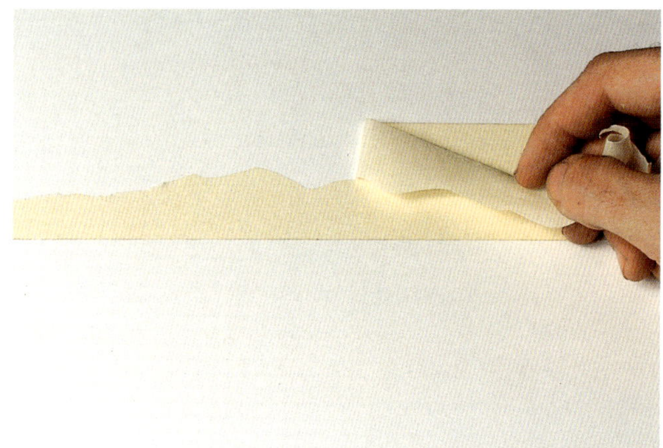

Masking tape

△ **1**   *Masking tape can be used to create a straight edge or cut to obtain a jagged or wavy edge. In this picture, the artist is cutting a jagged edge with a sharp scalpel.*

△ **2**   *The unwanted tape is removed by peeling it back from the support. The remaining cut edge – the mask – should be pressed down firmly on to the support.*

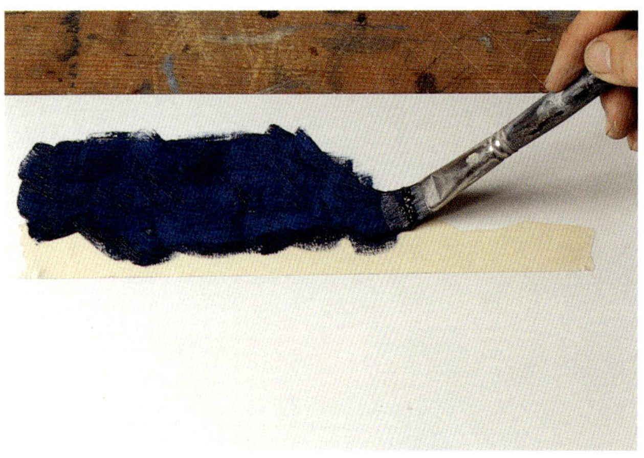

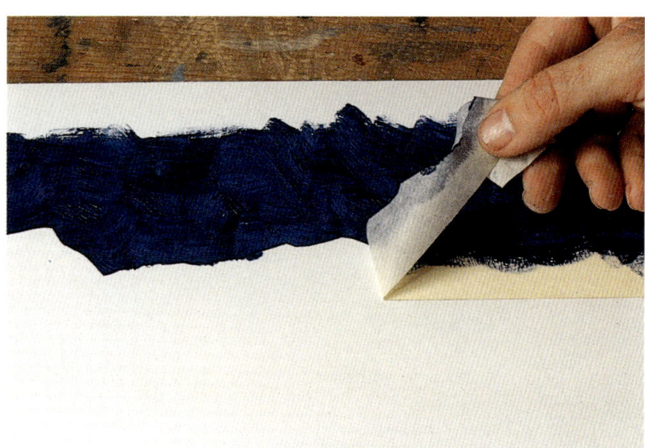

△ **3**   *Thick paint is applied up to and over the masked edge. If the colour is too thin, it will seep under the tape.*

△ **4**   *The mask is lifted clear of the surface, taking care not to smudge the wet paint.*

sharply ruled lines or mechanical shapes in your picture, even if most of the composition follows a freehand style.

You should not be inhibited about breaking away and using oils for sharper definitions but you have to be careful. Remember that straight edges can look out of place in freehand oil paintings.

When to mask

You may wish to divide a background with a particularly sharp line that requires emphasis. Your subject might be seen *contre-jour* – against the light – and you may want the dark silhouetted shapes to stand out particularly clearly against the bright background. The bottles and window frames in the painting overleaf are one such example, and the artist uses straight lines to emphasize the graphic qualities of the subject.

The quickest, most effective way of getting a cleanly painted edge to the colour is to use a mask. This protects the rest of the canvas, enabling you to paint right up to and over the edge of the masked area. When the mask is removed, you are left with a crisp mechanical line.

Masking materials

For a straight edge, use the special masking tape available at art shops and decorating stores. This is a soft, tacky tape that comes in various widths and can be removed without pulling the underlying paint away from the canvas. The tape will not adhere to wet paint, so the colour underneath must be dry before you start to mask.

A torn or jagged edge can be obtained by tearing or cutting the tape to the shape you want, then painting over it.

An alternative to masking tape is to use paper or card. Tear or cut this to the shape required, then hold it down firmly on the canvas as you paint over it. To remove the mask without smudging the paint, take one corner and carefully lift it clear of the surface without moving it across the canvas.

Paint for masking must always be fairly thick. If it is too runny, it will seep under the tape or paper mask and spoil the line.

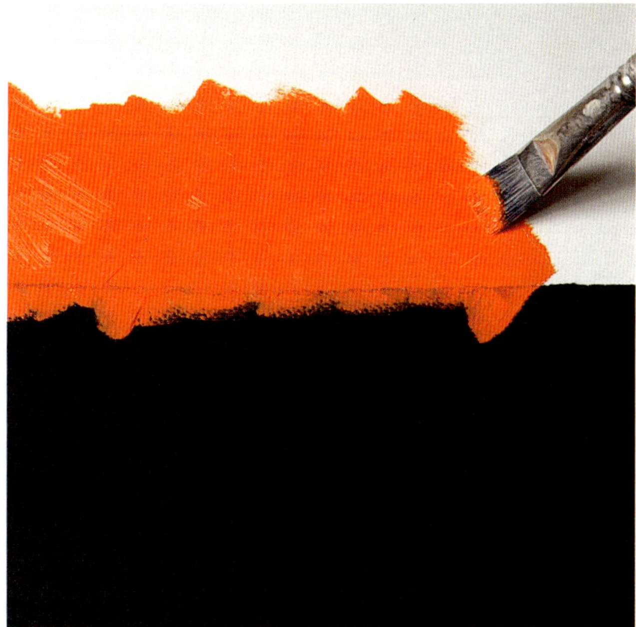

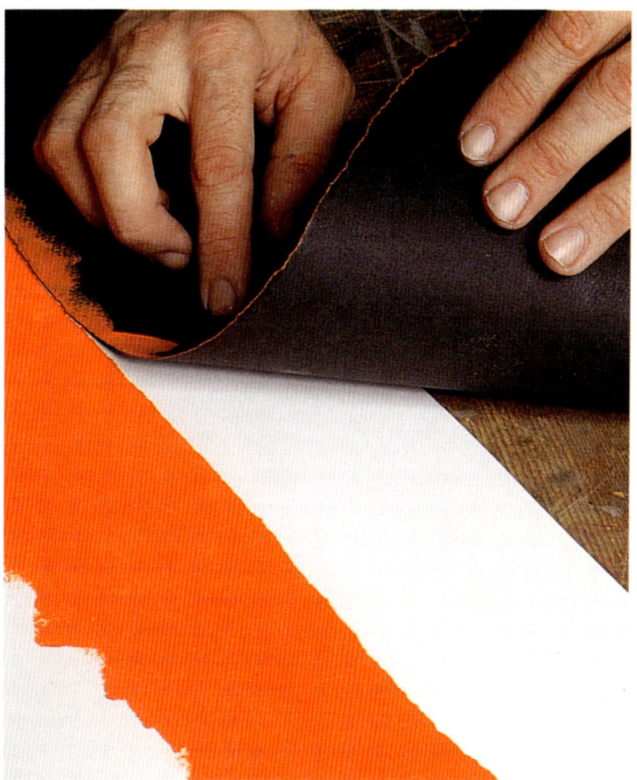

Paper mask

△ 1   *A mask can be made from a sheet of thick paper or thin card. Lay the sheet along the edge to be masked and apply thick colour up to and over the edge of the mask. Because the paper mask is not self-adhesive, it should be held firmly or taped in position as you paint.*

△ 2   *To remove the mask, take one corner and lift the sheet clear of the surface without touching the wet paint.*

PROJECTS

GLASS BOTTLES

A row of bottles standing against the sunlight is shown up as a pattern of stark shapes contained within the silhouetted frame of a sash window. It is an unusual subject in many respects, chosen by the artist for this reason. Rather than being changed in order to make a more conventional painting, the offbeat features have been deliberately emphasized.

Breaking the rules
An absence of obvious space within the subject is the first exceptional characteristic. A more conventional set-up would show the bottles grouped together, but here they are arranged side by side in a row on the window frame, and are therefore on the same plane. In addition to this, the bottles are viewed from a full-frontal position – you cannot see the sides of the bottles. Apart from the highlights on the glass, their volume is assumed rather than described.

Secondly, the composition is deliberately formal. The artist has placed the subject almost centrally on the canvas, and has used the window frame and panes to divide the picture symmetrically. A conventional approach would have been to offset these, to give the painting a more naturalistic appearance. The formality is further emphasized by the window frame, which is placed squarely on the canvas, with the horizontals parallel to the sides of the canvas.

The lack of space within the subject creates a flatness which is consciously accentuated by the artist, who chooses to paint the backgrounds as a flat colour instead of depicting the brick wall which is there in reality.

Masked bottles
The sharply defined bottles standing against the light are central to this painting. Each is different,

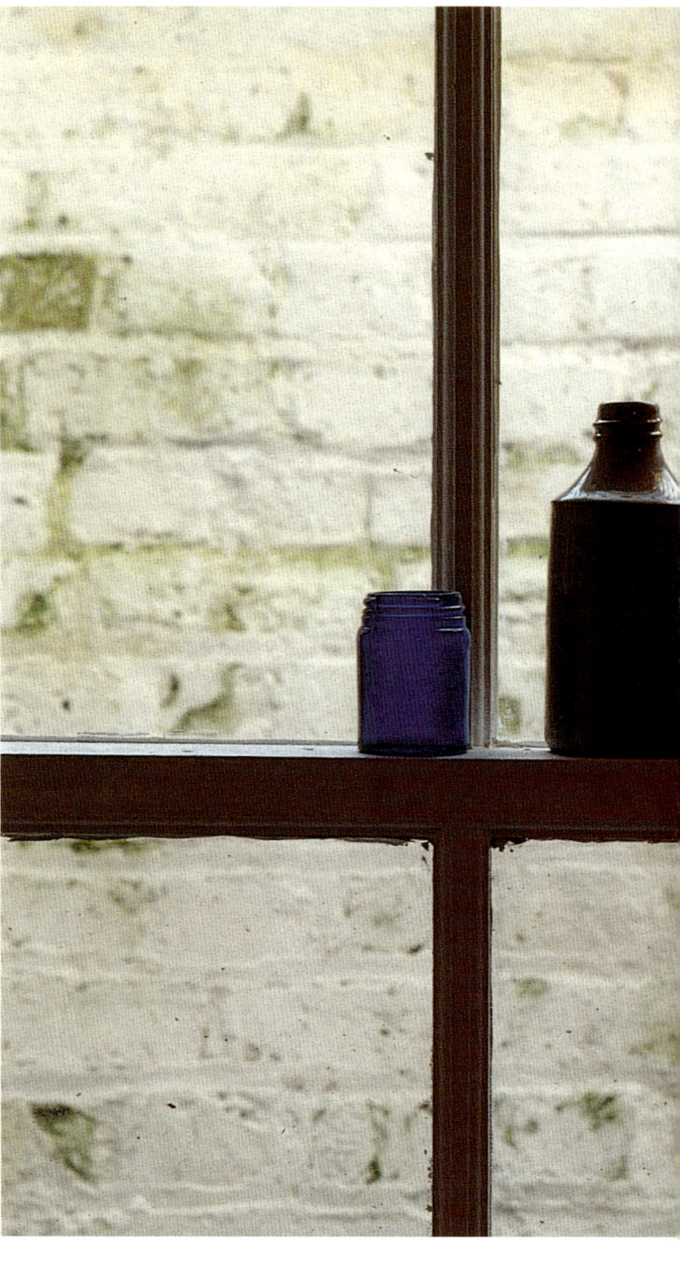

△ **1** *A row of bottles is lined up 'contre jour' – against the light. With the light behind them, the bottles stand out starkly, almost as silhouettes.*

both in shape and colour, giving the impression of a row of cut-out shapes. To re-create this starkness on the canvas, the artist uses masking tape to paint the straight edges of the bottles.

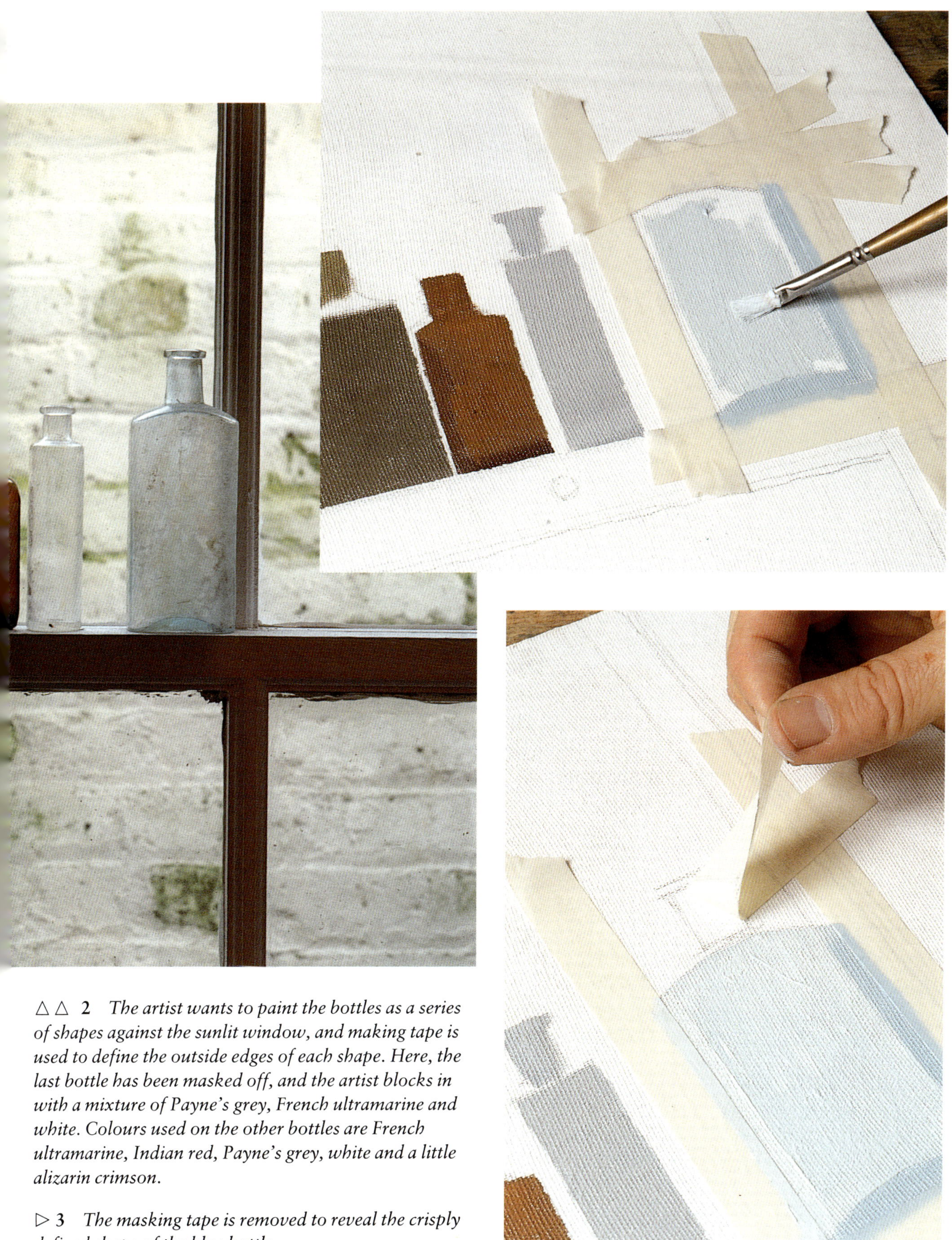

△ △ **2**   *The artist wants to paint the bottles as a series of shapes against the sunlit window, and making tape is used to define the outside edges of each shape. Here, the last bottle has been masked off, and the artist blocks in with a mixture of Payne's grey, French ultramarine and white. Colours used on the other bottles are French ultramarine, Indian red, Payne's grey, white and a little alizarin crimson.*

▷ **3**   *The masking tape is removed to reveal the crisply defined shape of the blue bottle.*

▷ **4** *Masking tape is used along the straight edges of the sash window, which are painted in Payne's grey and white, with a touch of Indian red.*

▽ **5** *Shadows and highlights are added in darker and lighter tones of the initial colour. These are painted as flat, cut-out shapes in order to retain the graphic qualities of the subject.*

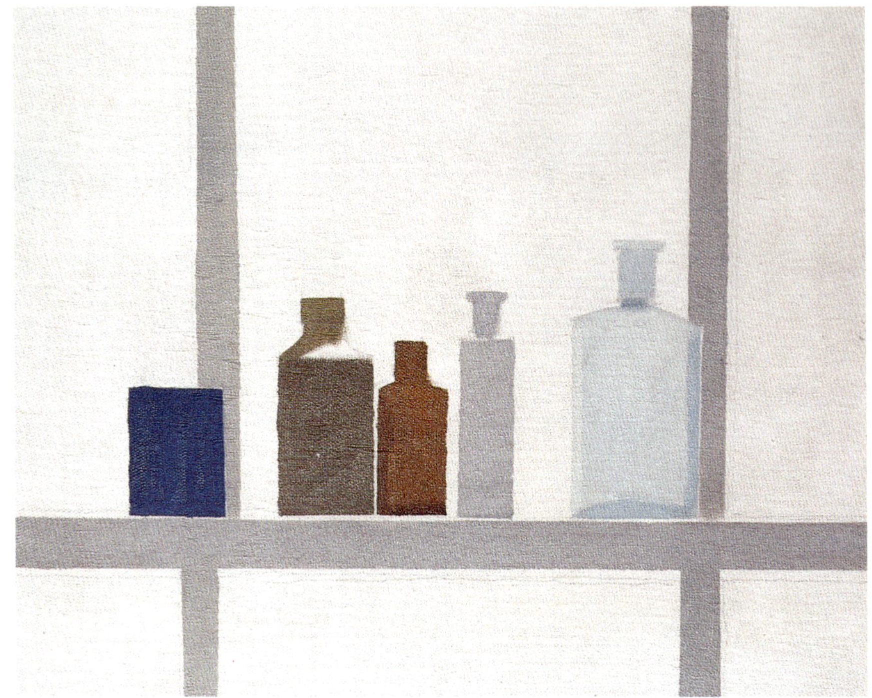

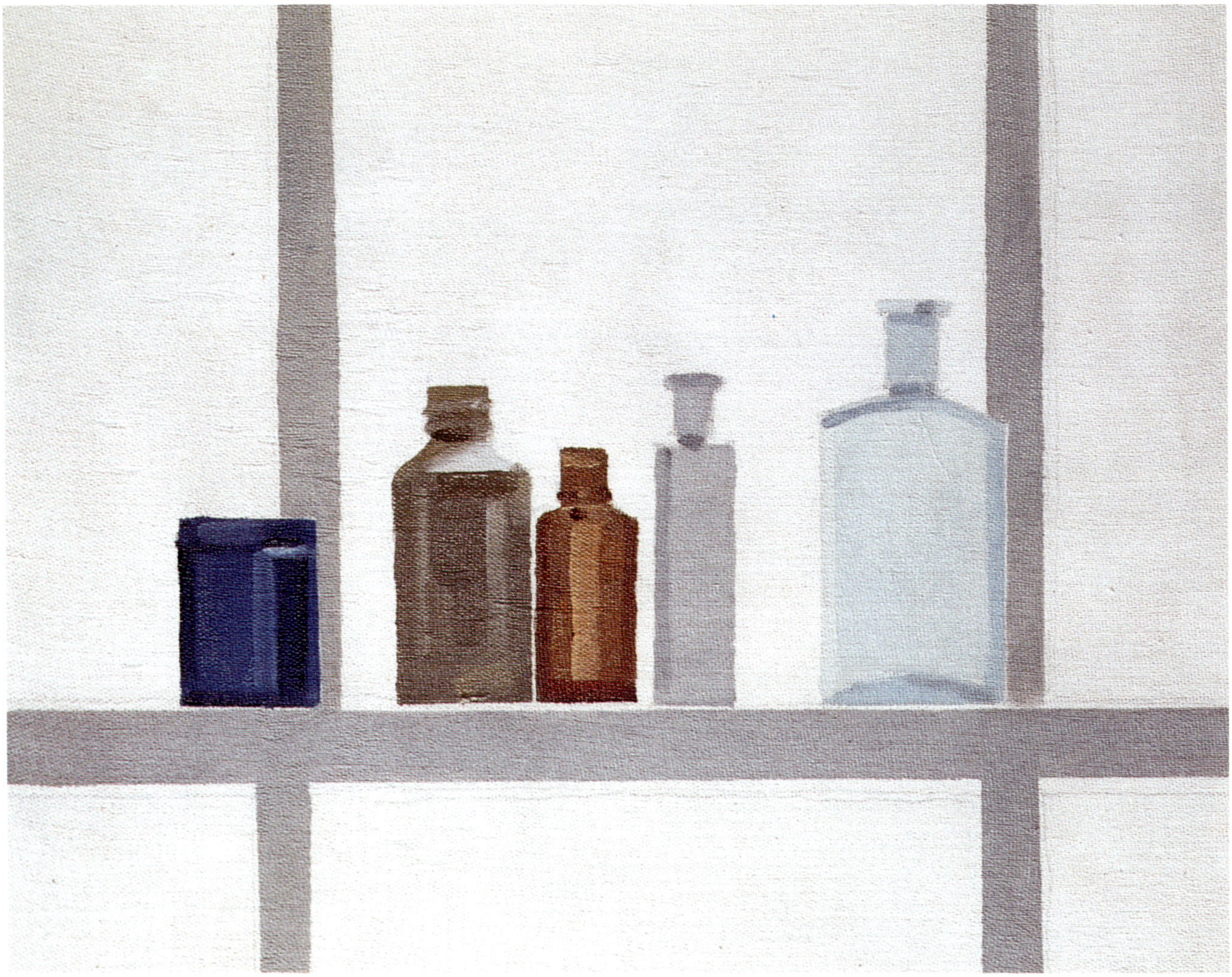

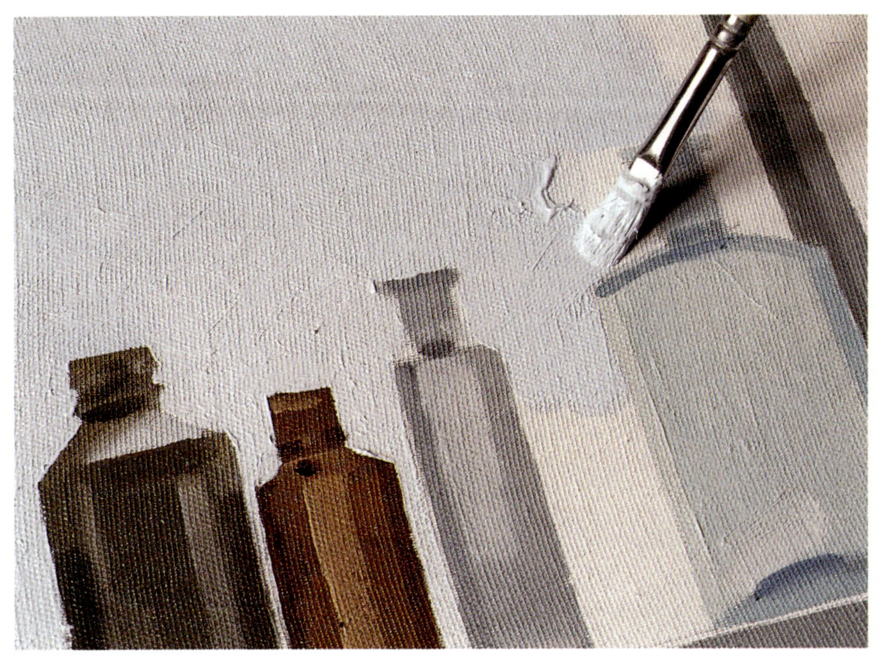

◁ **6** *The artist chooses to ignore the background bricks present in the actual subject. Instead, the background is painted in white mixed with a touch of Payne's grey.*

▽ **7** *In the completed painting, the subject has been simplified in order to re-create the essential elements of the subject. Straight lines and crisp shapes are created with masking tape; highlights and shadows are painted as simple, flat-shapes; and the bleached-out background has been rendered as a flat, light tone.*

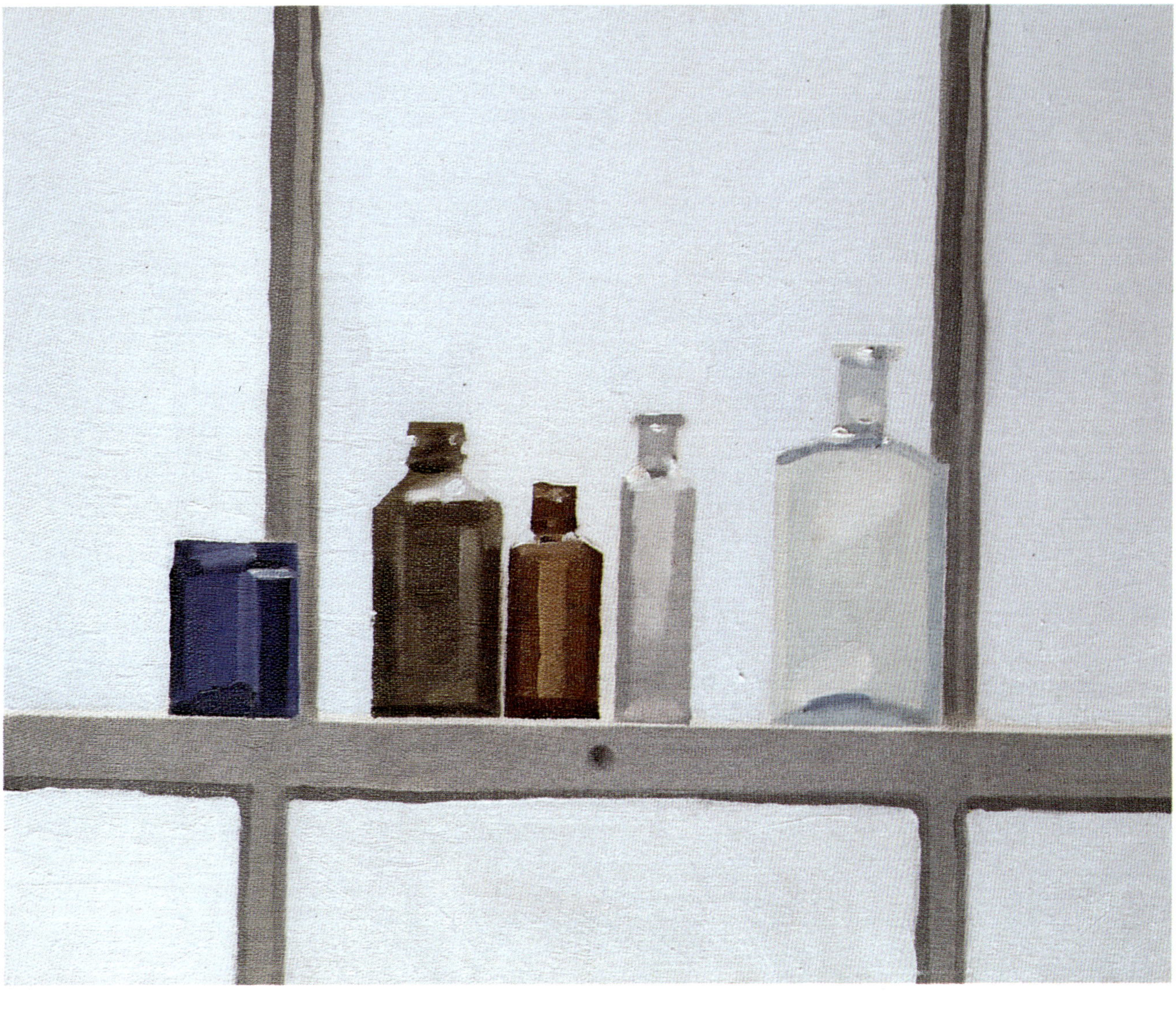

INDEX